The First Amendment

THE *May It Please the Court* SERIES

May It Please the Court
Live Recordings and Transcripts of the Supreme Court in Session
PETER IRONS AND STEPHANIE GUITTON, EDITORS

May It Please the Court
Arguments on Abortion: Live Recordings and Transcripts
of the Supreme Court Oral Arguments
STEPHANIE GUITTON AND PETER IRONS, EDITORS

May It Please the Court

The First Amendment

TRANSCRIPTS OF THE ORAL ARGUMENTS
MADE BEFORE THE SUPREME COURT IN
SIXTEEN KEY FIRST AMENDMENT CASES

Edited by Peter Irons

THE NEW PRESS

Library of Congress Catalog Card Number Number: 97-66268
ISBN 1-56584-330-4

Published in the United States by The New Press, New York
Distributed by W.W. Norton & Company, Inc., New York

The New Press was established in 1990 as a not-for-profit alternative to the large,
commercial publishing houses currently dominating the book publishing industry. The New Press operates in the public interest rather than for private gain,
and is committed to publishing, in innovative ways, works of educational, cultural, and community value that might not normally be commercially viable.

Book design by [sic]

Production management by Kim Waymer
Printed in the United States of America

9 8 7 6 5 4 3 2 1

CONTENTS

INTRODUCTION

This is the third set in the May It Please the Court series of edited and narrated tapes of Supreme Court oral arguments. The first set, published in 1993, included excerpts of arguments in 23 important cases, decided since the Court began taping all arguments in 1955. Cases in that set covered five areas of constitutional law: judicial power; First Amendment rights; criminal law; civil rights and equal protection; and privacy rights. The second set, issued in 1995, covered reproductive rights and abortion, and included arguments in eight cases, from *Griswold v. Connecticut* in 1965 to *Planned Parenthood v. Casey* in 1992.

The favorable response to the first two sets, particularly from students and teachers, has prompted the publication of this third set, which focuses on First Amendment cases. Four arguments from the initial set have been included, because of the importance of the issues and the quality of the arguments. These are: *Abington Township v. Schempp*, the school prayer case decided in 1963; *Tinker v. Des Moines*, which upheld in 1969 the right of students to wear black armbands to protest the Vietnam War; *Texas v. Johnson*, which struck down in 1989 a state law that made burning the American flag a criminal offense; and *New York Times v. United States*, the celebrated "Pentagon Papers" case of 1971, which barred the government from blocking the publication of a secret history of the Vietnam War.

I°n addition to these four arguments from the initial set, we have added twelve cases that span a wide range of First Amendment issues. Each new case—with two exceptions—involves a clash between an individual or private group and a government agency or official. This lineup—the individual against the state—characterizes almost every First Amendment case decided by the Supreme Court. The reasons for this lineup stem from the wording of the amendment itself. "Congress shall make no law," it begins, a negative check on federal power over expression that the Court has broadened to include state and local governments as well.

Although the constitutional prohibition on official action that infringes the exercise of First Amendment rights seems absolute, the Supreme Court has long made it clear that no rights are absolute and thus protected from any infringement. An exchange during oral argument of the celebrated "Pentagon Papers" case in 1971 illustrates this point. Solicitor General Erwin Griswold, arguing for the United States, looked up at Justice Hugo Black—known as a First Amendment "absolutist"—and said, "You say that 'no law' means 'no law,' and that should be obvious." Black replied drily, "I rather thought that." But Griswold continued, "And I can only say, Mr. Justice, that to me it is equally obvious that 'no law' does not mean 'no law.' And I would seek to persuade the Court that that is true."

In the "Pentagon Papers" case, Griswold did not persuade the Court to allow the government to block further publication of the secret Vietnam War history. But in dozens of other cases, the Court has recognized—and often crafted—exceptions to the 'no law' mandate of the First Amendment. Government may "accommodate" the interests of religious groups; it may penalize or punish the "free exercise" of religious practices such as polygamy or peyote use; it may punish speech that incites to "imminent lawless action" or that constitutes "fighting words"; it may criminalize obscenity and provide civil damages for libel; it may censor student publications; and it may impose "time, place, and manner" limitations on public assembly and demonstrations.

Most of the cases in this collection of oral arguments involve one or more of these "no law" exceptions, requiring the Court to weigh government claims for "reasonable" restrictions on expression against the claims of individuals that their First Amendment rights have been unduly infringed. These cases raise a wide variety of issues: school prayer; the burning of flags, crosses, and draft cards; the advertisement of pornography; nude dancing; ingesting peyote in a religious ceremony; wearing a jacket that says "Fuck the draft"; nativity scenes in a courthouse; and others that raise tempers and inflame passions.

Not all the cases in this collection are famous or notorious; some will be recognized only by First Amendment lawyers and scholars. And not all produced decisions and opinions that established new legal doctrine; some were decided with brief opinions that rested on settled law and precedent. However, each case reveals one of the many "fault lines" in American society that produce divisions over values and behavior: religion, patriotism, sexual mores, and respect for authority versus "do your own thing." And each case reached the Supreme Court for resolution of conflicts that could not be settled informally by the parties, by legislative bodies or official action, or by lower courts. However trivial the issues may seem in some cases, the Court exercised its discretion in choosing each case for argument and decision, from a docket that numbers four to five thousand potential cases each term. In that sense, none of the cases in this collection is "trivial," despite the occasional carping of dissenting justices that the Court has wasted its time in deciding a case of no great impact or import.

*   *   *

A word about the editing process in this collection is in order. The two prior sets in the May It Please the Court series included a few arguments (no more than four or five out of thirty) in which the temporal sequence of excerpts had been rearranged, simply for greater clarity and coherence. In other words, an excerpt from later in an argument was placed before one that came earlier (in one case, argument excerpts from two separate days were rearranged). A few critics (one in particular) complained about this practice, intimating that it "revised history" and had some sinister motivation. Whatever the propriety of this editing decision, the excerpts of every argument in this collection are presented in temporal order. Luckily, this did not cause any problems of clarity or coherence.

Thanks are due to many people who assisted in this project. In particular, Diane Wachtell and Jerome Chou of The New Press were supportive, helpful, and above all, patient in coping with unforeseen delays. Jerry Goldman of Northwestern University was very generous in providing taped copies of arguments; he has created a valuable resource in a World Wide Web site that allows anyone with RealAudio software to listen to complete and unedited Supreme Court arguments in close to seventy cases, as of January 1997. This resource can be accessed on the Web through http://oyez@nwu.edu. Goldman adds new arguments to his Web site as recordings become available from the National Archives. Students in my constitutional law seminar also helped with research on cases in this collection, and deserve thanks for their work.

As a member of the Supreme Court bar who has briefed (but not argued) one case thus far, I look forward to the prospect of oral argument if that case returns to the Court and is granted review. Should this happen, I hope that what I say after the ritual opening phrase, "Mr. Chief Justice, and may it please the Court," will approach the standards set by lawyers whose arguments I have heard on tape (and sometimes in person) and have admired, lawyers such as

Thurgood Marshall, Sarah Weddington, Erwin Griswold, Laurence Tribe, Anthony Amsterdam, and others of less reknown but equal skill. Oral argument before the United States Supreme Court remains the ultimate challenge of legal advocacy. I hope those who listen to the arguments in this collection will share my excitement at having this ear in the courtroom.

PETER IRONS
January 1997

The First Amendment

Abington
School District *v.*
Schempp

374 U.S. 203 (1963)

T he Pennsylvania legislature voted in 1959 that "ten verses from the Holy Bible shall be read" every day in each public school. Students could be excused on a written request from their parents. In Abington Senior High School near Philadelphia, Bible reading was followed by recitation of the Lord's Prayer. Roger and Donna Schempp were students at Abington and belonged to the Unitarian church, whose members reject the Christian Trinity. They sued the school district, claiming that Bible reading violated the establishment clause of the First Amendment. Trial testimony showed that New Testament passages offended Jewish and other non-Christian students. The Supreme Court ruled in 1963 that schools could not favor Christianity over other religions: "In the relationship between man and religion," Justice Tom Clark wrote, "the state is firmly committed to a position of neutrality."

Counsel for petitioners: Philip Ward, Philadelphia, Pennsylvania
Counsel for respondents: Henry Sawyer, Philadelphia, Pennsylvania

Chief Justice Earl Warren: Number 142, School District of Abington Township, Pennsylvania, et al., appellants, versus Edward Lewis Schempp, et al.

Narrator: It's February 27th, 1963. Chief Justice Earl Warren has called a case that challenges Bible reading and the Lord's Prayer in public schools. The issue is emotional and divisive. Polls show most Americans support classroom prayer. They feel it fosters morality and good behavior. Others argue that prayer should be personal and private. The New Testament and Lord's Prayer are Christian. Reading and reciting them could offend Jews and other non-Christians.

Today's argument goes to the beginning of the Bill of Rights, the first clause of the First Amendment. "Congress shall make no law respecting an establishment of religion." The Supreme Court applies this provision to all governments, federal, state, and local. The First Amendment is written in sweeping terms. "No law," Justice Hugo Black often said, "means no law." But what *is* an establishment of religion? America was settled by people who opposed the established church of England and religious orthodoxy. But most of the colonies set up established religions. They punished dissenters like Quakers, Baptists, and Catholics with fines, banishment, even death.

The establishment clause erected, the Supreme Court said, a "wall of separation" between church and state. Does that wall keep out any reference to God or public devotion? Our currency reads, "In God We Trust." The Pledge of Allegiance refers to "one nation, under God." Chaplains open sessions of Congress with prayer. And the Court has agreed that "we are a religious people whose institutions presuppose a Supreme Being."

But the Court has resisted efforts to bring the Bible and prayer into public schools. All children must attend school. But not all are Christian or even religious. In 1962 the Supreme Court ruled that New York teachers could not recite an official prayer in their classes. The establishment clause, Justice Black wrote, "put an end to governmental control of religion and of prayer." But the case did not end debate—often in loud voices—over school prayer.

Today's argument continues that debate, with quieter voices. The case began in a suburb of Philadelphia, Pennsylvania. Roger and Donna Schempp are students at Abington Senior High School. They belong to the Unitarian church, whose members reject the Christian Trinity. Pennsylvania law requires daily Bible reading in all schools. Roger and Donna challenged that law. They won in a lower court and the state appealed. Chief Justice Warren welcomes the state's lawyer, Philip Ward.

Warren: Mr. Ward.

Ward: May it please the Court. This case is here on an appeal from the decision of a three-judge district court that held Pennsylvania's Bible-reading statute to be an unconstitutional establishment of religion. We shall argue that the religious liberties of the Schempps, who are the appellees, the plaintiffs in this case, are not infringed; that this case doesn't concern the establishment of religion within the meaning of the Constitution; and that there is no requirement that Pennsylvania must give up an ancient custom simply because it involves the use of the Bible.

We also believe that this case is different from any of the cases, the church-state cases this Court has heretofore considered. We think we have a novel factual situation here. We think the question presented to this Court for the first time is, What does the Constitution require us to do with an old tradition that has undoubted secular value? It's noncompulsory, but yet, it in some ways reflects the religious origin of the country.

Narrator: Ward described what happens in Abington schools.

Ward: At Abington, this is the way it works: between 8:15 and 8:30 on every school day, all the children are in their home rooms, advisory sections. There's a public address system in each of their rooms. At 8:15 the morning exercise starts. First they have what's called an introduction, a "fact for the day." They pull something out of the World Almanac to gain the attention of the children— Mt. Everest is 29,000 feet high—something like that to get them thinking. This is followed by ten verses of the Bible, read without comment. The ten verses of the Bible is followed by the Lord's Prayer, which in turn is followed by the flag salute, which in turn is followed by the school announcements for the day— "The botany class will meet in room A instead of room B." Then you have a conclusion, at which they announce the children who read the preceding announcements. These announcements, this reading, the fact for the day, the Bible, the prayer, are done by the children of the, the students of the television and radio workshop, which is a regular course of the English department at Abington. There are about thirty students in this course, and it's voluntary.

Narrator: Ward defended the Bible as a source of common morality.
Ward: How do we use the Bible in the schools? We say, and the statute says, to

bring lessons in morality to the children. The Schempps say, no, you can't be doing this. How can you teach anything, how can you bring lessons in morality to the children, how is it a proper way to teach if you only use one source, we only use one book? If you don't allow any comment to be made on what is being read? If you don't select particular passages that are unusually good? They say, this can't be teaching morality. They say, you're not teaching morality. What in fact you're doing, they say, is you are teaching some kind of a public school creed that doesn't have religion, that's cut adrift from theology.

Gentlemen, that is precisely what we're doing. We're teaching morality without religion, cut adrift from theology. And that is proper for the people of Pennsylvania. We can bring to our children lessons of morality in their school days, as long as we're not bringing religion, not bringing theology. The people of Pennsylvania have wanted to do this, they have since the beginning wanted to bring these lessons in morality to the children. So what do they do? They pick a common source of morality, the Bible.

Narrator: Chief Justice Warren had a question.

Warren: Mr. Ward, may I ask you this, please? Suppose we accept your argument, that this ceremony is moral instruction and is not in any sense religious. And suppose the state next says: following these ceremonies each morning, there shall be one hour of instruction in morals, and during that hour of instruction, nothing shall be done except to read the Bible to the students, and all must attend except those whose parents object to it. Do you think that would be acceptable also?

Ward: I think, as the case before us now, ten verses is acceptable. I think I agree with you, Chief Justice, it could become so bad that you couldn't, reasonable men couldn't say, they are teaching morality. They would have to say, they are doing nothing but using the Bible to indoctrinate those children with religion.

Warren: Well, would an hour of instruction in morals be unconstitutional if a few moments of instruction would not be?

Ward: I think that would be a question of fact. I would think an hour, taken out of the school day, for morality—as Mr. Justice Brennan said, morality is a very important thing to teach. I don't know.

Warren: It is, it is, very important.

Ward: I don't know. I know if the people of Pennsylvania think that's a good way to teach morality, I think the problem would be for the Court to determine.

Narrator: Ward concluded his argument.

Ward: You can sum up our particular problem as this: Can you use, can you keep a tradition which has secular values? It does teach morality. It is noncompulsory; the child doesn't have to be there. But the only problem is, it involves part of the religious tradition of this country. It deals with a document that is of obvious religious origin and to many people an obviously religious book. Must the government rip out that document, that tradition, simply because it involves a religious book? Must the government, any time any tradition, in any way, reflects the fact that we are a religious people—must they rip out any tradition even, even if that tradition nobody has to abide by? The tradition isn't trying to teach anybody anything. The tradition isn't requiring a person to believe or disbelieve. The tradition has secular value; it has a purpose, like the Sunday closing. It has a purpose, to teach morality to the children.

Narrator: Chief Justice Warren welcomed the Schempp's lawyer, Henry Sawyer.

Warren: Mr. Sawyer.

Sawyer: Mr. Chief Justice, and may it please the Court.
    You cannot separate the moral leaven from the religious leaven in the Bible. I think the two go absolutely together. And it teaches—they say it doesn't proselytize—it *teaches*, the book teaches from the opening chapter of Genesis to the last chapter of Revelations. It teaches; it teaches the way the world was created, and it teaches in a sectarian sense from the opening. From the very opening it says, And lo, the Spirit was upon the waters. And in the King James Version, and I'm sure the Douay Version, that word is capitalized. It means the Holy Ghost. This is the beginning of a teaching of the concept of Trinity. It teaches.
    The New Testament is a teaching message. When Jesus said, "Others have said unto you, an eye for an eye and a tooth for a tooth, but I say unto you, thou shall resist not evil. If one smites thee upon one cheek," and so on. This is teaching. And it was highly controversial teaching then, and I submit to your honors, it's highly controversial teaching now. Men do not agree about these things.

Narrator: The First Amendment also protects the "free exercise" of religion. Sawyer's answer to claims that this clause allows school prayer drew questions from Justice Potter Stewart.

Sawyer: The question is, Is it a constitutional right under the free exercise clause to have the state conduct the prayer, or to pray, in other words, under the aegis of the state? And I think clearly not. Even if the overwhelming majority so feel, I think it probably has nothing to do with the question of majorities.

Stewart: Well, let's assume, let's assume there was no statute here, but that they had a student government in this Abington Township high school, which is fairly typical of many public high schools, and the students voted overwhelmingly that they wanted to begin their day by having one of their number—perhaps on a rotating basis—read ten verses from the Bible, whichever Bible the particular student, the reader chose that morning, to begin the school day. And this was attacked under the Constitution, and there was evidence from all of these people who voted that "our religious beliefs tell us we want to do this, in the free exercise of our religion." What kind of case would you have then?

Sawyer: May I ask a question just on the facts? Is this a case...

Stewart: I make up the facts as I go along. [*laughter*]

Sawyer: Yes, sir. Do the school authorities say, well then, certainly you can use the PA system and we'll get the children together?

Stewart: Well, yes, the children *are* together, they are together.

Sawyer: What would they be doing otherwise? In other words, I'll answer it this way. If, pursuant to that, the school authorities say, yes, you may use the PA system, we'll have the children not doing something else at the time in the classrooms, then I'd say that it's an establishment nonetheless.

Stewart: Isn't it a gross interference with the free exercise of their religion, of those, in my imaginary case, those ninety-eight percent of the student body who say, our religious beliefs tell us that this is what we want to do?

Sawyer: They have a right to do it, Your Honor, but they haven't got a right to get the state to help them.

Narrator: Dr. Solomon Grayzel, a Jewish scholar, told the lower court that parts of the New Testament were "offensive to Jewish tradition." Verses about Jesus as Messiah could be "psychologically harmful" to Jewish and other non-Christian students. Sawyer stressed this testimony.

Sawyer: The New Testament, the concept of Christ, a man who historically lived, as being the Son of God, is, as Dr. Grayzel testified, to Judaism a blasphemy. This was in fact Christ's crime. It is a blasphemy. You can't gloss this over by saying there's some minor differences. He pointed out that there's ridicule of the Jewish hierarchy throughout the New Testament. He pointed out, and think of it, gentlemen, the scene of the trial of Jesus before Pilate, where the multitude cries not for Barrabas but for Jesus, and Pilate washes his hands. And the version exculpates the Romans for the death of Christ. And then the Jews say, and they're so described, they say, his blood be upon us and our children. And Dr. Grayzel said that sentence has been responsible for more anti-Semitism than any single sentence in history, and I can't doubt it.

Narrator: Sawyer returned to the establishment clause.

Sawyer: Well, we say that there is an establishment. In addition to that, it's clear as crystal and just ingenuous to say that this doesn't prefer one religion over another. And how fine you chop it is another thing. But certainly at the grossest, and at the broadest, and in any sense of the word it prefers Christian religions over non-Christian religions. I think it goes further than that. And that you cannot do, and that the statute does. It is a religious exercise, it seems to me; it was intended to be a religious exercise. I think it's ingenuous to suggest that the legislature had anything else in mind but that. I don't think that you can use the word morality to encompass all that is purveyed to the minds of children by this book. There will be many, many things read, out of the King James Version, which will exclusively—if you can separate them, gentlemen—but it will exclusively concern religious concepts and ideas, without any distinguishable moral truth.

Narrator: Sawyer faced a final question.

Court: Mr. Sawyer, what do you say to Mr. Ward's argument that, well, even if it is religion, it's religious tradition?

Sawyer: I think tradition is not to be scoffed at. But let me say this very candidly. I think it is the final arrogance to talk constantly about "our religious tradition" in this country and equate it with this Bible. Sure, religious tradition. *Whose* religious tradition? It isn't any part of the religious tradition of a substantial number of Americans, of a great many, a great many things, and really some of the salient features of the King James Version, or the Douay Version, for that matter. And it's just to me a little bit easy and I say arrogant to keep talking about "our religious tradition." It suggests that the public schools, at least of Pennsylvania, are a kind of Protestant institution to which others are cordially invited. And I think to some extent they have been, in our state.

But we have here, in the schools of Pennsylvania, the conducting, man-

dated by statute, day after day, as an exercise, the reading of the sacred book of
Christianity.

Narrator: On June 17th, 1963, the Supreme Court ruled in favor of Roger and
Donna Schempp. Public schools could not use the Bible and prayer for classroom devotion. Justice Tom Clark wrote the Court's opinion. "The place of religion in our society," he said, "is an exalted one." But religion's proper place,
Clark added, is in "the home, the church, and…the individual heart and mind."
He restated the Court's earlier rulings: "In the relationship between man and
religion, the State is firmly committed to a position of neutrality."

Clark denied that Bible reading simply aided in teaching morality. He
noted "the pervading religious character" of the classroom ceremony and its
official endorsement of Christian belief. Clark emphasized that "the Bible is
worthy of study for its literary and historic qualities" in classes that do not
involve "religious exercises."

Only Justice Potter Stewart dissented. He focused on the First Amendment's "free exercise" clause. Stewart answered Justice Clark. "If schools are to
be truly neutral in the matter of religion," he wrote, they must accommodate
parents who "desire to have their children's school day open with the reading of
passages from the Bible."

Outside the Court, many Americans joined Stewart's dissent. "We are a
Christian nation, under God," one Congressman said. "These decisions do not
help us to be on God's side." Polls showed nearly seventy percent of the public
approved of school prayer. Reverend Billy Graham agreed. "I don't believe that a
small minority should rule the majority of the people." But other religious leaders supported the Court. "The decision is a good one, deeply rooted in the spirit
of the First Amendment," wrote the editors of a Protestant journal. A Catholic
journal praised the Court for protecting students against "religious values
which they do not accept." And almost all Jewish leaders praised the decision.

The Supreme Court decides constitutional questions. But it cannot
decide political controversies. The Court has reaffirmed its school prayer decisions many times since 1963. And yet, many teachers continue to lead students
in Bible reading and prayer. Few issues show such a collision of majority sentiment with minority sensitivity. Perhaps the best commentary comes from Justice Robert Jackson. His classic opinion in 1943 upheld the rights of students
who belong to religious minorities: "The very purpose of a Bill of Rights," he
said, "was to withdraw certain subjects from…political controversy, to place
them beyond the reach of majorities." Jackson understood that matters of faith
cannot be decided by majority vote.

EDITED SUPREME COURT OPINIONS
Abington School Dist. v. Schempp

MR. JUSTICE CLARK delivered the opinion of the Court.

Once again we are called upon to consider the scope of the provision of the First Amendment to the United States Constitution which declares that "Congress shall make no law respecting an establishment of religion, or prohibiting the free exercise thereof..." In light of the history of the First Amendment and of our cases interpreting and applying its requirements, we hold that the practices at issue and the laws requiring them are unconstitutional under the Establishment Clause, as applied to the States through the Fourteenth Amendment....

The Commonwealth of Pennsylvania by law...requires that "At least ten verses from the Holy Bible shall be read, without comment, at the opening of each public school on each school day. Any child shall be excused from such Bible reading, or attending such Bible reading, upon the written request of his parent or guardian." The Schempp family, husband and wife and two of their three children, brought suit to enjoin enforcement of the statute, contending that their rights under the Fourteenth Amendment to the Constitution of the United States are, have been, and will continue to be violated unless this statute be declared unconstitutional as violative of these provisions of the First Amendment.... A three-judge statutory District Court for the Eastern District of Pennsylvania held that the statute is violative of the Establishment Clause of the First Amendment as applied to the States by the Due Process Clause of the Fourteenth Amendment and directed that appropriate injunctive relief issue....

The appellees Edward Lewis Schempp, his wife Sidney, and their children, Roger and Donna, are of the Unitarian faith and are members of the Unitarian Church in Germantown, Philadelphia, Pennsylvania, where they, as well as another son, Ellory, regularly attend religious services....

At the first trial Edward Schempp and the children testified as to specific religious doctrines purveyed by a literal reading of the Bible "which were contrary to the religious beliefs which they held and to their familial teaching."... The children testified that all of the doctrines to which they referred were read to them at various times as part of the exercises. Edward Schempp testified at the second trial that he had considered having Roger and Donna excused from attendance at the exercises but decided against it for several reasons, including his belief that the children's relationships with their teachers and classmates would be adversely affected....

The trial court, in striking down the practices and the statute requiring them, made specific findings of fact that the children's attendance at Abington

Senior High School is compulsory and that the practice of reading ten verses from the Bible is also compelled by law. It also found that:

> The fact that some pupils, or theoretically all pupils, might be excused from attendance at the exercises does not mitigate the obligatory nature of the ceremony....The record demonstrates that it was the intention of...the Commonwealth...to introduce a religious ceremony into the public schools of the Commonwealth....

It is true that religion has been closely identified with our history and government. As we said in *Engel v. Vitale* (1962), "The history of man is inseparable from the history of religion. And...since the beginning of that history many people have devoutly believed that 'More things are wrought by prayer than this world dreams of.'"...We gave specific recognition to the proposition that "[w]e are a religious people whose institutions presuppose a Supreme Being." The fact that the Founding Fathers believed devotedly that there was a God and that the unalienable rights of man were rooted in Him is clearly evidenced in their writings, from the Mayflower Compact to the Constitution itself. This background is evidenced today in our public life through the continuance in our oaths of office from the Presidency to the Alderman of the final supplication, "So help me God." Likewise each House of the Congress provides through its Chaplain an opening prayer, and the sessions of this Court are declared open by the crier in a short ceremony, the final phrase of which invokes the grace of God....It can be truly said, therefore, that today, as in the beginning, our national life reflects a religious people who, in the words of Madison, are "earnestly praying, as...in duty bound, that the Supreme Lawgiver of the Universe...guide them into every measure which may be worthy of his [blessing....]"

This is not to say, however, that religion has been so identified with our history and government that religious freedom is not likewise as strongly imbedded in our public and private life. Nothing but the most telling of personal experiences in religious persecution suffered by our forebears...could have planted our belief in liberty of religious opinion any more deeply in our heritage.... The views of Madison and Jefferson, preceded by Roger Williams, came to be incorporated not only in the Federal Constitution but likewise in those of most of our States. This freedom to worship was indispensable in a country whose people came from the four quarters of the earth and brought with them a diversity of religious opinion. Today authorities list eighty-three separate religious bodies, each with membership exceeding fifty thousand, existing among our people, as well as innumerable smaller groups....

First, this Court has decisively settled that the First Amendment's mandate that "Congress shall make no law respecting an establishment of religion, or prohibiting the free exercise thereof" has been made wholly applicable to the States by the Fourteenth Amendment....

Second, this Court has rejected unequivocally the contention that the Establishment Clause forbids only governmental preference of one religion over another....

Finally, in *Engel v. Vitale*, only last year, these principles were so universally recognized that the Court...held that "it is no part of the business of government to compose official prayers for any group of the American people to recite as a part of a religious program carried on by government."... In discussing the reach of the Establishment and Free Exercise Clauses of the First Amendment the Court said:

> When the power, prestige and financial support of government is placed behind a particular religious belief, the indirect coercive pressure upon religious minorities to conform to the prevailing officially approved religion is plain....

And in further elaboration the Court found that the "first and most immediate purpose of the Establishment Clause rested on the belief that a union of government and religion tends to destroy government and to degrade religion."...

The conclusion follows that...the laws require religious exercises and such exercises are being conducted in direct violation of the rights of the appellees and petitioners. Nor are these required exercises mitigated by the fact that individual students may absent themselves upon parental request, for that fact furnishes no defense to a claim of unconstitutionality under the Establishment Clause....Further, it is no defense to urge that the religious practices here may be relatively minor encroachments on the First Amendment. The breach of neutrality that is today a trickling stream may all too soon become a raging torrent...

The place of religion in our society is an exalted one, achieved through a long tradition of reliance on the home, the church and the inviolable citadel of the individual heart and mind. We have come to recognize through bitter experience that it is not within the power of government to invade that citadel, whether its purpose or effect be to aid or oppose, to advance or retard. In the relationship between man and religion, the State is firmly committed to a position of neutrality. Though the application of that rule requires interpretation of a delicate sort, the rule itself is clearly and concisely stated in the words of the First Amendment. Applying that rule to the facts of these cases, we affirm the judgment....

MR. JUSTICE STEWART, dissenting.

The First Amendment declares that "Congress shall make no law respecting an establishment of religion, or prohibiting the free exercise thereof...." It is, I think, a fallacious oversimplification to regard these two provisions as establishing a single constitutional standard of "separation of church and state," which can be mechanically applied in every case to delineate the required boundaries between government and religion. We err in the first place if we do not recognize, as a matter of history and as a matter of the imperatives of our free society, that religion and government must necessarily interact in countless ways. Secondly, the fact is that while in many contexts the Establishment Clause and the Free Exercise Clause fully complement each other, there are areas in which a doctrinaire reading of the Establishment Clause leads to irreconcilable conflict with the Free Exercise Clause.

A single obvious example should suffice to make the point. Spending federal funds to employ chaplains for the armed forces might be said to violate the Establishment Clause. Yet a lonely soldier stationed at some faraway outpost could surely complain that a government which did *not* provide him the opportunity for pastoral guidance was affirmatively prohibiting the free exercise of his religion. And such examples could readily be multiplied. The short of the matter is simply that the two relevant clauses of the First Amendment cannot accurately be reflected in a sterile metaphor which by its very nature may distort rather than illumine the problems involved in a particular case....

Unlike other First Amendment guarantees, there is an inherent limitation upon the applicability of the Establishment Clause's ban on state support to religion....

That the central value embodied in the First Amendment—and, more particularly, in the guarantee of "liberty" contained in the Fourteenth—is the safeguarding of an individual's right to free exercise of his religion has been consistently recognized....

It is this concept of constitutional protection embodied in our decisions which makes the cases before us such difficult ones for me. For there is involved in this case a substantial free exercise claim on the part of those who affirmatively desire to have their children's school day open with the reading of passages from the Bible....It might be argued here that parents who wanted their children to be exposed to religious influences in school could...send their children to private or parochial schools. But the consideration which renders this contention too facile to be determinative has already been recognized by the Court: "Freedom of speech, freedom of the press, freedom of religion are available to all, not merely to those who can pay their own way." (*Murdock* v. *Pennsylvania*)

It might also be argued that parents who want their children exposed to religious influences can adequately fulfill that wish off school property and outside school time. With all its surface persuasiveness, however, this argument seriously misconceives the basic constitutional justification for permitting the exercises at issue in these cases. For a compulsory state educational system so structures a child's life that if religious exercises are held to be an impermissible activity in schools, religion is placed at an artificial and state-created disadvantage. Viewed in this light, permission of such exercises for those who want them is necessary if the schools are truly to be neutral in the matter of religion. And a refusal to permit religious exercises thus is seen, not as the realization of state neutrality, but rather as the establishment of a religion of secularism, or at the least, as government support of the beliefs of those who think that religious exercises should be conducted only in private....

In the *Schempp* case the record shows no more than a subjective prophecy by a parent of what he thought would happen if a request were made to be excused from participation in the exercises under the amended statute. No such request was ever made, and there is no evidence whatever as to what might or would actually happen, nor of what administrative arrangements the school actually might or could make to free from pressure of any kind those who do not want to participate in the exercises....

What our Constitution indispensably protects is the freedom of each of us, be he Jew or Agnostic, Christian or Atheist, Buddhist or Freethinker, to believe or disbelieve, to worship or not worship, to pray or keep silent, according to his own conscience, uncoerced and unrestrained by government. It is conceivable that these school boards, or even all school boards, might eventually find it impossible to administer a system of religious exercises during school hours in such a way as to meet this constitutional standard—in such a way as completely to free from any kind of official coercion those who do not affirmatively want to participate. But I think we must not assume that school boards so lack the qualities of inventiveness and good will as to make impossible the achievement of that goal.

BIBLIOGRAPHY

KEYNES, EDWARD. *The Court v. Congress.* Duke University Press, 1989.

LAUBACH, JOHN H. *School Prayers: Congress, the Courts, and the Public.* Public Affairs Press, 1969.

POLLAK, LOUIS H. "The Supreme Court 1962 Term—Foreword: Public Prayers in Public Schools." *Harvard Law Review* 77, no. 1 (November 1963): 62.

SCANLON, JOHN. "Prayer or Pluralism in the Schools?" *The Saturday Review.* July 18, 1964, p. 41.

"The Bible—Better in School than in Court." *Life.* April 12, 1963, p. 62.

SMITH, RODNEY K. *Public Prayer and the Constitution.* Scholarly Resources, 1987.

County of Allegheny
v. ACLU

492 U.S. 573 (1989)

Beginning in the early 1980s, officials in Pittsburgh, Pennsylvania, allowed the Holy Name Society of the Catholic Church to display a Christmas nativity creche in the main rotunda of the Allegheny county courthouse. One block away, outside the City-County administration building, members of Chabad, an Orthodox Jewish group, erected an 18-foot-high menorah next to a large Christmas tree to celebrate the Chanukah holiday. Pittsburgh residents of several religious faiths—and of no religion—joined the American Civil Liberties Union in suing the county and city, claiming the display of the nativity scene and menorah violated the "establishment of religion" clause of the First Amendment. A closely divided Supreme Court ruled, 5-to-4, that the nativity scene must be removed but the justices—by the same margin—allowed the menorah to stay. The Court's rulings closely examined the "context" of the challenged displays, and gave local officials broad latitude to allow religious displays that include secular objects like Santa Claus candy canes and Christmas trees.

TRANSCRIPT OF EDITED AND NARRATED ARGUMENTS IN
County of Allegheny v. ACLU Greater Pittsburgh Chapter, 492 U.S. 573 (1989)

Counsel for petitioner, Allegheny County: Peter Buscemi, Washington, D.C.
Counsel for petitioner, Chabad: Nathan Lewin, Washington, D.C.
Counsel for respondent, ACLU: Roslyn Litman, Pittsburgh, Pennsylvania

Chief Justice Rehnquist: We'll hear argument now in No. 87-2050, County of Allegheny *v.* American Civil Liberties Union and related cases.

Narrator: It's February 22, 1989. We're in the chamber of the United States Supreme Court in Washington, D.C. Chief Justice William Rehnquist has called for argument a set of cases that challenge the display of religious scenes and symbols on public property. Most Americans enjoy displays of nativity creches and Christmas trees during the Christmas season. They don't see any conflict with the Constitution.

Not everyone, however, agrees with religious displays on public property. Some people—both religious believers and nonbelievers—feel that government should avoid any connection with religious symbols and ceremonies. They believe the Establishment of Religion clause of the First Amendment prohibits such activities.

Today's arguments involve two separate displays in Pittsburgh, Pennsylvania. One is a nativity creche in the lobby of the Allegheny County courthouse, which is a setting for Christmas caroling by many groups. Above the creche is a sign that reads "Gloria in Excelsis Deo." The creche is owned by a Catholic group, the Holy Name Society. The other display is an 18-foot-high Jewish menorah, a candelabrum that symbolizes the Chanukah holiday. The menorah, which is owned by an Orthodox Jewish group called Chabad, is placed next to a Christmas tree, outside the City-County building in downtown Pittsburgh.

Both displays were challenged by the local chapter of the American Civil Liberties Union and citizens who were Christian, Jewish, Muslim, and of no religion. The county and city defended both displays, and Chabad entered the case to support its menorah. After a federal judge ruled against the challengers, a federal appeals court reversed his decision by a 2-1 vote.

The city and county are represented by Peter Buscemi, whose firm in Washington, D.C., handles many Supreme Court cases. He first points the justices to a 1984 case, *Lynch v. Donnelly*. The appeals court in the Pittsburgh cases rejected this decision as precedent. Chief Justice Rehnquist welcomes Buscemi.

Rehnquist: Mr. Buscemi, you may proceed whenever you're ready.

Buscemi: Thank you, Mr. Chief Justice, and may it please the Court. Five years ago this Court decided a case called *Lynch* against *Donnelly*. In that case, the Court upheld a Christmas display in Pawtucket, Rhode Island, against a First Amendment challenge. The display contained a rather large nativity scene with figures as big as five feet tall. The city of Pawtucket owned the display, erected it, and maintained it each year as part of a display in the vicinity of the City Hall and a private park near the downtown shopping center.

The Court rejected the establishment clause challenge in *Lynch* and held that the display did not compel or seek to compel adherence to any religious belief and did not violate the establishment clause.

The way in which the Court put the issue to be decided in *Lynch* is significant for today's case. The Court said that the issue for decision in *Lynch* was whether the establishment clause prohibits a municipality from including a creche or nativity scene in its annual Christmas display. That is how the Court began its opinion.

Narrator: Buscemi outlined the facts of the two displays.

Buscemi:This case is here on certiorari to the Third Circuit and it involves displays in the Allegheny County Courthouse and in the City-County Building which is directly across the street from the Allegheny County Courthouse in downtown Pittsburgh. The Allegheny County Courthouse display consists of a nativity scene which is surrounded by Christmas trees, poinsettia plants, wreaths on the windows behind the staircase, and is used as the site for a choral program that takes place throughout the Christmas season each year.

I might add, just so that the facts are clear, the second display is in the front of the City-County Building. It consists of a 45-foot Christmas tree. There is an 18-foot menorah attached to the pillar next to the Christmas tree. And there are—there is a sign from the mayor of the city of Pittsburgh, the text of which is reprinted in the briefs—talks about a salute to liberty and a reminder that the festive lights remind us that we are the keepers of the flame of liberty and our legacy of freedom.

Narrator: Christians and Jews are the two major religious groups in Pittsburgh. But many residents belong to other faiths. Justice Antonin Scalia presses Buscemi on this issue.

Scalia: What does the city do for Moslems? I don't know what an equivalently important celebration for Moslems would be—Ramadan, I don't think they celebrate Ramadan. It's a penitential season. But—

Buscemi: I'm not aware that—

Scalia: Pick a Moslem holiday. What if it were shown that the city here did not put up a similar display for the Moslem holiday?
Buscemi: I'm not aware that the city does put up a similar display for any holiday. One of the named respondents in this case is a Moslem, Mr. Tunador. He testified at the hearing in this case that the Moslem faith does not use outward symbols and, indeed, regards them as improper.

Scalia: Uh-huh.

Buscemi: So, just to answer your specific question—

Scalia: Well, pick another faith. Or make one up. You see my point. In order to avoid endorsing or appearing to favor one sect or religion over another, which I think the Constitution does not permit, does the city have to do this for every group?

Buscemi: The key point in the *Lynch* case and the key point in my answer to your question would be the Christmas holiday season itself. That is, distinction that I would make between this case and the case that you pose is that Christmas has already been recognized as a national and a state holiday. Christmas—and that is, in fact, the central thrust of the Court's opinion in *Lynch*.

Christmas, with its name derived from Christ and Christ's mass, has been recognized as a holiday. It's celebrated. The public employees are paid for not— even though they don't work on that day. And the recognition of the historical origins of the holiday was seen by the Court in *Lynch* as having, at least in part, a secular purpose.

Scalia: Well, that explains the creche but not the menorah.

Buscemi: The menorah, I think, Your Honor, is part and parcel of the holiday season, as it is celebrated by the residents of Pittsburgh. And that, indeed, is what was said by the district court in this case, and it was also what was testified to by the witnesses called by petitioners in the case.

The Chanukah holiday occurs on [the] calendar at approximately the time of Christmas. The menorah was designed to—for the purposes set forth in the mayor's message, to remind the people in Pittsburgh of the light of liberty and our legacy of freedom, and there was a secular component to that symbol.

Narrator: Peter Buscemi limited his argument to the nativity scene in the county courthouse. He yields the podium to Nathan Lewin, who defends the menorah display for Chabad. The Jewish community is divided in this case. Several Reform Jewish groups oppose the menorah display, while Orthodox groups support it.

Lewin: Mr. Chief Justice, and may it please the Court. The irony of this case, insofar as it applies to the menorah, is that an apparently successful effort on the part of the city of Pittsburgh to demonstrate to its population neutrality with regard to all religions, by displaying a symbol which is religious as well as nonreligious to the Jewish community, is being attacked as violating the establishment clause.

The holiday season that is involved here is, of course, a season which is recognized throughout the United States, and throughout the world indeed, but principally because its focus is a day that has become a secular holiday but has very substantial religious overtones to the majority population in this country. It is not, from the vantage point of the Jewish faith, a time of a principal holiday that Jews celebrate. It happens to be a time when there is also a minor Jewish festival, which is the festival of Chanukah.

And, therefore, to demonstrate to the citizens of Pittsburgh its respect for minority faiths, the city erected immediately adjacent to a very large Christmas tree—and we have a photograph at page 4 of our petition of the scene—a forty-five-foot-high Christmas tree. Immediately adjacent to that, an eighteen-foot-high menorah. And we submit that, given the context, that is a perfectly appropriate and permissible educational effort on the part of the state.

Narrator: Justice John Paul Stevens picks up the line of questions that Justice Scalia had asked Buscemi about minority religions.

Stevens: If then you have two religions represented, would you have a constitutional obligation to satisfy the request of a third or fourth and a fifth that might have different—pagan symbols or whatever they might be?

Lewin: We think that a city that has a place, such as the steps of city hall or something, where it could put other symbols, should not discriminate among religions and should—

Stevens: Then, how large—

Lewin:—in fact—

Stevens:—how large—

Lewin:—put other symbols there as well.

Stevens: How large must the religious group be to be entitled to that kind of representation?

Lewin: Well, frankly, I think a religious group that is a bona fide religious group—it needn't be very large. It may say, at that time, we would like to have some indication of our faith, at that time.

Stevens: I suppose three or four persons who sincerely believed in the particular faith would be sufficient.

Lewin: Well, again—

Stevens: Well, why not?

Lewin: I think it's—

Stevens: Why not?

Lewin: It's—

Stevens: Is this a majority rule kind of thing?

Lewin: No, I don't—it's not a majority rule, Justice Stevens. But I think it's really a question—I think an impracticality—

Stevens: I mean, there can be a very large religion from, you know, another country where they have only three or four representatives in Pittsburgh, but they may feel just as deeply about it.

Lewin: And I think that for—indeed, if, for example, the city of Pittsburgh had a public forum which was open to religious faiths to conduct meetings on, it would be guided by the same standard.

Narrator: No one disputes that the nativity scene is religious for all Christians. Lewin asks the justices to separate the creche from the menorah. He faces a skeptical question.

Court: Is it not correct that the whole premise of your argument is that the creche itself conveys a religious message?

Lewin: The creche conveys a religious message. We believe the Christmas tree contains an element of a religious message. And the menorah is—conveys a religious message although we—there is evidence in the record that the menorah has significance other than religious significance as well.

Narrator: Roslyn Litman practices law in Pittsburgh and serves on the ACLU's national board. Like Peter Buscemi, she discusses the *Lynch* case, and tries to distinguish it from the Pittsburgh displays. She fields questions from Chief Justice Rehnquist and Justices Harry Blackmun and Antonin Scalia.

Litman: Mr. Chief Justice, and may it please the Court. The issue posed—the question posed in this case is whether the establishment clause limits at all the government's display of religious symbols during not only Christmas Day but during the period, in this case, of forty-five days, including, preceding, and following Christmas.

Now, the view taken by the petitioners, the city, and county, apparently is that somehow by reason of the fact that Congress has recognized that December 25th is a federal holiday, and because presidents have made proclamations, and the state has recognized it as a state holiday, that somehow the action trumps the establishment clause.

We don't think there is any necessity for this Court to take that view. We don't think this Court said that in *Lynch*, and it is perfectly appropriate to view these recognitions of Christmas as a holiday in terms of the states being allowed to celebrate its secular aspects, but not in terms of, as counsel has argued, having a mass in the courthouse, having symbols in the courthouse.

I think it's important for this Court to understand that there are two displays here. Justice Stevens, in terms of your question about does the creche require the menorah, the Court should understand that the creche stands as one. It is in the courthouse and it is in the most prominent and most public place in the courthouse.

The second display is the display involving the menorah. That is in another building by another governmental body. The creche is the county, the menorah is by the city of Pittsburgh—and that menorah is not on the steps of, but on the face of the building itself.

Rehnquist: And it is with the Christmas tree?

Litman: That is exactly correct, Justice Rehnquist. Now, we take from *Lynch* that the key question in evaluating governmental displays is whether the display amounts to government endorsement of religion, of a particular—or of a particular religious message. That is to say, does that display send a message to nonadherents that they are outsiders, not full members of the political community, and the accompanying message to adherents, that they are insiders, favored members of the political community?

This Court in *Lynch* held that a nativity scene did not do that. These displays do, and they do so for reasons that are constitutionally important and meaningful. And I'd like to just briefly identify three of those. First—

Blackmun: Well, the two displays are somewhat different, aren't they, Mrs. Litman?

Litman: They are totally different displays, Justice Blackmun.

Blackmun: But you take the position that you're supporting both of them in your position?

Litman: We take the same position as to both of them. That is, that both of them violate the establishment clause. Unlike *Lynch*, these displays are at government headquarters where the presence of government is pervasive and unmistakable. Not only that, the buildings are courthouses much like this one where certain classes of citizens are compelled to come, under compulsion of law, and which constitutes buildings, we would think that, irrespective of whether they bear a sign such as this one does, "Equal Access Under Law," that every citizen should come to and does come to with the expectation—

Scalia: Well, where—

Litman:—that he or she will be treated equally, irrespective of religion.

Scalia: Where was it in *Lynch*?

Litman: In—

Scalia: I had the impression it was in a place that it would be even more difficult to avoid.

Litman: It—it—

Scalia: And it was clear that that was a governmental display, wasn't it? You really want us to make a distinction on the basis of whether it's in a—on government property even though the display is obviously government display, is obviously in a place where a lot of people have to see it?

Litman: Justice Scalia, I think that the decision in this case should hinge on the confluence, the combination of all three factors. And that is to say whether here, in these buildings where you have government engaged in—what the Court said in *Ball* was a symbolic embrace between church and state where you have the kind of fusion of church and state that this Court has struck down in *Larson*. And where you have symbols that are undilutedly, intensely religious.

Narrator: Justices Kennedy and Scalia continue the questioning.

Kennedy: If we ban Christmas carols in all public buildings, could that be interpreted reasonably by some people as hostility to religion?
Litman: I think, Justice Kennedy, that there comes a point at which this Court must say that the Establishment Clause does prohibit government from making certain religious pronouncements. That point is not always easy to reach. In this case it is because it is so far to whatever the point should be. But, obviously, in cases there are balances required between free exercise and establishment. What makes this case easy is there is no tension between free exercise and establishment. In this case, this is not accommodation. This is promotion. This is not neutrality. This is favoritism. And to address the question of would the government have to put up a menorah of a certain size, or the question of Justice Scalia of what does the government do for Moslems, the answer is the government does nothing for Moslems. And even the—that is, the county, and the city of Pittsburgh doesn't either. But the display of the city of Pittsburgh, this frankly Judeo-Christian symbol, certainly conveys—

Scalia: Did Moslems request that something be done for them?

Litman: No, they did not, Your Honor. But that brings into question the issue of in order for a government to be neutral, as this Court has insisted it must be, may it take the position that it can sit back and wait for religions to ask?

Scalia: Well, certainly one thing—one way it could justify doing that is, we were told by opposing counsel that the Moslems simply do not want something like that. So that perhaps if they don't ask, it means they are not in the least bit desirous of having a public display.

Litman: That might be the case, but what the record showed in this case, what

Malik Tunador testified, was that in his religion personification of the deity—and he included Jesus Christ as one of the figures that one should not profane—that personification by figures is a profanation of his symbol.

Narrator: Justice Scalia poses a final question.

Scalia: I don't understand your endorsement point, at least with respect to the Christmas tree and the menorah. How could you possibly be endorsing either Christianity or Judaism when you have symbols of either? Now, I can understand how you might say you are endorsing religiousness by acknowledging the religiousness of the people, and this is a significant religious holiday for both of these groups. But as for endorsing one sect rather than another, how could you possibly be?

Litman: We think what you're endorsing in that case, Justice Scalia, is Judeo-Christian symbols that totally ignore in an appalling lack of appreciation for the Moslems, the Hindus, the Buddhists in the population of Pittsburgh, the ever-increasing number of Asian-Americans whom we are in the process of welcoming to our country who don't adhere to the Judeo-Christian symbols, but who are nevertheless part of what is, we believe, embraced and protected by the prohibitions of the Establishment Clause.

And we think that by adhering to the concept that government must remain neutral—we have managed—this country has managed over the last two hundred years to preserve a very important right that the Framers set for us when they wrote the First Amendment. And to say, as counsel does, that we can now kick over all of the jurisprudence of this Court on the establishment clause, that suddenly we put in a new provision talking about coercion—and he neglects to mention to the Court that the same kind of indirect coercion is present here, as the Court found in Engel—but this Court has never required coercion.

Their interpretation means that this Court would say that the Framers, in enacting the establishment clause, enacted a total redundancy because, of course, it would have no meaning.

Narrator: On July 3, 1989, the Supreme Court decided the nativity scene and menorah cases in a way that satisfied only one of the nine justices. Spread across five separate opinions that cover more than 100 pages, the Court's profound division over issues of religion reflects the difficulty of accommodating religious majorities, minorities, and nonbelievers.

Four justices voted to ban both the nativity scene and menorah from public display. Four other justices would allow both to stand during the holiday season. Justice Harry Blackmun cast the deciding vote. Allegheny County officials must remove the nativity scene, but the menorah remains next to the Christmas tree. His fellow justices picked over the parts of Blackmun's opinion like picky eaters faced with a strange menu. Two sections of his opinion found no takers on the entire Court.

Blackmun reached back to the *Lynch* case for his central propositions that "the government's use of religious symbolism is unconstitutional if it has the effect of endorsing religious beliefs," and that the effect of each display "depends on its context." The nativity creche, standing alone in the courthouse lobby, gives the county's endorsement of its Christian message. On the other hand, placing a menorah next to a Christmas tree creates an "overall holiday setting" that is primarily secular in nature.

Justice William Brennan agreed with Blackmun that the nativity scene did not belong in the courthouse, but differed on the menorah. He wrote that "the menorah is indisputably a religious symbol, used ritually in a celebration that has deep religious significance." Justice Anthony Kennedy wrote for three colleagues who would allow both displays. Kennedy chided the five justices who evicted the nativity scene for displaying "hostility toward religion" and failing to acknowledge that government support for religion is "an accepted part of our political and cultural heritage."

The Allegheny County case shows that Thomas Jefferson's famous "wall of separation" between church and state is now more like a picket fence, with loose slats and many gates. Government officials now make sure that Santa Claus and Christmas trees surround each religious display in public buildings and parks. This compromise may not fill everyone with holiday cheer, but the Supreme Court has never pleased everyone in religion cases.

EDITED SUPREME COURT OPINIONS
County of Allegheny v. ACLU
Argued February 22, 1989—Decided July 3, 1989

JUSTICE BLACKMUN announced the judgment of the Court and delivered the opinion of the Court with respect to Parts III-A, IV, and V, an opinion with respect to Parts I and II, in which JUSTICE STEVENS and JUSTICE O'CONNOR join, an opinion with respect to Part III-B, in which JUSTICE STEVENS joins, an opinion with respect to Part VII, in which JUSTICE O'CONNOR joins, and an opinion with respect to Part VI.

This litigation concerns the constitutionality of two recurring holiday displays located on public property in downtown Pittsburgh. The first is a creche placed on the Grand Staircase of the Allegheny County Courthouse. The second is a Chanukah menorah placed just outside the City-County Building, next to a Christmas tree and a sign saluting liberty. The Court of Appeals for the Third Circuit ruled that each display violates the Establishment Clause of the First Amendment because each has the impermissible effect of endorsing religion. 842 F. 2d 655 (1988). We agree that the creche display has that unconstitutional effect but reverse the Court of Appeals' judgment regarding the menorah display....

We turn first to the county's creche display. There is no doubt, of course, that the creche itself is capable of communicating a religious message....

Indeed, the creche in this lawsuit uses words, as well as the picture of the nativity scene, to make its religious meaning unmistakably clear. "Glory to God in the Highest!" says the angel in the creche—Glory to God because of the birth of Jesus. This praise to God in Christian terms is indisputably religious—indeed sectarian—just as it is when said in the Gospel or in a church service.

Under the Court's holding in *Lynch*, the effect of a creche display turns on its setting. Here, unlike in *Lynch*, nothing in the context of the display detracts from the creche's religious message. The *Lynch* display comprised a series of figures and objects, each group of which had its own focal point. Santa's house and his reindeer were objects of attention separate from the creche, and had their specific visual story to tell. Similarly, whatever a "talking" wishing well may be, it obviously was a center of attention separate from the creche. Here, in contrast, the creche stands alone: it is the single element of the display on the Grand Staircase.

The floral decoration surrounding the creche cannot be viewed as somehow equivalent to the secular symbols in the overall *Lynch* display. The floral frame, like all good frames, serves only to draw one's attention to the message inside the frame. The floral decoration surrounding the creche contributes to, rather than detracts from, the endorsement of religion conveyed by the creche....

Furthermore, the creche sits on the Grand Staircase, the "main" and "most beautiful part" of the building that is the seat of county government. No viewer could reasonably think that it occupies this location without the support and approval of the government. Thus, by permitting the "display of the creche in this particular physical setting," *Lynch*, 465 U.S., at 692 (O'CONNOR, J., concurring), the county sends an unmistakable message that it supports and promotes the Christian praise to God that is the creche's religious message.

The fact that the creche bears a sign disclosing its ownership by a Roman Catholic organization does not alter this conclusion. On the contrary, the sign simply demonstrates that the government is endorsing the religious message of that organization, rather than communicating a message of its own. But the Establishment Clause does not limit only the religious content of the government's own communications. It also prohibits the government's support and promotion of religious communications by religious organizations....

Finally, the county argues that it is sufficient to validate the display of the creche on the Grand Staircase that the display celebrates Christmas, and Christmas is a national holiday. This argument obviously proves too much. It would allow the celebration of the Eucharist inside a courthouse on Christmas Eve. While the county may have doubts about the constitutional status of celebrating the Eucharist inside the courthouse under the government's auspices,…this Court does not. The government may acknowledge Christmas as a cultural phenomenon, but under the First Amendment it may not observe it as a Christian holy day by suggesting that people praise God for the birth of Jesus….

In sum, *Lynch* teaches that government may celebrate Christmas in some manner and form, but not in a way that endorses Christian doctrine. Here, Allegheny County has transgressed this line. It has chosen to celebrate Christmas in a way that has the effect of endorsing a patently Christian message: Glory to God for the birth of Jesus Christ. Under *Lynch*, and the rest of our cases, nothing more is required to demonstrate a violation of the Establishment Clause. The display of the creche in this context, therefore, must be permanently enjoined….

The display of the Chanukah menorah in front of the City-County Building may well present a closer constitutional question. The menorah, one must recognize, is a religious symbol: it serves to commemorate the miracle of the oil as described in the Talmud. But the menorah's message is not exclusively religious. The menorah is the primary visual symbol for a holiday that, like Christmas, has both religious and secular dimensions.

Moreover, the menorah here stands next to a Christmas tree and a sign saluting liberty. While no challenge has been made here to the display of the tree and the sign, their presence is obviously relevant in determining the effect of the menorah's display. The necessary result of placing a menorah next to a Christmas tree is to create an "overall holiday setting" that represents both Christmas and Chanukah—two holidays, not one….

The mere fact that Pittsburgh displays symbols of both Christmas and Chanukah does not end the constitutional inquiry. If the city celebrates both Christmas and Chanukah as religious holidays, then it violates the Establishment Clause. The simultaneous endorsement of Judaism and Christianity is no less constitutionally infirm than the endorsement of Christianity alone.

Conversely, if the city celebrates both Christmas and Chanukah as secular holidays, then its conduct is beyond the reach of the Establishment Clause. Because government may celebrate Christmas as a secular holiday, it follows that government may also acknowledge Chanukah as a secular holiday. Simply put, it would be a form of discrimination against Jews to allow Pittsburgh to celebrate Christmas as a cultural tradition while simultaneously disallowing the city's acknowledgment of Chanukah as a contemporaneous cultural tradition….

Accordingly, the relevant question for Establishment Clause purposes is whether the combined display of the tree, the sign, and the menorah has the effect of endorsing both Christian and Jewish faiths, or rather simply recognizes that both Christmas and Chanukah are part of the same winter holiday season, which has attained a secular status in our society. Of the two interpretations of this particular display, the latter seems far more plausible and is also in line with *Lynch*.

The Christmas tree, unlike the menorah, is not itself a religious symbol. Although Christmas trees once carried religious connotations, today they typify the secular celebration of Christmas....

Numerous Americans place Christmas trees in their homes without subscribing to Christian religious beliefs, and when the city's tree stands alone in front of the City-County Building, it is not considered an endorsement of Christian faith. Indeed, a 40-foot Christmas tree was one of the objects that validated the creche in *Lynch*. The widely accepted view of the Christmas tree as the preeminent secular symbol of the Christmas holiday season serves to emphasize the secular component of the message communicated by other elements of an accompanying holiday display, including the Chanukah menorah....

Lynch v. *Donnelly* confirms, and in no way repudiates, the long-standing constitutional principle that government may not engage in a practice that has the effect of promoting or endorsing religious beliefs. The display of the creche in the county courthouse has this unconstitutional effect. The display of the menorah in front of the City-County Building, however, does not have this effect, given its "particular physical setting."

The judgment of the Court of Appeals is affirmed in part and reversed in part, and the cases are remanded for further proceedings.

It is so ordered.

JUSTICE BRENNAN, with whom JUSTICE MARSHALL and JUSTICE STEVENS join, concurring in part and dissenting in part.

According to the Court, the creche display sends a message endorsing Christianity because the creche itself bears a religious meaning, because an angel in the display carries a banner declaring "Glory to God in the highest!" and because the floral decorations surrounding the creche highlight it rather than secularize it. The display of a Christmas tree and Chanukah menorah, in contrast, is said to show no endorsement of a particular faith or faiths, or of religion in general, because the Christmas tree is a secular symbol which brings out the secular elements of the menorah....

And, JUSTICE BLACKMUN concludes, even though the menorah has religious aspects, its display reveals no endorsement of religion because no other symbol could have been used to represent the secular aspects of the holiday of Chanukah without mocking its celebration.

Rather than endorsing religion, therefore, the display merely demonstrates that "Christmas is not the only traditional way of observing the winter-holiday season," and confirms our "cultural diversity."

Thus, the decision as to the menorah rests on three premises: the Christmas tree is a secular symbol; Chanukah is a holiday with secular dimensions, symbolized by the menorah; and the government may promote pluralism by sponsoring or condoning displays having strong religious associations on its property. None of these is sound....

The first step toward JUSTICE BLACKMUN'S conclusion is the claim that, despite its religious origins, the Christmas tree is a secular symbol....

In my view, this attempt to take the "Christmas" out of the Christmas tree is unconvincing. That the tree may, without controversy, be deemed a secular symbol if found alone does mean that it will be so seen when combined with other symbols or objects. Indeed, JUSTICE BLACKMUN admits that "the tree is capable of taking on a religious significance if it is decorated with religious symbols."...

The second premise on which today's decision rests is the notion that Chanukah is a partly secular holiday, for which the menorah can serve as a secular symbol. It is no surprise and no anomaly that Chanukah has historical and societal roots that range beyond the purely religious. I would venture that most, if not all, major religious holidays have beginnings and enjoy histories studded with figures, events, and practices that are not strictly religious. It does not seem to me that the mere fact that Chanukah shares this kind of background makes it a secular holiday in any meaningful sense. The menorah is indisputably a religious symbol, used ritually in a celebration that has deep religious significance. That, in my view, is all that need be said. Whatever secular practices the holiday of Chanukah has taken on in its contemporary observance are beside the point....

Nor do I discern the theory under which the government is permitted to appropriate particular holidays and religious objects to its own use in celebrating "pluralism." The message of the sign announcing a "Salute to Liberty" is not religious, but patriotic; the government's use of religion to promote its own cause is undoubtedly offensive to those whose religious beliefs are not bound up with their attitude toward the Nation.

The uncritical acceptance of a message of religious pluralism also ignores the extent to which even that message may offend. Many religious faiths are hostile to each other, and indeed, refuse even to participate in ecumenical services designed to demonstrate the very pluralism JUSTICES BLACKMUN and

O'CONNOR extol. To lump the ritual objects and holidays of religions together without regard to their attitudes toward such inclusiveness, or to decide which religions should be excluded because of the possibility of offense, is not a benign or beneficent celebration of pluralism: it is instead an interference in religious matters precluded by the Establishment Clause....

JUSTICE KENNEDY, with whom THE CHIEF JUSTICE, JUSTICE WHITE, and JUSTICE SCALIA join, concurring in the judgment in part and dissenting in part.

The majority holds that the County of Allegheny violated the Establishment Clause by displaying a creche in the county courthouse, because the "principal or primary effect" of the display is to advance religion within the meaning of Lemon v. Kurtzman, 403 U.S. 602, 612–613 (1971). This view of the Establishment Clause reflects an unjustified hostility toward religion, a hostility inconsistent with our history and our precedents, and I dissent from this holding. The creche display is constitutional, and, for the same reasons, the display of a menorah by the city of Pittsburgh is permissible as well....

Rather than requiring government to avoid any action that acknowledges or aids religion, the Establishment Clause permits government some latitude in recognizing and accommodating the central role religion plays in our society....

Any approach less sensitive to our heritage would border on latent hostility toward religion, as it would require government in all its multifaceted roles to acknowledge only the secular, to the exclusion and so to the detriment of the religious. A categorical approach would install federal courts as jealous guardians of an absolute "wall of separation," sending a clear message of disapproval. In this century, as the modern administrative state expands to touch the lives of its citizens in such diverse ways and redirects their financial choices through programs of its own, it is difficult to maintain the fiction that requiring government to avoid all assistance to religion can in fairness be viewed as serving the goal of neutrality....

There is no suggestion here that the government's power to coerce has been used to further the interests of Christianity or Judaism in any way. No one was compelled to observe or participate in any religious ceremony or activity. Neither the city nor the county contributed significant amounts of tax money to serve the cause of one religious faith. The creche and the menorah are purely passive symbols of religious holidays. Passersby who disagree with the message conveyed by these displays are free to ignore them, or even to turn their backs, just as they are free to do when they disagree with any other form of government speech....

The approach adopted by the majority contradicts important values embodied in the Clause. Obsessive, implacable resistance to all but the most carefully scripted and secularized forms of accommodation requires this Court to act as a censor, issuing national decrees as to what is orthodox and what is not. What is orthodox, in this context, means what is secular; the only Christmas the State can acknowledge is one in which references to religion have been held to a minimum. The Court thus lends its assistance to an Orwellian rewriting of history as many understand it. I can conceive of no judicial function more antithetical to the First Amendment....

A further contradiction arises from the majority's approach, for the Court also assumes the difficult and inappropriate task of saying what every religious symbol means. Before studying these cases, I had not known the full history of the menorah, and I suspect the same was true of my colleagues. More important, this history was, and is, likely unknown to the vast majority of people of all faiths who saw the symbol displayed in Pittsburgh. Even if the majority is quite right about the history of the menorah, it hardly follows that this same history informed the observers' view of the symbol and the reason for its presence. This Court is ill equipped to sit as a national theology board, and I question both the wisdom and the constitutionality of its doing so. Indeed, were I required to choose between the approach taken by the majority and a strict separationist view, I would have to respect the consistency of the latter.

The suit before us is admittedly a troubling one. It must be conceded that, however neutral the purpose of the city and county, the eager proselytizer may,seek to use these symbols for his own ends. The urge to use them to teach or to taunt is always present. It is also true that some devout adherents of Judaism or Christianity may be as offended by the holiday display as are nonbelievers, if not more so. To place these religious symbols in a common hallway or sidewalk, where they may be ignored or even insulted, must be distasteful to many who cherish their meaning.

For these reasons, I might have voted against installation of these particular displays were I a local legislative official. But we have no jurisdiction over matters of taste within the realm of constitutionally permissible discretion. Our role is enforcement of a written Constitution. In my view, the principles of the Establishment Clause and our Nation's historic traditions of diversity and pluralism allow communities to make reasonable judgments respecting the accommodation or acknowledgment of holidays with both cultural and religious aspects. No constitutional violation occurs when they do so by displaying a symbol of the holiday's religious origins.

Barnes v.
Glen Theatre, Inc.

501 U.S. 560 (1991)

Darlene Miller was a "go-go" dancer at the Kitty Kat Lounge in South Bend, Indiana, and Gayle Sutro danced in a coin-operated booth at the nearby Chippewa Bookstore. Both women were forced by Indiana's "public indecency" law to wear "pasties" and "G-strings" to cover their nipples and pubic areas. They felt that shedding their skimpy costumes and dancing nude would encourage patrons to spend more on drinks and tips. Supported by their striptease club owners, Darlene and Gayle sued the crusading county prosecutor, Michael Barnes, who had directed raids of clubs with nude dancers. They claimed the Indiana law infringed their First Amendment right to "expression" of an erotic message; the state argued that nude dancing promoted prostitution and other social evils. By a vote of 5-to-4, the Supreme Court upheld the law as a means to protect "morals and public order," over the dissenting view that nude dancing before "consenting adults" is a form of protected expression.

Counsel for petitioner: Wayne E. Uhl, Deputy Attorney General of Indiana
Counsel for respondent: Bruce J. Ennis, Washington, D.C.

Chief Justice Rehnquist: We'll hear argument next in No. 90-26, *Michael Barnes v. Glen Theatre, Inc.*

Narrator: It's January 8, 1991. We're in the chamber of the United States Supreme Court in Washington, D.C. Chief Justice William Rehnquist has called for argument a case the Framers of the Bill of Rights probably never anticipated. This case began in 1985, in South Bend, Indiana, not far from the tree-shaded campus of Notre Dame University. Darlene Miller sells drinks and dances at the Kitty Kat Lounge, and Gayle Sutro dances in a coin-operated booth at the Chippewa Bookstore. Both women dance in the skimpiest costume of "pasties" and "G-strings." But they feel they could make more money, in drink commissions and tips, by dancing nude.

Darlene and Gayle, and other striptease dancers in South Bend, are afraid to shed their tiny costumes. Prodded by Michael Barnes, the crusading county prosecutor, local police have raided several clubs and arrested dancers for performing nude. Indiana law, like that of most states, prohibits nudity in public places. A group of club owners and dancers sued Barnes and other officials in federal court, claiming the law violates the dancers' right to free speech under the First Amendment.

This case bounced up and down the lower federal courts for six years before it reached the Supreme Court. A federal judge struck down the nudity law as "overbroad" for banning nude dancing in clubs where only adult customers were admitted. After an appeals court reversed this ruling, another judge viewed a videotape of the striptease dancers, from fully clothed to totally nude. He decided that nude dancing was "not expressive activity" protected by the First Amendment. The appeals court reversed that ruling, holding that nude dancing communicates an "emotional" theme of "eroticism and sensuality."

County attorney Barnes asked the Supreme Court to uphold the nudity law, arguing in his brief that it was necessary to prevent "adultery, prostitution, degradation of women, sexual assault, and other crime." The lawyers for Darlene Miller and Gayle Sutro responded that nude dancing conveys the message that "the human body is not shameful" and the dancers' feelings about "human life and movement." Both sides may have overstated their cases, leaving the Supreme Court to decide if the First Amendment covers a naked body in a striptease club. Chief Justice Rehnquist welcomes the Indiana deputy attorney general, Wayne Uhl, who defends the nudity law. He spends several minutes sparring with Justice Antonin Scalia.

Rehnquist: Mr. Uhl.

Uhl: Thank you, Mr. Chief Justice, and may it please the Court. In Indiana under Indiana code, Section 35-45-4-1, a person cannot leave his home naked and walk down the street. He cannot give a political speech in a park without—

Scalia: Without being in trouble.

Uhl: That's correct. [General laughter.] He would get in trouble, Your Honor, if he walked into a public place such as a bar or a bookstore without his clothes on. Once inside the bar, he could not walk naked up and down the aisles in the bar, nor could he sit down at a table without his clothes on, nor could he stand up on the bar or on a stage at the front of that public establishment without his clothes on.

Scalia: He can evidently sing in an opera without his clothes on.

Uhl: Well, our point, Your Honor, is that the plaintiffs say that if he starts dancing when he gets up on that stage or up on that bar, then he can do anything—or anything that can be defined as dancing—then he's privileged under the First Amendment to appear naked, notwithstanding Indiana's public indecency statute.

Scalia: What about seeing an opera? Am I correct in my understanding of what Indiana law is? That there is an exception to the nudity law somehow for artistic performances, is that right?

Uhl: The Indiana Supreme Court, in order to avoid an overbreadth challenge, has held that the statute does not affect activity which cannot be restricted by the First Amendment. And the term that the court used in that case was "a larger form of expression." So—

Scalia: Which includes opera but not go-go dancing?

Uhl: That's correct, Your Honor.

Scalia: Is there-where does that come from?

Uhl: Your Honor, the court looked at cases such as *Southeastern Promotions* where this Court implied that the production of *Hair*, for example, needed to include nudity. And I think, drawing from that line of cases, presumed that the First Amendment—

Scalia: It is the good-taste clause of the Constitution? How does one draw that line between Salome and the Kitty Kat Lounge? I don't—

Uhl: The line is drawn the same way the line is drawn anytime conduct is involved, and that is whether or not the conduct communicates. If the conduct communicates, then the conduct is speech. If the conduct does not communicate, then the conduct is not speech.

Scalia: Communicates what? An idea?

Uhl: Communicates a particularized message or an idea.

Scalia: What about a particularized message and an idea of sensuality?

Uhl: That could be communicated. However, the plaintiffs in this case did not establish—did not carry their burden of proving that that was the particularized message that they were sending by their dancing.

Scalia: Because they were not good enough dancers?

Uhl: No, it didn't have anything to do with the quality of the dance, Your Honor. It had to do with—

Scalia: Well, could a dance communicate that?

Uhl: Yes, a dance could communicate that.

Scalia: But this one didn't?

Uhl: These dances did not.

Scalia: Because they were not good enough dancers?

Uhl: No, Your Honor, it wasn't the quality of the dancing. Go-go dancing can be good or bad, but in either instance it's [not] speech.

Narrator: Chief Justice Rehnquist cut into this verbal fandango.

Rehnquist: Well, Mr. Uhl, are you conceding that if conduct does communicate, then it can't be regulated at all under the First Amendment?

Uhl: No, Your Honor, our second issue in the case is that even if this dance is speech, then it can be restricted under the First Amendment. And basically, we've drawn on two lines of cases for that argument. First, we've argued that our statute is a general criminal prohibition on public nudity that applies—that is not directed at speech and is content neutral in the sense that it is—irrelevant what message might be sent by the conduct.

Narrator: Justices Byron White and Sandra O'Connor joined the dance.

White: [S]uppose the dancers were clothed and suppose the state of Indiana or a police official attempted to prohibit that performance, a clothed performance, would the First Amendment protect the performer?

Uhl: No, not these performances in this case.

White: Then you're saying it would be permissible to pass a statute prohibiting tap dancing?

Uhl: Unless tap dancing were shown to be speech under the First Amendment, that's correct.

White: Well, but under your view it doesn't convey any particular message so you could prohibit it.

Uhl: That's correct, Your Honor.

White: Well, you might not be able to prohibit under some other provision in the Constitution. You just say it wouldn't be protected by the First Amendment.

Uhl: That's correct. Obviously due-process and equal-protection concerns would be—

O'Connor: Could the state prohibit rock music?

Uhl: Your Honor, this Court found in the *Ward* case that rock music is speech under the First Amendment, so no, it could not. But—

O'Connor: Well, how is it that music is protected but dance is not?

Uhl: Music is different—

O'Connor: Could you explain that?

Uhl: Music is different from dance in that the very nature of the medium is communicative. But by the definition of dance that's been submitted by the respondents—

O'Connor: Do you think some of the rock music played in the *Ward* case conveyed a message? [General laughter.]

Uhl: An artistic message.

O'Connor: An artistic message?

Uhl: An artistic message. Yes, Your Honor. Whereas not all dance conveys an artistic message.

O'Connor: Well, I suggest not all music does either.

Uhl: That may be a case-by-case determination and this Court hasn't addressed that except in *Ward* to say that music in general is communicative and therefore is speech under the First Amendment.

O'Connor: Well, dance in general might be communicative under that test, might it not?

Uhl: We would resist that, Your Honor, because dance can be so broadly defined as to include perhaps what I'm doing here today. Dance can be any—

Court: Song and dance. [General laughter.]

Uhl: Well, not that kind of song and dance. [General laughter].

Narrator: Uhl waits for the laughter to subside, and continues.

Uhl: The respondents have suggested that a production in which nudes simply stand nude on a stage would be dance or that—if someone were to simply—

rhythm is not important to the definition of a dance. Improvisation can be dance according to the respondents. Any movement can be defined as dance. And if this Court were to hold that all dance as it's defined there is speech, then the First Amendment would be trivialized to include any kind of movement or motion that expresses some kind of emotion.

Narrator: A popular slogan of the Sixties was "the medium is the message." One justice wants to know if this applies to nude dancing.

Court: If we were to find that an emotional communication as opposed to a particularized message were protectable, what would you then say to the argument on the other side that they simply cannot communicate the message in any other way except by nude dancing? I think what they're saying in effect is that [this is] some kind of a medium-is-the-message argument.

Uhl: If the medium is the message, Your Honor, then it's our contention that the nudity is not an essential part of that particular medium. The dance can be communicated just as effectively, or almost as effectively, with pasties and G-strings covering the vital parts of the body that are at issue under the statute. And it's our contention that alternative means of communication are open to these plaintiffs and that the mere requirement of—that the certain parts of the body be covered is not essential to their communication.

Court: So you're saying they cannot define their activity by saying the medium and the message are identical and thereby evade the possibility of otherwise permissible First Amendment regulation?

Uhl: That's correct, Your Honor. In one sense their claim that nudity is an inherent part of their dance is no different than someone who might be putting on a play and decide that the use of marijuana during the play is also protected because it's connected with this protected play. I think the Court would immediately reject that argument out of hand, that that kind of criminal conduct, even though it's in the context of a protected production, can be criminalized by a state.

Narrator: Wayne Uhl ended his argument by claiming that Darlene Miller and Gayle Sutro could express their erotic message just as well in pasties and G-strings. Their lawyer, Bruce Ennis, disagreed.

Ennis: Mr. Chief Justice, and may it please the Court. Nude dancing is suffi-

ciently expressive to at least trigger First Amendment analysis for two independent reasons. First, nude dancing is expressive, because performance dance is
inherently expressive of emotions and ideas, and second, because nude dancing
communicates a particularized message of sensuality and eroticism. First, performance dance, like music, is one of the oldest forms of human communication and is inherently expressive of emotions and ideas. In *Ward*, this Court
found that music is expressive without bothering to determine whether the
music at issue did or did not communicate a particularized message. A particularized message test applied only to conduct that is not ordinarily expressive,
such as flag burning. Even that kind of conduct can be found expressive if in
context it communicates a particularized message. But the Court has never
used that test to determine whether marching or picketing or other traditionally considered expressive forms of activity are expressive or not. The Court's
decisions made clear that if expressive—if conduct is otherwise expressive and
protected by the First Amendment, the fact that the conduct involves nudity
does not shed that protection.

Narrator: Justice Scalia asked Ennis to define his terms.

Scalia: You began by using a term—was it dance performance?

Ennis: Performance dance. By that I mean dance which is intended as a performance in front of an audience, to distinguish that from recreational dance or
dancing at home in your own room.

Scalia: Suppose someone wanted to increase business at the car wash or in a bar
and they hired a woman and said, now, you sit in this glass case—and this is an
adults-only car wash. [General laughter.] You sit in this glass case and attract
the customers. Is that permitted?

Ennis: Your Honor, I think it would—if it was intended as expressive activity, if
it was performance dance.

Scalia: No, it's just what I said. The employer says this is the job, you sit up there.

Ennis: I think that that would trigger First Amendment analysis. Whether the
state could ban it or not would depend on the state's justifications.

Scalia: Well, suppose he said, I've heard the arguments in the Supreme Court
and you have to dance. And she said, I can't dance. And he said, just wander
around when the music starts to play. [General laughter.]

Ennis: Well, Your Honor—

Scalia: I mean, that's the point, isn't it? It's a question of what is performance dance. What is it?.

Ennis: What is performance dance is a question in this case. The main way that that is answered, if you'll look at the material cited in the briefs, *Encyclopedia Britannica* and others, is where there is an intention to perform in front of an audience through dancing. That the district court found as a fact, and that was not disputed here, that all of these respondents did intend to dance as communication and as expression.

Narrator: A question from Justice Scalia prompted Ennis to discuss cases that dealt with burning draft cards and the American flag.

Scalia: The statute here, Mr. Ennis, isn't addressed to dancing at all. It's addressed to public nudity.

Ennis: The statute in *O'Brien* was not—the statute in many of the cases, like the flag-burning cases, was not addressed to expressive activity on its face. It was addressed only to the conduct of burning or mutilating the flag.

Scalia: But the equivalent here would be addressing it to dancing. In the flag-burning case, the equivalent to what happened here would be a statute that banned burning anything in the street, a flag or anything else. And then people would have come in and said, well, you know, it's a ban on expression, because what I wanted to burn was a flag, and I think we would have said in the flag case—in fact I think we did say in dictum that if it was that kind of a statute it would be a totally different question. And it's that kind of a statute you have here.

Ennis: Justice Scalia—

Scalia: It's not nude dancing. It's not dancing. It's nudity, period.

Ennis: Justice Scalia, the Court's opinion in *O'Brien* and all the flag-burning cases uses the same analysis. It says the state must justify the application of an otherwise content-neutral statute to expressive activity for reasons unrelated to expression. In this case, you can look at the state's briefs. The state has acknowledged its fear that nude dancing is, quote, "likely to inspire patrons to solicit sex from performers or contemplate rape or adultery." The state has admitted it has concerns about the effect of nude dancing on attitudes toward women and has argued that it should be free to ban nude dancing because it, quote, "encourages activities which break down family structure and advocates adultery, licentiousness, prostitution, and crime."

Narrator: The next point Ennis made prompted questions that stemmed from the famous statement of Justice Oliver Wendell Holmes that "the most stringent protection of free speech would not protect a man in falsely shouting fire in a theatre."

Ennis: The state seems to feel that if nude dancing is artistic, it has one effect on the audience and does not incite the audience to prostitution, rape, or adultery, but that if nude dancing is not artistic, it does have that effect on the audience.

Court: I suppose there are some things the state can prohibit even if—just because it has an effect on the audience. What about shouting fire in a crowded room?

Ennis: Your Honor, I think that there are certainly some categorical exceptions to otherwise First Amendment protections that the state could argue here. They have not. That state's justifications here—they've said over and over again in their briefs, and in fact in the oral argument—

Court: Well, you just recited that the state thought that nude dancing would have some unsatisfactory [effect] on the audience and you say that's not permissible because that means it's really expressive.

Ennis: It means that it is a content-based statute.

Court: Well, what about fire? A fire in a theater?

Ennis: Fire in a theater has an effect regardless of whether the listeners agree or disagree with the message.

Court: Well, it depends exactly on what you say.

Ennis: Pardon me, Your Honor?

Court: It depends exactly on what you said. You said, fire, rather than no fire.

Ennis: Your Honor, I that there are—the distinction is that there—what the state is concerned about is that the consenting adults in the audience will agree with this message, will follow what they take the message to be, and will go out and have bad attitudes about women or commit prostitution, rape, or adultery. It depends upon the state—the listeners' reactions of being persuaded by the message that the state wants to suppress. That is not true in the shouting-fire-in-the-theater context. It doesn't matter whether the people in the theater think there's really a fire or not. There's a stampede and people get hurt. That's a very different case.

Narrator: Ennis argued that the Indiana law was "overbroad" and should be more narrowly drawn.

Ennis: One point I think is worth mentioning is that even if this decision is affirmed, the state of Indiana would be left with ample authority to regulate or perhaps prohibit nude dancing in a constitutional manner. The state could certainly prohibit all obscene dancing, whether in public or in private. It could—the state could certainly prohibit all obscene, nude dancing. That would not be affected by affirmance here. That state could certainly under the Twenty-first Amendment prohibit dancing where alcohol is served, whether the dancers are nude or clothed. The state could certainly regulate nude dancing under the *Sable* analysis in truly public places before unconsenting adults, captive audiences, or children.

Narrator: Ennis concluded with a reference to a case in which the Court struck down a conviction for wearing a jacket with the slogan, "Fuck the Draft" painted on it.

Ennis: In fact as Justice Harlan wrote in *Cohen v. California*, one man's lyric is another's vulgarity. And as Justice Harlan said, it is precisely because governments cannot make principled decisions between those kinds of communications, that the First Amendment leaves judgments in matters of taste to the individual. Thank you very much.

Narrator: On June 21, 1991, the Supreme Court decided—by a bare majority of one vote—that Darlene Miller and Gayle Sutro could not dance nude in their striptease clubs. There was, in fact, no majority opinion for the Court. The five justices who voted to uphold Indiana's public nudity law produced three separate opinions, with very different reasoning.

Chief Justice William Rehnquist pronounced the Court's judgment in an opinion joined only by Justices Sandra O'Connor and Anthony Kennedy. Rehnquist sounded like Anthony Comstock, the 19th century crusader against public vice. The Indiana law, he wrote, "furthers a substantial government interest in protecting order and morality." The state was free to protect its citizens against the "evil" of public nudity. Rehnquist conceded that the First Amendment protects erotic messages from complete prohibition, but concluded that the Indiana law was the "bare minimum" necessary to protect against "public indecency."

Justice Antonin Scalia joined the majority with a typically sarcastic opinion. He differed from Rehnquist in claiming that the Indiana law "is not subject to First Amendment scrutiny at all." Scalia argued that some behavior is legally prohibited, not because it harms others but simply because society considers it immoral. The purpose of Indiana's public nudity law would be violated, he wrote, "if 60,000 fully consenting adults crowded into the Hoosier Dome to display their genitals to one another, even if there were not an offended innocent in the crowd."

The fifth and deciding vote to uphold the law came from mild-mannered and soft-spoken Justice David Souter. He agreed with Rehnquist that nude dancing enjoys some degree of First Amendment protection, but wrote that "dropping the final stitch is prohibited," because total nudity is not essential in expressing an erotic message.

Justice Byron White wrote for the four dissenters. He accused the majority of "transparently erroneous" reasoning. The First Amendment prohibits censorship based on the content of the message. What Indiana wanted to ban, White claimed, was not nudity but erotic messages. "The nudity of the dancer," he wrote, "is an integral part of the emotions and thoughts" that she hopes to arouse in those who watch her perform.

The Supreme Court decision in this case gives each state the power to ban nude dancing. Patrons of the Kitty Kat Lounge in South Bend still watch dancers in pasties and G-strings. Or they can make the short drive to Chicago and watch totally nude dancers. The First Amendment covers less—or is it more—in Indiana than Illinois.

EDITED SUPREME COURT OPINIONS
Barnes v. Glen Theatre, Inc.
Argued January 8, 1991—Decided June 21, 1991

CHIEF JUSTICE REHNQUIST announced the judgment of the Court and delivered an opinion, in which JUSTICE O'CONNOR and JUSTICE KENNEDY join.

Respondents are two establishments in South Bend, Indiana, that wish to provide totally nude dancing as entertainment, and individual dancers who are employed at these establishments. They claim that the First Amendment's guarantee of freedom of expression prevents the State of Indiana from enforcing its public indecency law to prevent this form of dancing. We reject their claim.

The facts appear from the pleadings and findings of the District Court and are uncontested here. The Kitty Kat Lounge, Inc. (Kitty Kat), is located in the city of South Bend. It sells alcoholic beverages and presents "go-go dancing." Its proprietor desires to present "totally nude dancing," but an applicable Indiana statute regulating public nudity requires that the dancers wear "pasties" and "G-strings" when they dance. The dancers are not paid an hourly wage, but work on commission. They receive a 100 percent commission on the first $60 in drink sales during their performances. Darlene Miller, one of the respondents in the action, had worked at the Kitty Kat for about two years at the time this action was brought. Miller wishes to dance nude because she believes she would make more money doing so.

Respondent Glen Theatre, Inc., is an Indiana corporation with a place of business in South Bend. Its primary business is supplying so-called adult entertainment through written and printed materials, movie showings, and live entertainment at an enclosed "bookstore." The live entertainment at the "bookstore" consists of nude and seminude performances and showings of the female body through glass panels. Customers sit in a booth and insert coins into a timing mechanism that permits them to observe the live nude and seminude dancers for a period of time. One of Glen Theatre's dancers, Gayle Ann Marie Sutro, has danced, modeled, and acted professionally for more than 15 years, and in addition to her performances at the Glen Theatre, can be seen in a pornographic movie at a nearby theater....

We granted certiorari, 498 U.S. 807 (1990) and now hold that the Indiana statutory requirement that the dancers in the establishments involved in this case must wear pasties and G-strings does not violate the First Amendment.

Several of our cases contain language suggesting that nude dancing of the kind involved here is expressive conduct protected by the First Amendment....

Indiana, of course, has not banned nude dancing as such, but has proscribed public nudity across the board. The Supreme Court of Indiana has construed the Indiana statute to preclude nudity in what are essentially places of public accommodation such as the Glen Theatre and the Kitty Kat Lounge. In such places, respondents point out, minors are excluded and there are no non-consenting viewers. Respondents contend that while the State may license establishments such as the ones involved here, and limit the geographical area in which they do business, it may not in any way limit the performance of the dances within them without violating the First Amendment....

This public indecency statute is clearly within the constitutional power of the State and furthers substantial governmental interests. It is impossible to discern, other than from the text of the statute, exactly what governmental interest the Indiana legislators had in mind when they enacted this statute, for Indiana does not record legislative history, and the State's highest court has not shed additional light on the statute's purpose. Nonetheless, the statute's purpose of protecting societal order and morality is clear from its text and history. Public indecency statutes of this sort are of ancient origin and presently exist in at least 47 States. Public indecency, including nudity, was a criminal offense at common law, and this Court recognized the common-law roots of the offense of "gross and open indecency" in *Winters v. New York*, 333 U.S. 507, 515 (1948). Public nudity was considered an act *malum in se. Le Roy v. Sidney*, 1 Sid. 168, 82 Eng. Rep. 1036 (K. B. 1664). Public indecency statutes such as the one before us reflect moral disapproval of people appearing in the nude among strangers in public places.

This public indecency statute follows a long line of earlier Indiana statutes banning all public nudity. The history of Indiana's public indecency statute shows that it predates barroom nude dancing and was enacted as a general prohibition. At least as early as 1831, Indiana had a statute punishing "open and notorious lewdness, or...any grossly scandalous and public indecency."...

Respondents contend that even though prohibiting nudity in public generally may not be related to suppressing expression, prohibiting the performance of nude dancing is related to expression because the State seeks to prevent its erotic message....

But we do not think that when Indiana applies its statute to the nude dancing in these nightclubs it is proscribing nudity because of the erotic message conveyed by the dancers. Presumably numerous other erotic performances are presented at these establishments and similar clubs without any interference from the State, so long as the performers wear a scant amount of clothing. Likewise, the requirement that the dancers don pasties and G-strings does not deprive the dance of whatever erotic message it conveys; it simply makes the message slightly less graphic. The perceived evil that Indiana seeks to address is not erotic dancing, but public nudity. The appearance of people of all shapes, sizes and ages in the nude at a beach, for example, would convey little if any erotic message, yet the State still seeks to prevent it, whether or not it is combined with expressive activity....

As indicated in the discussion above, the governmental interest served by the text of the prohibition is societal disapproval of nudity in public places and among strangers. The statutory prohibition is not a means to some greater end, but an end in itself. It is without cavil that the public indecency statute is "narrowly tailored"; Indiana's requirement that the dancers wear at least pasties and G-strings is modest and the bare minimum necessary to achieve the State's purpose.

The judgment of the Court of Appeals accordingly is

Reversed.

JUSTICE SCALIA, concurring in the judgment.

I agree that the judgment of the Court of Appeals must be reversed. In my view, however, the challenged regulation must be upheld, not because it survives some lower level of First Amendment scrutiny, but because, as a general law regulating conduct and not specifically directed at expression, it is not subject to First Amendment scrutiny at all....

Indiana's statute is in the line of a long tradition of laws against public nudity, which have never been thought to run afoul of traditional understanding of "the freedom of speech." Public indecency—including public nudity—has long been an offense at common law. ... .

The dissent confidently asserts...that the purpose of restricting nudity in public places in general is to protect nonconsenting parties from offense; and argues that since only consenting, admission-paying patrons see respondents dance, that purpose cannot apply and the only remaining purpose must relate to the communicative elements of the performance. Perhaps the dissenters believe that "offense to others" *ought* to be the only reason for restricting nudity in public places generally, but there is no basis for thinking that our society has ever shared that Thoreauvian "you-may-do-what-you-like-so-long-as-it-does-not-injure-someone-else" beau ideal—much less for thinking that it was written into the Constitution. The purpose of Indiana's nudity law would be violated, I think, if 60,000 fully consenting adults crowded into the Hoosier Dome to display their genitals to one another, even if there were not an offended innocent in the crowd. Our society prohibits, and all human societies have prohibited, certain activities not because they harm others but because they are considered, in the traditional phrase, "*contra bonos mores*," i.e., immoral. In American society, such prohibitions have included, for example, sadomasochism, cockfighting, bestiality, suicide, drug use, prostitution, and sodomy. While there may be great diversity of view on whether various of these prohibitions should exist (though I have found few ready to abandon, in principle, all of them), there is no doubt that, absent specific constitutional protection for the conduct involved, the Constitution does not prohibit them simply because they regulate "morality."

JUSTICE SOUTER, concurring in the judgment.

Not all dancing is entitled to First Amendment protection as expressive activity. This Court has previously categorized ballroom dancing as beyond the Amendment's protection, *Dallas v. Stanglin*, 490 U.S. 19, 24-25 (1989), and dancing as aerobic exercise would likewise be outside the First Amendment's concern. But dancing as a performance directed to an actual or hypothetical audience gives expression at least to generalized emotion or feeling, and where the dancer is nude or nearly so the feeling expressed, in the absence of some contrary clue, is eroticism, carrying an endorsement of erotic experience. Such is the expressive content of the dances described in the record.

Although such performance dancing is inherently expressive, nudity *per se* is not. It is a condition, not an activity, and the voluntary assumption of that condition, without more, apparently expresses nothing beyond the view that the condition is somehow appropriate to the circumstances. But every voluntary act implies some such idea, and the implication is thus so common and minimal that calling all voluntary activity expressive would reduce the concept of expression to the point of the meaningless. A search for some expression beyond the minimal in the choice to go nude will often yield nothing: a person may choose nudity, for example, for maximum sunbathing. But when nudity is combined with expressive activity, its stimulative and attractive value certainly can enhance the force of expression, and a dancer's acts in going from clothed to nude, as in a striptease, are integrated into the dance and its expressive function. Thus I agree with the plurality and the dissent that an interest in freely engaging in the nude dancing at issue here is subject to a degree of First Amendment protection....

I nonetheless write separately to rest my concurrence in the judgment, not on the possible sufficiency of society's moral views to justify the limitations at issue, but on the State's substantial interest in combating the secondary effects of adult entertainment establishments of the sort typified by respondents' establishments....

[T]he State of Indiana could reasonably conclude that forbidding nude entertainment of the type offered at the Kitty Kat Lounge and the Glen Theatre's "bookstore" furthers its interest in preventing prostitution, sexual assault, and associated crimes....

It is possible, for example, that the higher incidence of prostitution and sexual assault in the vicinity of adult entertainment locations results from the concentration of crowds of men predisposed to such activities, or from the simple viewing of nude bodies regardless of whether those bodies are engaged in expression or not. In neither case would the chain of causation run through the persuasive effect of the expressive component of nude dancing.

Because the State's interest in banning nude dancing results from a simple correlation of such dancing with other evils, rather than from a relationship between the other evils and the expressive component of the dancing, the interest is unrelated to the suppression of free expression. ... .

Pasties and a G-string moderate the expression to some degree, to be sure, but only to a degree. Dropping the final stitch is prohibited, but the limitation is minor when measured against the dancer's remaining capacity and opportunity to express the erotic message. Nor, so far as we are told, is the dancer or her employer limited by anything short of obscenity laws from expressing an erotic message by articulate speech or representational means; a pornographic movie featuring one of respondents, for example, was playing nearby without any interference from the authorities at the time these cases arose.

JUSTICE WHITE, with whom JUSTICE MARSHALL, JUSTICE BLACK-MUN, and JUSTICE STEVENS join, dissenting.

The first question presented to us in this case is whether nonobscene nude dancing performed as entertainment is expressive conduct protected by the First Amendment. The Court of Appeals held that it is, observing that our prior decisions permit no other conclusion. Not surprisingly, then, the plurality now concedes that "nude dancing of the kind sought to be performed here is expressive conduct within the outer perimeters of the First Amendment...."

The plurality acknowledges that it is impossible to discern the exact state interests which the Indiana Legislature had in mind when it enacted the Indiana statute, but the plurality nonetheless concludes that it is clear from the statute's text and history that the law's purpose is to protect "societal order and morality."

[T]he plurality and JUSTICE SCALIA's simple references to the State's general interest in promoting societal order and morality are not sufficient justification for a statute which concededly reaches a significant amount of protected expressive activity....

Closer inquiry as to the purpose of the statute is surely appropriate.

Legislators do not just randomly select certain conduct for proscription; they have reasons for doing so and those reasons illuminate the purpose of the law that is passed. Indeed, a law may have multiple purposes. The purpose of forbidding people to appear nude in parks, beaches, hot dog stands, and like public places is to protect others from offense. But that could not possibly be the purpose of preventing nude dancing in theaters and barrooms since the viewers are exclusively consenting adults who pay money to see these dances. The purpose of the proscription in these contexts is to protect the viewers from what the State believes is the harmful message that nude dancing communicates....

The perceived evil is not erotic dancing but public nudity, which may be prohibited despite any incidental impact on expressive activity. This analysis is transparently erroneous.

In arriving at its conclusion, the plurality concedes that nude dancing conveys an erotic message and concedes that the message would be muted if the dancers wore pasties and G-strings. Indeed, the emotional or erotic impact of the dance is intensified by the nudity of the performers....

This being the case, it cannot be that the statutory prohibition is unrelated to expressive conduct. Since the State permits the dancers to perform if they wear pasties and G-strings but forbids nude dancing, it is precisely because of the distinctive, expressive content of the nude dancing performances at issue in this case that the State seeks to apply the statutory prohibition. It is only because nude dancing performances may generate emotions and feelings of eroticism and sensuality among the spectators that the State seeks to regulate such expressive activity, apparently on the assumption that creating or emphasizing such thoughts and ideas in the minds of the spectators may lead to increased prostitution and the degradation of women. But generating thoughts, ideas, and emotions is the essence of communication. The nudity element of nude dancing performances cannot be neatly pigeonholed as mere "conduct" independent of any expressive component of the dance....

That the performances in the Kitty Kat Lounge may not be high art, to say the least, and may not appeal to the Court, is hardly an excuse for distorting and ignoring settled doctrine. The Court's assessment of the artistic merits of nude dancing performances should not be the determining factor in deciding this case. In the words of Justice Harlan: "It is largely because governmental officials cannot make principled decisions in this area that the Constitution leaves matters of taste and style so largely to the individual." *Cohen v. California*, 403 U.S. 15, 25 (1971).

Branzburg *v.* Hayes

408 U.S. 665 (1972)

Paul Branzburg was a reporter in 1969 for the Louisville, Kentucky, *Courier-Journal*, a highly respected newspaper. Even in Kentucky, the 1960s were a time of protest, alternative lifestyles, and drug use. Branzburg wrote an article that described in detail the activities of two young men who turned marijuana into hashish, a more potent hallucinogenic drug. The article stated that Branzburg had agreed to protect the identities of his informants. A local prosecutor called Branzburg before a county grand jury and demanded that he identify his confidential sources. Branzburg refused to answer, and filed suit against the judge who issued a grand jury subpoena. Along with two similar cases, the Supreme Court heard arguments on whether news reporters may claim a First Amendment privilege against disclosing their sources. By a five-to-four vote, the justices ruled that the Court "cannot seriously entertain the notion that the First Amendment protects a newsman's agreement to conceal the criminal conduct of his source" from grand jurors. The dissenters argued that news sources would "dry up" if they feared disclosure. Reporters in many states continue to face the choice of disclosing sources or risking contempt citations and jail.

Counsel for petitioner: Edgar A. Zingman, Louisville, Kentucky
Counsel for respondent: Edwin A. Schroering, Jr., Commonwealth's Attorney,
Louisville, Kentucky
Counsel for United States as amicus curiae: William B. Reynolds, Dept. of Justice, Washington, D.C.

Chief Justice Warren Burger: The Court will now hear arguments in Number 70-85, *Branzburg* against *Hayes*.

Narrator: It's February 23, 1972. We're in the chamber of the United States Supreme Court in Washington, D.C. Chief Justice Warren Burger has called for argument a case that involves freedom of the press. The First Amendment prohibits both federal and state governments from infringing press freedom. The Supreme Court has consistently upheld the right of the news media to publish or broadcast without censorship, and has protected the media from most libel actions.

One area of press freedom, however, remains murky and unsettled. The justices accepted today's case—and two companion cases—to answer this question: Does the First Amendment prohibit a grand jury from compelling a reporter to disclose confidential information received by him in the course of his news-gathering activities? Put another way, does the First Amendment provide reporters with a privilege to protect their sources from disclosure? In most states, husbands and wives, doctors, lawyers, and members of the clergy can assert privileges against disclosing confidential information in court. Should reporters have a similar privilege?

The reporter in this case is Paul Branzburg of the Louisville, Kentucky, *Courier-Journal*, a highly respected newspaper. In 1969, Branzburg wrote an article about two young men who produced and sold hashish, a powerful hallucinogenic drug. Branzburg wrote that he had agreed not to publish their names. He was then called before the county grand jury and asked to identify his sources. Branzburg refused, citing both the First Amendment and a Kentucky law that protected reporters from disclosing "sources of information." A county judge ordered Branzburg to testify, and Branzburg filed suit to overturn the order. Kentucky's highest court ruled that state law did not protect Branzburg from testifying about what he observed, including his sources' names.

State and federal judges have issued conflicting rulings in reporters' privilege cases, and the Supreme Court will hear argument today in three cases with different facts but similar issues. In Branzburg's case, the defendant is now county judge John Hayes. Edgar Zingman, a prominent Louisville attorney, argues for Branzburg. Chief Justice Burger welcomes him to the podium.

Chief Justice Burger: Mr. Zingman, you may proceed whenever you're ready.

Zingman: Mr. Chief Justice, and may it please the Court:

We appear here in behalf of the petitioner, Paul Branzburg, a professional journalist employed by the *Courier-Journal*, a daily newspaper published in Louisville, Kentucky. The petitioner seeks reversal on First and Fourteenth Amendment grounds of two cases decided by the Court of Appeals of Kentucky.

In the first of these, involving the respondent Hayes, a judge in the trial court in Jefferson County, Kentucky, following upon publication in the *Courier-Journal* of an article authorized by the petitioner, which described the manufacture of hashish by two individuals in Louisville, Kentucky, and which in the body of the article contained the statement that a promise had been given by the petitioner that the identities of the two individuals would be maintained confidential and would not be disclosed, the petitioner was subpoenaed before a grand jury sitting in Jefferson County, Kentucky, and was asked by that grand jury two questions relating to the identity of the person that he had described in the newspaper article.

The petitioner refused to answer these questions and was brought before the predecessor in office of the respondent Hayes, a trial judge by the name of Pound, and upon the questions being read to the judge, the petitioner was directed to answer the questions. At that time we appeared on behalf of the petitioner and asserted First and Fourteenth Amendment grounds under the concept of freedom of the press, for the petitioner's refusal to answer the questions. We also asserted the provisions of a Kentucky shield statute, K.R.S.—Kentucky Revised Statutes—421.100, which is phrased in language that protects a newsman from revealing the source of any information published by him.

Narrator: Zingman moves from the facts of the case to the constitutional issues.

Zingman: We are asking here only for that historical protection against governmental interference—excuse me—with exercise of First Amendment rights which this Court has always provided. While the factual setting may be novel, these cases seek nothing more than the application here of this Court's salutary and oft-repeated requirement that there is imposed upon the Government the burden of demonstrating a compelling and overriding need and the lack of alternatives less destructive of First Amendment rights, before Government interference with the exercise of First Amendment rights will be countenanced.

The rule that we urge upon the Court is that the freedom of the press guaranteed by the First and Fourteenth Amendments encompasses not only publication, but all meaningful preconditions to publication, not the least of which is the ability to gather and obtain information. To ensure these rights, we believe that it is necessary for this Court to declare that the First Amendment protects the newsman from being compelled to enter a closed proceeding and from being compelled to disclose confidential information obtained by him as a newsman, unless there has been a prior demonstration by the Government in an open hearing of a compelling and overriding need for the disclosure.

Narrator: Justice Byron White has a question for Zingman. Chief Justice Burger continues with another question.

Burger: What do you think in this case, just as a practical matter: A reporter goes and sees what he says, and reports it. As a practical matter, why would the people he saw running this hashish laboratory permit him to publish the fact that there was this laboratory operating, but say "please don't publish our names?"

Zingman: Well this, Mr. Justice White, I think goes to the heart of what we're talking about and why this is so important. There are dissident elements in the society today which for the first time, historically, the news media are really dealing with. Traditionally, the news media—and historically—have reported what is going on in the general community, the orthodox community. But, more and more, through investigative reporting they're dealing with the unorthodox, the rebellious, the youth, the drug culture, the hippies, the dissidents. Now these people do want to get their positions across to the community at large, and it is important to the community at large to understand their positions. There's great controversy in this country today about the question of legalization of marijuana. It's important for the public in determining that question to understand the attitude of those who use—

Court: Shouldn't the public have a right to know the sources of that information?

Zingman: Well, I think the important thing is for the public to have the right to know. And, if having the right to know the sources will destroy the ability to obtain the information, then it leads us no place.

Court: Isn't the public going to make its evaluation of the information depending on the credibility of the source, and the possible self-interest of the source?

Zingman: Well that's part of it. And I suppose, in that quantum, the public will also weigh the fact that these people wanted to remain unidentified. But, obviously, if you're going to print news about what is presently an illegal activity, you are not going to get information voluntarily from those who are participating in such activity if it's going to immediately lead to their arrest and prosecution. It's a question of cutting off the information at the very start.

Narrator: Zingman proposes that reporters be required to identify sources only when their testimony is necessary to prevent "direct, immediate, and irreparable prospective damage to national security, human life, or liberty." Justice William Rehnquist has a question about Zingman's proposal.

Rehnquist: Under your test, Mr. Zingman, supposing that the reporter had witnessed a murder, but there was no reason to believe that the man was in the business of murdering people. It was a one-time offense. Could the grand jury subpoena him to testify?

Zingman: Subpoena the reporter?

Court: Yes.

Zingman: Under our balancing test, that would be possible, yes.

Court: But I thought it was "danger to national security, liberty, or"—you would regard the prosecution of an already completed offense as a way of, in effect, averting that sort of danger?

Zingman: I would say that would come in under the balancing act and might be permissible for a court using the standards we have applied, if he felt that it fit the definition of prospective damage to human life or liberty.

Narrator: Zingman concludes with these words.

Zingman: We think that the failure to ensure to newsmen a First Amendment right here would result in self-censorship, prior restraint, the drying up of sources of information, and would result in a total loss to the general public of the kinds and scope and extent of information which the First Amendment was designed to achieve. I think the record demonstrates very clearly the chilling effect upon the newsman's ability to operate that these subpoenas and compelling testimony induces.

Narrator: Edwin Schroering of the state attorney's office argues for Judge Hayes and the grand jury.

Schroering: Mr. Chief Justice, may it please the Court: As I see it, the newsman has no more privilege under the law than the average citizen. There is, of course, a chilling effect upon any use of the law. If the grand jury goes out and subpoenas someone and asks them a question, and citizens observe that person going before the grand jury, certainly there's some effect that might develop from this. But isn't this something that we have to accept as a part of our obligation as citizens?

I would call the attention of the Court to the procedure which has been suggested by counsel in his discussion of how you would have this open hearing to determine whether a newsman would be subpoenaed, in which they referred to the same type of procedure that we would use in determining Fifth Amendment privileges. The Fifth Amendment applies to everyone. The Fifth Amendment does not merely apply to newsmen or any group of newsmen.

Also, we'd like to call the attention of the Court to the reasons why the informants gave their information to the newsman—and it's in the brief—he "wanted to bug the narcotics agents involved in the community." This—it appears to be a reason not quite as important as some of the reasons that have developed in other privileges under the law that we've noted. Certainly "bugging the narcotics agents"—his purpose in giving the information—is not the type of a privilege, or should not go to consider the type of privilege that's being requested here.

Narrator: Schroering takes issue with the "balancing test" that Edgar Zingman proposed.

Schroering: The petitioner has suggested these different tests to be made. I would take the position that this would fetter the grand jury process to the point that it would have a substantial effect upon the operation of the grand jury. The grand jury certainly has deep roots in constitutional law. They have a constitutional duty to investigate, just as the press has the freedom as any other citizen. When these two meet under these circumstances, certainly doesn't the grand jury that acts for all of the people, doesn't their constitutional duty carry heavier weight in this connection than the corresponding privilege which is advanced here by counsel?

Narrator: Justice Thurgood Marshall has questions for Schroering. His tone suggests a skeptical attitude.

Marshall: Well, if this judgment is affirmed, then every place in the country, once a story appears in the press which shows confidential information concerning a crime, wouldn't it automatically follow that the grand jury would subpoena that reporter?

Schroering: Not necessarily.

Court: Well, how—you say they're so great—how can they be doing their job, if they didn't?

Schroering: If the newspaper reporters observed a crime, the commission of a crime, they become witnesses and they have a duty and a responsibility to testify in a court of law.

Court: Well, then, wouldn't it be true that once they publish the story they volunteer as a witness?

Schroering: They are subject to being subpoenaed before the grand jury.

Court: And wouldn't they be?

Schroering: That's correct. Just like you would subpoena a husband in Kentucky, or a wife, in connection with a case, or you would subpoena someone else with some privilege. They would raise the privilege in the particular communication involved in a court of law, whether it be before the grand jury or whether it be before the petit jury.

Narrator: Schroering has divided his time with William Bradford Reynolds of the Federal Justice Department. The Reagan administration sides with the state in this case.

Reynolds: Mr. Chief Justice, may it please the Court: Our position is essentially that to allow this type of wholesale interference—and it would be wholesale interference—with the grand jury, is contrary and undercuts the specific protections that the framers of the Constitution intended by the Fifth Amendment. The Fifth Amendment provides that a grand jury shall be the sole method for preferring charges in criminal cases—serious criminal cases. Our grand jury is modeled after the English grand jury, as a body of laymen with very broad powers to investigate, in secret, alleged criminal acts, not only for determining probable guilt, but also for the purpose of protecting innocent people of false prosecution.

Narrator: Reynolds addresses the claim that forcing reporters to identify their confidential sources will deter people from talking with the media.

Reynolds: Now we've heard a lot this morning about the fact that a holding by this Court to the effect that there is no privilege in the First Amendment is going to dry up news sources. The news media in this country have, of course, existed for almost 200 years without a constitutional privilege of the sort that's being argued here. Confidential sources have long been used in the news gathering process.

We think that if there is—if there is really a difficulty with respect to drying up of sources—and we point out again that the news media have been able to exist for 200 years without any constitutional privilege and without a drying up of sources—but if there is a difficulty along those lines, we think that it's for the legislature to determine on an informed judgment, looking at the different particular problems with respect to different media, and to meet that difficulty in that way. We don't believe that the right approach is a constitutional privilege that is to be confined to a particular class of citizenry—that is, news reporters, as such.

Narrator: The Court decided *Branzburg* and its companion cases on June 29, 1972. The vote in all three was narrow: five to four. The result in all three was the same: Paul Branzburg and his fellow reporters must testify before grand juries and, if asked, identify their confidential sources. In other words, reporters must break promises of confidentiality to help grand juries investigate crime and bring charges.

Justice Byron White wrote for the majority. His opinion, like his questions at oral argument, had a tone of skepticism toward the media and reporters. The Court "cannot seriously entertain the notion that the First Amendment protects a newsman's agreement to conceal the criminal conduct of his source," White wrote, "on the theory that it is better to write about crime than to do something about it." White dismissed claims that news sources would "dry up" as "speculative."

White also wrote that the "preference for anonymity" of news sources involved in criminal activity "is presumably a product of their desire to escape criminal prosecution" and is "hardly deserving of constitutional protection." White concluded that Paul Branzburg's "claim of privilege under the First Amendment presents no substantial question" to the Court.

The four dissenters did see a substantial question. Justice William O. Douglas, the Court's staunchest defender of press freedom, bristled with indignation. Just two weeks before this decision, police arrested White House operatives for the Watergate break-in, and Washington *Post* reporters began cultivating the ultimate confidential source, "Deep Throat." "A reporter is no better than his source of information," Douglas wrote. "Unless he has a privilege to withhold the identity of his source, he will be the victim of governmental intrigue or aggression."

In the years since the Court decided *Branzburg v. Hayes*, more than twenty reporters have gone to jail—some for weeks or months—for refusing to identify confidential sources. On the other hand, several states have adopted "shield" laws to protect reporters against forced disclosure of their sources. How much news has "dried up" as a result of *Branzburg* still remains a matter of speculation.

EDITED SUPREME COURT OPINIONS
Branzburg v. Hayes et al.
Argued February 23,1972—Decided June 29, 1972*

Opinion of the Court by MR. JUSTICE WHITE, announced by THE CHIEF JUSTICE.

The issue in these cases is whether requiring newsmen to appear and testify before state or federal grand juries abridges the freedom of speech and press guaranteed by the First Amendment. We hold that it does not....

The writ of certiorari in No 70-85, *Branzburg v. Hayes* and *Meigs*, brings before us two judgments of the Kentucky Court of Appeals, both involving petitioner Branzburg, a staff reporter for the *Courier-Journal*, a daily newspaper published in Louisville, Kentucky.

On November 15, 1969, the *Courier-Journal* carried a story under petitioner's by-line describing in detail his observations of two young residents of Jefferson County synthesizing hashish from marijuana, an activity which, they asserted, earned them about $5,000 in three weeks. The article included a photograph of a pair of hands working above a laboratory table on which was a substance identified by the caption as hashish. The article stated that petitioner had promised not to reveal the identity of the two hashish makers. Petitioner was shortly subpoenaed by the Jefferson County grand jury; he appeared, but refused to identify the individuals he had seen possessing marihuana or the persons he had seen making hashish from marijuana. A state trial court judge ordered petitioner to answer these questions and rejected his contention that the Kentucky reporters' privilege statute, Ky Rev Stat § 421 100 (1962), the First Amendment of the United States Constitution, or §§ 1, 2, and 8 of the Kentucky Constitution authorized his refusal to answer. Petitioner then sought prohibition and mandamus in the Kentucky Court of Appeals on the same grounds, but the Court of Appeals denied the petition.

---

* Together with No. 70-94, In re Pappas, on certiorari to the Supreme Judicial Court of Massachusetts, also argued February 23, 1972, and No. 70-57, *United States v. Caldwell*, on certiorari to the United States Court of Appeals for the Ninth Circuit, argued February 22, 1972.

Petitioners Branzburg and Pappas and respondent Caldwell press First Amendment claims that may be simply put that to gather news it is often necessary to agree either not to identify the source of information published or to publish only part of the facts revealed, or both; that if the reporter is nevertheless forced to reveal these confidences to a grand jury, the source so identified and other confidential sources of other reporters will be measurably deterred from furnishing publishable information, all to the detriment of the free flow of information protected by the First Amendment. Although the newsmen in these cases do not claim an absolute privilege against official interrogation in all circumstances, they assert that the reporter should not be forced either to appear or to testify before a grand jury or at trial until and unless sufficient grounds are shown for believing that the reporter possesses information relevant to a crime the grand jury is investigating, that the information the reporter has is unavailable from other sources, and that the need for the information is sufficiently compelling to override the claimed invasion of First Amendment interests occasioned by the disclosure....

We do not question the significance of free speech, press, or assembly to the country's welfare. Nor is it suggested that news gathering does not qualify for First Amendment protection; without some protection for seeking out the news, freedom of the press could be eviscerated. But these cases involve no intrusions upon speech or assembly, no prior restraint or restriction on what the press may publish, and no express or implied command that the press publish what it prefers to withhold. No exaction or tax for the privilege of publishing, and no penalty, civil or criminal, related to the content of published material is at issue here. The use of confidential sources by the press is not forbidden or restricted; reporters remain free to seek news from any source by means within the law. No attempt is made to require the press to publish its sources of information or indiscriminately to disclose them on request. The sole issue before us is the obligation of reporters to respond to grand jury subpoenas as other citizens do and to answer questions relevant to an investigation into the commission of crime. Citizens generally are not constitutionally immune from grand jury subpoenas; and neither the First Amendment nor any other constitutional provision protects the average citizen from disclosing to a grand jury information that he has received in confidence. The claim is, however, that reporters are exempt from these obligations because if forced to respond to subpoenas and identify their sources or disclose other confidences, their informants will refuse or be reluctant to furnish newsworthy information in the future. This asserted burden on news gathering is said to make compelled testimony from newsmen constitutionally suspect and to require a privileged position for them....

This we decline to do. Fair and effective law enforcement aimed at provid-

ing security for the person and property of the individual is a fundamental function of government, and the grand jury plays an important, constitutionally
mandated role in this process. On the records now before us, we perceive no
basis for holding that the public interest in law enforcement and in ensuring
effective grand jury proceedings is insufficient to override the consequential,
but uncertain, burden on news gathering that is said to result from insisting
that reporters, like other citizens, respond to relevant questions put to them in
the course of a valid grand jury investigation or criminal trial.

This conclusion itself involves no restraint on what newspapers may publish or on the type or quality of information reporters may seek to acquire, nor
does it threaten the vast bulk of confidential relationships between reporters
and their sources. Grand juries address themselves to the issues of whether
crimes have been committed and who committed them. Only where news
sources themselves are implicated in crime or possess information relevant to
the grand jury's task need they or the reporter be concerned about grand jury
subpoenas. Nothing before us indicates that a large number or percentage of all
confidential news sources falls into either category and would in any way be
deterred by our holding that the Constitution does not, as it never has, exempt
the newsman from performing the citizen's normal duty of appearing and furnishing information relevant to the grand jury's task.

The preference for anonymity of those confidential informants involved in
actual criminal conduct is presumably a product of their desire to escape criminal prosecution, and this preference, while understandable, is hardly deserving
of constitutional protection....

Thus, we cannot seriously entertain the notion that the First Amendment
protects a newsman's agreement to conceal the criminal conduct of his source,
or evidence thereof, on the theory that it is better to write about crime than to
do something about it. Insofar as any reporter in these cases undertook not to
reveal or testify about the crime he witnessed, his claim of privilege under the
First Amendment presents no substantial question. The crimes of news sources
are no less reprehensible and threatening to the public interest when witnessed
by a reporter than when they are not....

The argument that the flow of news will be diminished by compelling
reporters to aid the grand jury in a criminal investigation is not irrational, nor
are the records before us silent on the matter. But we remain unclear how often
and to what extent informers are actually deterred from furnishing information
when newsmen are forced to testify before a grand jury. The available data indicate that some newsmen rely a great deal on confidential sources and that some
informants are particularly sensitive to the threat of exposure and may be
silenced if it is held by this Court that, ordinarily, newsmen must testify pur-

suant to subpoenas, but the evidence fails to demonstrate that there would be a significant constriction of the flow of news to the public if this Court reaffirms the prior common-law and constitutional rule regarding the testimonial obligations of newsmen. Estimates of the inhibiting effect of such subpoenas on the willingness of informants to make disclosures to newsmen are widely divergent and to a great extent speculative. It would be difficult to canvass the views of the informants themselves; surveys of reporters on this topic are chiefly opinions of predicted informant behavior and must be viewed in the light of the professional self-interest of the interviewees.

Reliance by the press on confidential informants does not mean that all such sources will in fact dry up because of the later possible appearance of the newsman before a grand jury. The reporter may never be called and if he objects to testifying, the prosecution may not insist. Also, the relationship of many informants to the press is a symbiotic one which is unlikely to be greatly inhibited by the threat of subpoena quite often; such informants are members of a minority political or cultural group that relies heavily on the media to propagate its views, publicize its aims, and magnify its exposure to the public....

Accepting the fact, however, that an undetermined number of informants not themselves implicated in crime will nevertheless, for whatever reason, refuse to talk to newsmen if they fear identification by a reporter in an official investigation, we cannot accept the argument that the public interest in possible future news about crime from undisclosed, unverified sources must take precedence over the public interest in pursuing and prosecuting those crimes reported to the press by informants and in thus deterring the commission of such crimes in the future....

It is said that currently press subpoenas have multiplied, that mutual distrust and tension between press and officialdom have increased, that reporting styles have changed, and that there is now more need for confidential sources, particularly where the press seeks news about minority cultural and political groups or dissident organizations suspicious of the law and public officials. These developments, even if true, are treacherous grounds for a far-reaching interpretation of the First Amendment, fastening a nationwide rule on courts, grand juries, and prosecuting officials everywhere. The obligation to testify in response to grand jury subpoenas will not threaten these sources not involved with criminal conduct and without information relevant to grand jury investigations, and we cannot hold that the Constitution places the sources in these two categories either above the law or beyond its reach.

MR. JUSTICE DOUGLAS, dissenting in No 70-57, *United States v. Caldwell*.

Today's decision will impede the wide-open and robust dissemination of ideas and counterthought which a free press both fosters and protects and which is essential to the success of intelligent self-government. Forcing a reporter before a grand jury will have two retarding effects upon the fear and the pen of the press. Fear of exposure will cause dissidents to communicate less openly to trusted reporters and fear of accountability will cause editors and critics to write with more restrained pens.

I see no way of making mandatory the disclosure of a reporter's confidential source of the information on which he bases his news story.

The press has a preferred position in our constitutional scheme, not to enable it to make money, not to set newsmen apart as a favored class, but to bring fulfillment to the public's right to know. The right to know is crucial to the governing powers of the people, to paraphrase Alexander Meiklejohn. Knowledge is essential to informed decisions....

The people who govern are often far removed from the cabals that threaten the regime; the people are often remote from the sources of truth even though they live in the city where the forces that would undermine society operate. The function of the press is to explore and investigate events, inform the people what is going on, and to expose the harmful as well as the good influences at work. There is no higher function performed under our constitutional regime. Its performance means that the press is often engaged in projects that bring anxiety or even fear to the bureaucracies, departments, or officials of government. The whole weight of government is therefore often brought to bear against a paper or a reporter.

A reporter is no better than his source of information. Unless he has a privilege to withhold the identity of his source, he will be the victim of governmental intrigue or aggression. If he can be summoned to testify in secret before a grand jury, his sources will dry up and the attempted exposure, the effort to enlighten the public, will be ended. If what the Court sanctions today becomes settled law, then the reporter's main function in American society will be to pass on to the public the press releases which the various departments of government issue....

The intrusion of government into this domain is symptomatic of the disease of this society. As the years pass the power of government becomes more and more pervasive. It is a power to suffocate both people and causes. Those in power, whatever their politics, want only to perpetuate it. Now that the fences of the law and the tradition that has protected the press are broken down, the people are the victims. The First Amendment, as I read it, was designed precisely to prevent that tragedy. I would also reverse the judgments in No 70-85, *Branzburg v. Hayes*, and No. 70-94, In re Pappas, for the reasons stated in the above dissent in No. 70-57, *United States v. Caldwell*.

MR. JUSTICE STEWART, with whom MR. JUSTICE BRENNAN and MR. JUSTICE MARSHALL join, dissenting.

The Court's crabbed view of the First Amendment reflects a disturbing insensitivity to the critical role of an independent press in our society. The question whether a reporter has a constitutional right to a confidential relationship with his source is of first impression here, but the principles that should guide our decision are as basic as any to be found in the Constitution....

It is obvious that informants are necessary to the news-gathering process as we know it today. If it is to perform its constitutional mission, the press must do far more than merely print public statements or publish prepared handouts. Familiarity with the people and circumstances involved in the myriad background activities that result in the final product called "news" is vital to complete and responsible journalism, unless the press is to be a captive mouthpiece of "newsmakers."

It is equally obvious that the promise of confidentiality may be a necessary prerequisite to a productive relationship between a newsman and his informants. An officeholder may fear his superior; a member of the bureaucracy, his associates; a dissident, the scorn of majority opinion. All may have information valuable to the public discourse, yet each may be willing to relate that information only in confidence to a reporter whom he trusts, either because of excessive caution or because of a reasonable fear of reprisals or censure for unorthodox views. The First Amendment concern must not be with the motives of any particular news source, but rather with the conditions in which informants of all shades of the spectrum may make information available through the press to the public....

After today's decision, the potential informant can never be sure that his identity or off-the-record communications will not subsequently be revealed through the compelled testimony of a newsman. A public-spirited person inside government, who is not implicated in any crime, will now be fearful of revealing corruption or other governmental wrongdoing, because he will now know he can subsequently be identified by use of compulsory process. The potential source must, therefore, choose between risking exposure by giving information or avoiding the risk by remaining silent.

The reporter must speculate about whether contact with a controversial source or publication of controversial material will lead to a subpoena. In the event of a subpoena, under today's decision, the newsman will know that he must choose between being punished for contempt if he refuses to testify, or violating his profession's ethics and impairing his resourcefulness as a reporter if he discloses confidential information.

Cohen *v.* California

403 U.S. 15 (1971)

Protests against the Vietnam War escalated in the late 1960s as Viet Cong attacks reached the heart of Saigon and thousands of American soldiers returned home in body bags. Most of those who protested were peaceful, standing in silent vigils or parading through public streets and parks. Some protests, however, disrupted public order or became violent, leading to arrests and criminal convictions. Several Vietnam protest cases reached the Supreme Court, which tried to distinguish "speech" from "conduct" that crossed the line between protected advocacy and criminal action. One case testing this distinction began in April 1968 when Paul Robert Cohen entered a Los Angeles courthouse wearing a jacket on which was painted the slogan, "Fuck the Draft." Cohen was convicted of disturbing the peace and sentenced to 30 days in jail. The Supreme Court reversed his conviction, holding that the best remedy for Cohen's "distasteful" slogan was the "powerful medicine" of free speech in a diverse and divided country.

Counsel for petitioner: Melville B. Nimmer, Los Angeles, California
Counsel for respondent: Michael T. Sauer, Deputy City Attorney, Los Angeles, California

Chief Justice Burger: We will hear arguments next in Number 299, *Cohen* against *California*.

Narrator: It's February 22, 1971. We're in the chamber of the United States Supreme Court in Washington, D.C. Chief Justice Warren Burger has called for argument a case that may seem trivial to some, an appeal from a disturbing the peace conviction that resulted in a 30-day jail sentence. This case involves just three words, painted on the back of a denim jacket worn by Paul Robert Cohen. A 19-year-old store clerk, Cohen wore his jacket in the Los Angeles county courthouse on April 26, 1968.

One of the words on Cohen's jacket offended police sergeant Huston Splawn, who arrested him for engaging in "tumultuous and offensive conduct." The words that brought Cohen a jail sentence and a Supreme Court hearing were "Fuck the Draft," a sentiment shared by many Vietnam war opponents during this tumultuous period in American history. The day of Cohen's arrest, a Los Angeles Times headline read "GIs Battle Viet Cong in Saigon Outskirts." More than 20,000 GIs had already come back from Vietnam in body bags, and the Pentagon announced a draft call of 347,000 young men for the year. Paul Cohen's opposition to the draft, expresed in words that many find offensive, was mild in comparison to the loud and sometimes violent protests that rocked college campuses across the country.

A trial judge found Cohen guilty, holding that his jacket expressed an "obscene" message. State appellate judges rejected this ruling, but upheld the conviction on grounds that Cohen's jacket expressed "fighting words" that might provoke violence. After the California Supreme Court refused to hear Cohen's appeal, his lawyers asked the U.S. Supreme Court to review the case. Cohen is represented by Melville Nimmer, a UCLA law professor who volunteered for the American Civil Liberties Union.

Chief Justice Burger welcomes Nimmer to the podium and urges him to keep Cohen's offensive words out of the Court's records and recordings. Nimmer politely but pointedly declines, explaining later that he did not want to concede "that I was dealing with an unspeakable word." He responds to Justice Potter Stewart's question about the facts of the case.

Nimmer: Mr. Chief Justice, and may it please the Court. At Mr. Chief Justice's suggestion, I certainly will keep very brief the statement of facts. But, fundamentally, we do have here the appellant charged and convicted of engaging in tumultuous and offensive conduct, in violation of the California Disturbing the Peace statute, Penal Code Section 415.

What this young man did was to walk through a courthouse corridor in Los Angeles County, on his way to a courtroom where he had some business.... While walking through that corridor, he was wearing a jacket on which were inscribed the words "Fuck the Draft." Also inscribed were the words "Stop War," and several peace symbols.

When he entered the courtroom, he took off his jacket and held it folded. When he left the courtroom he was arrested for disturbing the peace. Specifically, engaging in tumultuous and offensive conduct.

Stewart: Now you say he took his jacket off in the courtroom? Did he put it in a place that was prominently on view?

Nimmer: No, Mr. Justice Stewart. He held it folded over his arm and it was not on view there. Furthermore, the policeman who observed him walking through the corridor before he went into the courtroom—this is in the record—requested the judge in the courtroom to hold the young man in contempt. The judge refused to hold the young man in contempt, because there was nothing to be seen in the courtroom—I shouldn't say that. I don't know what would have been done if he did see anything, but there was nothing to be seen. And then he left, and at that point he was arrested.

Narrator: Nimmer addresses the issue of whether the words on Cohen's jacket would provoke violence by those who were offended.

Nimmer: I think it's important at the outset to point out to the Court that there was no violence—no component of violence—present. It was stated in the Settled Statement signed by the trial judge that the appellant did not engage in violence, did not threaten violence; that no one observing him engaged in violence or threatened violence, so the "violence" component is completely out.

And I suggest that that is terribly significant for the broader significance of this case, pointing out as it can do, depending upon this Court's decision, the very vital distinction between "dissent" which may be offensive to people— some people may not like it—but, "non-violent dissent" and "violent dissent;" a distinction which all too often members of the younger generation tend to forget. They tend to equate violent dissent with dissent that may be regarded as objectionable or offensive. It is terribly important, we submit to Your Honors, that this Court make clear the distinction that "dissent" by its very nature involves a right to be "offensive." Non-offensive dissent is almost a contradiction in terms. Because if it's non-offensive, it means you agree with it; but, on the other hand, violent dissent is something quite different.

Narrator: Justice Byron White questions Nimmer about the "fighting words" doctrine, established by the Supreme Court in its 1942 decision in *Chaplinsky v. New Hampshire*. Walter Chaplinsky was a Jehovah's Witness who was arrested for calling a police officer a "damned Fascist" and "racketeer." The Supreme Court defined "fighting words" in *Chaplinsky* as those which "inflict injury or tend to incite an immediate breach of the peace."

White: Would it be your position that your client could have—would have had a First Amendment right to say these words orally, face-to-face, to any person in the hall outside the courtroom?

Nimmer: Mr. Justice White, I don't think the distinction lies in whether it's oral or written. But, if you are suggesting a distinction based upon the "fighting words" concept—

White: I'm not suggesting anything. I just asked the question. Would your position be the same?

Nimmer: Yes, if you used these precise words, namely, relating to the draft—

White: Yes. To any person, face-to-face, in the hallway. Do you think he has a First Amendment right to do that?

Nimmer: Yes, I do, Your Honor.

White: And if he didn't, there might be some trouble? You might have some trouble in this case?

Nimmer: Uh, I don't, offhand, see a viable distinction between the written and the oral, yes.

White: Yes.

Nimmer: But, Your Honor, I think it's terribly important. This suggests—perhaps you were not suggesting, but it suggests to me this line of the "fighting words" concept taken from the *Chaplinsky* case decided by this Court some years ago where this Court suggested that in certain circumstances words may be regarded as "fighting words" because men will reasonable know they will result in violence. And, hence, that those words are outside of the First Amendment.

White: Is your view of "fighting words" different than—do you think "fighting words" are different than "insulting words"?

Nimmer: No, Your Honor. That's precisely my point; I think they're synonymous. And hence these are not fighting words, because they're—well, perhaps I should be more specific. Insulting words are insulting to the hearer. They are insulting the person to whom the words are addressed, is what the basic concept of "fighting words" refers to—as in *Chaplinsky*, "damned racketeer" and "Fascist." Here there was no attack on the hearer. There was an "opposition"—verbal attack, if you will, on an institution, the Selective Service System—but not as against any of the viewers of this sign. Hence, we submit this does not at all come under the *Chaplinsky* "fighting words" concept.

Narrator: Nimmer faces questions from Justice Thurgood Marshall.

Nimmer: This is an ordinary free—exercise, in freedom of expression. Certainly, one is not limited, in one's freedom of expression, to expressing—

Marshall: Well, could he have stood in the court hallways and yelled those words?

Nimmer: Certainly not. That would have been highly improper, Your Honor. But that raises another non-speech element.

Marshall: Well, it says that he had it "emblazoned on his jacket." We can't tell whether that's loud, or what, can we?

Nimmer: Well, Your Honor, it was on his jacket, which meant that a person, if he wishes to, could see it on his jacket. But a person was not forced to continue to observe that, as in terms of a loud noise where one can't help but hear it.

Marshall: Does it mean that somebody walking up the hall, directly behind him, couldn't help from seeing it?

Nimmer: For the moment, but—

Marshall: I mean, obviously that's why he did it.

Nimmer: Yes, Your Honor.

Marshall: He didn't want people to see it?

Nimmer: No. I'm certainly not stating that, at all. Quite definitely he did want to pass that message, but it's a somewhat different question as to what his motive was in wearing it. And, in part, it was to convey this message, although he was not "parading" or "picketing" or anything of the sort. He was making his way to the courtroom, and then made his way back; but he did want people to see this.

Narrator: Nimmer admits that Cohen's jacket had an "emotive" content that might upset or offend those who saw it. He argues that the First Amendment protects the form of expression as well as its substance.

Nimmer: Now we get to what the First Amendment is all about, and what it is all about, of course, is competition in the marketplace of ideas—what ideas are going to prevail. We subscribe to the democratic faith that the ideas that prevail by a majority are the ideas which should be followed. But, in order for that system to work, it's important that the State not step in and try to censor either emotive content, or intellectual content. Because, depending on the emotive content—particular emotive content—the message will appeal to various groups of citizens. And, by determining what the emotive—by censoring the emotive content, even if not the intellectual content, the State is thereby enabled, to a great degree, to determine what group will buy this idea, to what group the idea will appeal, and hence, ultimately, will be able to determine what ideas will prevail in the competition of the market. And so for that reason, we respectfully submit to the Court that emotive content, just as much as intellectual content—or, to put it another way—that the offensiveness of form, no less than the offensiveness of substance, must be preserved by the First Amendment, if the First Amendment is to be meaningful.

Narrator: Michael Sauer, a deputy city attorney in Los Angeles, argues for the state of California. Chief Justice Burger welcomes him.

Chief Justice Burger: Mr. Sauer?

Sauer: Mr. Chief Justice, and may it please the Court. As an issue developed in appellant's opening argument, I don't believe there's any difference in whether the appellant wore it in a courtroom, or in a corridor. If the defendant were protesting the decisions of this Court, and carried a similar sign, and walked across the plaza and up the marble staircase and down the corridor here, I don't think it's be any different if he stopped and took his jacket off at the curtain, or if he entered the courtroom here with the same type sign. I believe the same violation would have occurred; that that would have been engaging in offensive conduct—or, if the man wore it in a public street, I would say the same type of conviction should stand.

Narrator: Sauer faces questions about the form of Cohen's protest against the draft.

Court: There was "offensive" conduct?

Sauer: Correct. "Conduct" by displaying the—

Court: The "conduct" was what?

Sauer:—by wearing the jacket, and walking in the corridor.

Court: Well, wearing the—was it—the "conduct" was, precisely, what?

Sauer: Displaying the sign on the jacket. By the fact that he was walking with the sign displayed on his jacket.

Court: Well, the "walking" wasn't offensive conduct? Just the "walking," was it?

Sauer: Walking with the sign. Merely "walking," no.

Court: No. And, so, what was the "conduct"?

Sauer: Displaying the sign.

Court: "Displaying"?

Sauer: Yes. His conduct of displaying the sign.

Court: The words?

Sauer: Yes, where other persons were present—

Court: The words were painted on, or sewn on, or whatever it was, on his jacket?

Sauer: Right. They were painted on.

Court: The jacket?

Sauer: Correct. That is our contention.

Court: The display of the words?

Sauer: Correct.

Narrator: Justice Marshall turns to the facts of the case. Justice Harry Blackmun rescues Sauer from Marshall's questions.

Marshall: Well, what is there in the record—in testimony—that shows that these words were offensive to any person in the building at that time?

Sauer: There's nothing in the record, Mr. Justice Marshall. We just said "the effect on the average person." As I go back and read *Chaplinsky*, there's no showing that Major Browerlein, when the man yelled at him, "You damn fascist," or "you damn racketeer," was offended by the statement. There's no showing that Major Browerlein was going to react against it.

Marshall: Well, who in the building was interested in the draft? Does the record show?

Sauer: There's no showing. Even appellant admits the man was there just because citizens who would be present—

Marshall: Well, my great difficulty is as to what's the difference between the man whispering something in the corner to somebody, and wearing a jacket that so far as this record shows only one person saw?

Sauer: No, I believe three people saw it. There was a Sergeant Spawn. There was someone named Alexander; and there was one other person, I believe.

Marshall: Well, was it offensive to them?

Blackmun: Mr. Sauer, may I read from the Settled Statement on appeal? "Sergeant Shauler and Officer Alexander corroborated Sergeant Spawn's testimony as to defendant's presence in the corridor; his wearing of the jacket; his entering the courtroom; and as to the presence in the corridor of women and children." Isn't that the answer?

Sauer: Correct, Mr. Justice Blackmun, yes. I said the record shows that there were other individuals present, as well as three specifically named individuals. There were women and children present in the corridor.

Narrator: Justice Marshall returns to the offending word on Cohen's jacket.

Sauer: I believe you have to—if you take "offensive" as defined in *Chaplinsky*, you have to apply it as what the "average man" would think. And I would say that these words would be offensive to the average man.

Marshall: You mean the one word, don't you? Suppose he had on his jacket, "I don't like the draft"—no—

Sauer: Then I don't believe—

Marshall:—no—"I dislike the draft"?

Sauer: Then I doubt we would be here, Mr. Justice Marshall.

Marshall: It's the word, isn't it?

Sauer: Yes.

Marshall: Isn't that all you have?

Sauer: "A" word, yes. I think collectively, throughout the case, it's referred to as "the three words."

Narrator: Sauer points the justices to earlier cases that allowed punishment of offensive and obscene speech.

Sauer: The terms "offensive" have been upheld by this Court in the past. In *Feiner v. New York*, the defendant was charged, among other things, with using "offensive" language, conduct, or behavior; "acting in a manner so as to be offensive to others." In *Chaplinsky*, the man was charged with using offensive words. This word has stood the test of time in the past. In other cases—in *Beauharnais* and *Roth*—in discussing an area of obscene speech—if these words are determined to be obscene speech—the Court, it was said that certainly no one would contend that obscene speech may be punished only upon a showing of circumstances of a clear and present danger. In *Roth* and in *Beauharnais* it seemed to indicate that someone used obscene speech in public, that would be a sufficient violation.

Narrator: Sauer faces another round of questions from Justices Stewart and Marshall.

Stewart: I don't have so much problem with the "tumultuous or offensive" as I do with what the "conduct" is here.

Sauer: The conduct is wearing the jacket, displaying the sign.

Stewart: Just displaying the words? That's all the conduct there is, isn't it?

Sauer: Yes. Correct, if the man had "yelled" the word, Mr. Justice Stewart. That part of the statute is not before us, but it says if he "yells it in a loud and boisterous manner"—

Stewart: Well, we're not talking about decibels here, at all.

Sauer: Okay.

Stewart: That would be quite a different case. This is a "displaying of message," and that's the only conduct involved, isn't it?

Sauer: That's correct. Displaying a term that we would contend is not accepted for public display. The fact that it appears in best sellers, I don't believe is sufficient reason to allow it to be displayed in public. There are people who may wish to read a best seller. That is their choice. But here individuals were a captive audience, with the words foisted upon them. They could not avoid it, other than to close their eyes. But they had the right to be in the corridor, also.

Stewart: If these words had been "nuts to the draft," would this case have been here?

Sauer: No, I don't—I do not believe so.

Stewart: So, it's not the—it narrows down to this one four-letter word? Is that it?

Sauer: That is correct. A word that we contend, and the Court of Appeal said, is not generally accepted for public display. I would say that if persons were in front of the White House, picketing the President, using this word in relation to the President, or picketing this Court with the word in relation to the Court, it would still be offensive conduct in words that are not accepted at this time.

Marshall: Is everyone in Los Angeles walking down the street who might use that word, subject to being arrested?

Sauer: If they were "displaying" the word, we would consider that to be offensive conduct.

Marshall: Have you got jails big enough? [Laughter].

Narrator: Sauer tries to distinguish Paul Cohen from the civil rights demonstrators whose speech and signs and songs offended white segregationists in the Deep South.

Sauer: The argument's been made that we should have a democratic dialogue. I agree that, you know, conversation's important. The streets are to be used for public argument. I don't believe this type of language has to be subjected upon an unwilling public. I think, in the past, we've seen candidates for public office, you know, who've been subjected to offensive signs, language being yelled at them, things that at the moment are not accepted by all the public. I don't believe this is the same as an individual in *Edwards*, or some of the sit-in cases from the South—the fact that some white individuals may have objected to the fact that these people were peacefully protesting—because there's no showing that they displayed such signs. Many of them sang freedom songs and engaged in, say, conduct like that. But in this case, the man has displayed a sign that the State of California has found to be offensive by its decisions.

Narrator: Sauer concludes by invoking the *Chaplinsky* case. Chief Justice Burger ends the argument.

Sauer: We would just repeat, as I cited in our brief, and going back to *Chaplinsky*, it's been well urged—paraphrasing—that words of this type are no essential part of any exposition of ideas, and citing social value as a step to the truth, that any benefit that may be derived from them is clearly outweighed by the social interests in order and morality. We believe the conviction of the California Court of Appeal is valid, and the judgment should stand. Thank you, Mr. Justices.

Burger: Thank you, Mr. Sauer.

Narrator: On June 7, 1971, the Supreme Court reversed Paul Cohen's conviction and erased his jail sentence. The five-to-four decision shuffled the normal lineup of liberals and conservatives in First Amendment cases. Justice John Marshall Harlan, one of the Court's most conservative members, wrote for the majority, joined by another conservative justice, Potter Stewart. Harlan began by admitting that Cohen's case may seem "too inconsequential to find its way into our books, but the issue it presents is of no small constitutional significance."

Harlan stressed that Cohen was convicted solely for the speech that was scrawled on his jacket, not for any conduct that might provoke violence. He distinguished this case from *Chaplinsky*, where the insulting or "fighting" words were directed personally at a police officer. Harlan conceded that Cohen's words would offend many, but he countered that "the constitutional right of free expression is powerful medicine in a society as diverse and populous as ours."

Harlan added a phrase to his opinion that upset Chief Justice Burger and other defenders of verbal decorum. While the four-letter word on Paul Cohen's jacket was perhaps "distasteful," Harlan wrote, "it is nevertheless often true that one man's vulgarity is another's lyric."

Four justices did not like the lyrics in Harlan's opinion. Justice Harry Blackmun wrote for the dissenters, who included Hugo Black, normally a First Amendment "absolutist" in speech cases. Blackmun was brief and pungent. "Cohen's absurd and immature antic," he wrote, "was mainly conduct and little speech." Blackmun also claimed that *Cohen* was "well within the sphere of *Chaplinsky v. New Hampshire*," although he did not explain how the two cases fit the same constitutional mold.

Since the Court decided *Cohen v. California*, the justices have never upheld a conviction under the "fighting words" doctrine of *Chaplinsky*. But they have not reversed that decision, leaving the expression of offensive speech at risk in future cases.

EDITED SUPREME COURT OPINIONS
Cohen v. California

MR. JUSTICE HARLAN delivered the opinion of the Court.

This case may seem at first blush too inconsequential to find its way into our books, but the issue it presents is of no small constitutional significance.

Appellant Paul Robert Cohen was convicted in the Los Angeles Municipal Court of violating that part of California Penal Code § 415 which prohibits "maliciously and willfully disturb[ing] the peace or quiet of any neighborhood or person…by…offensive conduct…." He was given 30 days' imprisonment. The facts upon which his conviction rests are detailed in the opinion of the Court of Appeal of California, Second Appellate District, as follows:

"On April 26, 1968, the defendant was observed in the Los Angeles County Courthouse in the corridor outside of division 20 of the municipal court wearing a jacket bearing the words 'Fuck the Draft' which were plainly visible. There were women and children present in the corridor. The defendant was arrested. The defendant testified that he wore the jacket knowing that the words were on the jacket as a means of informing the public of the depth of his feelings against the Vietnam War and the draft.

"The defendant did not engage in, nor threaten to engage in, nor did anyone as the result of his conduct in fact commit or threaten to commit any act of violence. The defendant did not make any loud or unusual noise, nor was there any evidence that he uttered any sound prior to his arrest." 1 Cal. App. 3d 94, 97–08, 81 Cal. Rptr. 503, 505 (1969).

In affirming the conviction the Court of Appeal held that "offensive conduct" means "behavior which has a tendency to provoke others to acts of violence or to in turn disturb the peace," and that the State had proved this element because, on the facts of this case, "[i]t was certainly reasonably foreseeable that such conduct might cause others to rise up to commit a violent act against the person of the defendant or attempt to forceably remove his jacket." 1 Cal. App. 3d, at 99–100, 81 Cal. Rptr., at 506. The California Supreme Court declined review by a divided vote. We brought the case here, postponing the consideration of the question of our jurisdiction over this appeal to a hearing of the case on the merits. 399 U.S. 904. We now reverse….

In order to lay hands on the precise issue which this case involves, it is useful first to canvass various matters which this record does *not* present.

The conviction quite clearly rests upon the asserted offensiveness of the *words* Cohen used to convey his message to the public. The only "conduct" which the State sought to punish is the fact of communication. Thus, we deal here with a conviction resting solely upon "speech," cf. *Stromberg v. California*,

283 U.S. 359 (1931), not upon any separately identifiable conduct which allegedly was intended by Cohen to be perceived by others as expressive of particular views but which, on its face, does not necessarily convey any message and hence arguably could be regulated without effectively repressing Cohen's ability to express himself. Cf. *United States v. O'Brien*, 391 U.S. 367 (1968). Further, the State certainly lacks power to punish Cohen for the underlying content of the message the inscription conveyed. At least so long as there is no showing of an intent to incite disobedience to or disruption of the draft, Cohen could not, consistently with the First and Fourteenth Amendments, be punished for asserting the evident position on the inutility or immorality of the draft his jacket reflected. *Yates v. United States*, 354 U.S. 298 (1957).

Appellant's conviction, then, rests squarely upon his exercise of the "freedom of speech protected from arbitrary governmental interference by the Constitution and can be justified, if at all, only as a valid regulation of the manner in which he exercised that freedom, not as a permissible prohibition on the substantive message it conveys. This does not end the inquiry, of course, for the First and Fourteenth Amendments have never been thought to give absolute protection to every individual to speak whenever or wherever he pleases, or to use any form of address in any circumstances that he chooses. In this vein, too, however, we think it important to note that several issues typically associated with such problems are not presented here.

In the first place, Cohen was tried under a statute applicable throughout the entire state. Any attempt to support this conviction on the ground that the statute seeks to preserve an appropriately decorous atmosphere in the courthouse where Cohen was arrested must fail in the absence of any language in the statute that would have put appellant on notice that certain kinds of otherwise permissible speech or conduct would nevertheless, under California law, not be tolerated in certain places. See *Edwards v. South Carolina*, 372 U.S. 229, 236–237, and n. 11 (1963). Cf. *Adderley v. Florida*, 385 U.S. 39 (1966). No fair reading of the phrase "offensive conduct" can be said sufficiently to inform the ordinary person that distinctions between certain locations are thereby created.

In the second place, as it comes to us, this case cannot be said to fall within those relatively few categories of instances where prior decisions have established the power of government to deal more comprehensively with certain forms of individual expression simply upon a showing that such a form was employed. This is not, for example, an obscenity case. Whatever else may be necessary to give rise to the States' broader power to prohibit obscene expression, such expression must be, in some significant way, erotic. *Roth v. United States*, 354 U.S. 476 (1957). It cannot plausibly be maintained that this vulgar allusion to the Selective Service System would conjure up such psychic stimulation in anyone likely to be confronted with Cohen's crudely defaced jacket.

This Court has also held that the States are free to ban the simple use, without a demonstration of additional justifying circumstances, of so-called "fighting words," those personally abusive epithets which, when addressed to the ordinary citizen, are, as a matter of common knowledge, inherently likely to provoke violent reaction. *Chaplinsky v. New Hampshire*, 315 U.S. 568 (1942). While the four-letter word displayed by Cohen in relation to the draft is not uncommonly employed in a personally provocative fashion, in this instance it was clearly not "directed to the person of the hearer." *Cantwell v. Connecticut*, 310 U.S. 296, 309 (1940). No individual actually or likely to be present could reasonably have regarded the words on appellant's jacket as a direct personal insult. Nor do we have here an instance of the exercise of the State's police power to prevent a speaker from intentionally provoking a given group to hostile reaction. Cf. *Feiner v. New York*, 340 U.S. 315 (1951); *Terminiello v. Chicago*, 337 U.S. 1 (1949). There is, as noted above, no showing that anyone who saw Cohen was in fact violently aroused or that appellant intended such a result.

Finally, in arguments before this Court much has been made of the claim that Cohen's distasteful mode of expression was thrust upon unwilling or unsuspecting viewers, and that the State might therefore legitimately act as it did in order to protect the sensitive from otherwise unavoidable exposure to appellant's crude form of protest. Of course, the mere presumed presence of unwitting listeners or viewers does not serve automatically to justify curtailing all speech capable of giving offense. Sec. e. 9., *Organization for a Better Austin v. Keefe*, 402 U.S. 415 (1971). While this Court has recognized that government may properly act in many situations to prohibit intrusion into the privacy of the home of unwelcome views and ideas which cannot be totally banned from the public dialogue, *e. g., Rowan v. Post Office Dept.*, 397 U.S. 728 (1970), we have at the same time consistently stressed that "we are often 'captives' outside the sanctuary of the homes and subject to objectionable speech." *Id.*, at 738. The ability of governments consonant with the Constitution, to shut off discourse solely to protect others from hearing it is, in other words, dependent upon a showing that substantial privacy interests are being invaded in an essentially intolerable manner. Any broader view of this authority would effectively empower a majority to silence dissidents simply as a matter of personal predilections.

In this regard, persons confronted with Cohen's jacket were in a quite different posture than, say, those subjected to the raucous emissions of sound trucks blaring outside their residences. Those in the Los Angeles courthouse could effectively avoid further bombardment of their sensibilities simply by

averting their eyes. And, while it may be that one has a more substantial claim
to a recognizable privacy interest when walking through a courthouse corridor
than, for example, strolling through Central Park, surely it is nothing like the
interest in being free from unwanted expression in the confines of one's own
home. Cf. *Keefe, supra.* Given the subtlety and complexity of the factors
involved, if Cohen's "speech" was otherwise entitled to constitutional protection, we do not think the fact that some unwilling "listeners" in a public building may have been briefly exposed to it can serve to justify this breach of the
peace conviction where, as here, there was no evidence that persons powerless
to avoid appellant's conduct did in fact object to it, and where that portion of
the statute upon which Cohen's conviction rests evinces no concern, either on
its face or as construed by the California courts, with the special plight of the
captive auditor, but, instead, indiscriminately sweeps within its prohibitions all
"offensive conduct" that disturbs "any neighborhood or person." Cf. *Edwards* v.
South Carolina, supra.

II

Against this background, the issue flushed by this case stands out in bold relief.
It is whether California can excise, as "offensive conduct," one particular scur-
rilous epithet from the public discourse, either upon the theory of the court
below that its use is inherently likely to cause violent reaction or upon a more
general assertion that the States, acting as guardians of public morality, may
properly remove this offensive word from the public vocabulary.

The rationale of the California court is plainly untenable. At most it
reflects an "undifferentiated fear or apprehension of disturbance [which] is not
enough to overcome the right to freedom of expression." *Tinker* v. *Des Moines
Indep. Community School Dist.*, 393 U.S. 503, 508 (1969). We have been shown
no evidence that substantial numbers of citizens are standing ready to strike out
physically at whoever may assault their sensibilities with execrations like that
uttered by Cohen. There may be some persons about with such lawless and violent proclivities, but that is an insufficient base upon which to erect, consistently with constitutional values, a governmental power to force persons who
wish to ventilate their dissident views into avoiding particular forms of expression. The argument amounts to little more than the self-defeating proposition
that to avoid physical censorship of one who has not sought to provoke such a
response by a hypothetical coterie of the violent and lawless, the States may
more appropriately effectuate that censorship themselves. Cf. *Ashton* v. *Kentucky*, 384 U.S. 195, 200 (1966); *Cox* v. *Louisiana*, 379 U.S. 536, 550–551 (1965).

Admittedly, it is not so obvious that the First and Fourteenth Amendments must be taken to disable the States from punishing public utterance of this unseemly expletive in order to maintain what they regard as a suitable level of discourse within the body politic. We think, however, that examination and reflection will reveal the shortcomings of a contrary viewpoint.

At the outset, we cannot overemphasize that, in our judgment, most situations where the State has a justifiable interest in regulating speech will fall within one or more of the various established exceptions, discussed above but not applicable here, to the usual rule that governmental bodies may not prescribe the form or content of individual expression. Equally important to our conclusion is the constitutional backdrop against which our decision must be made. The constitutional right of free expression is powerful medicine in a society as diverse and populous as ours. It is designed and intended to remove governmental restraints from the arena of public discussion putting the decision as to what views shall be voiced largely into the hands of each of us, in the hope that use of such freedom will ultimately produce a more capable citizenry and more perfect polity and in the belief that no other approach would comport with the premise of individual dignity and choice upon which our political system rests. See *Whitney v. California*, 274 U.S. 357, 375–377 (1927) (Brandeis, J., concurring).

To many, the immediate consequence of this freedom may often appear to be only verbal tumult, discord, and even offensive utterance. These are, however, within established limits, in truth necessary side effects of the broader enduring values which the process of open debate permits us to achieve. That the air may at times seem filled with verbal cacophony is, in this sense not a sign of weakness but of strength. We cannot lose sight of the fact that, in what otherwise might seem a trifling and annoying instance of individual distasteful abuse of a privilege, these fundamental societal values are truly implicated. That is why "[w]holly neutral futilities...come under the protection of free speech as fully as do Keats' poems or Donne's sermons," *Winters v. New York*, 333 U.S. 507, 528 (1948) (Frankfurter, J., dissenting), and why "so long as the means are peaceful, the communication need not meet standards of acceptability," *Organization for a Better Austin v. Keefe*, 402 U.S. 415, 419 (1971).

Against this perception of the constitutional policies involved, we discern certain more particularized considerations that peculiarly call for reversal of this conviction. First, the principle contended for by the State seems inherently boundless. How is one to distinguish this from any other offensive word? Surely the State has no right to cleanse public debate to the point where it is grammatically palatable to the most squeamish among us. Yet no readily ascertainable general principle exists for stopping short of that result were we to affirm the judgment below. For, while the particular four-letter word being litigated here is perhaps more distasteful than most others of its genre, it is nevertheless often true that one man's vulgarity is another's lyric. Indeed, we think it is largely because governmental officials cannot make principled distinctions in this area that the Constitution leaves matters of taste and style so largely to the individual.

Additionally, we cannot overlook the fact, because it is well illustrated by the episode involved here, that much linguistic expression serves a dual communicative function: it conveys not only ideas capable of relatively precise, detached explication, but otherwise inexpressible emotions as well. In fact, words are often chosen as much for their emotive as their cognitive force. We cannot sanction the view that the Constitution, while solicitous of the cognitive content of individual speech, has little or no regard for that emotive function which, practically speaking, may often be the more important element of the overall message sought to be communicated....

Finally, and in the same vein, we cannot indulge the facile assumption that one can forbid particular words without also running a substantial risk of suppressing ideas in the process. Indeed, governments might soon seize upon the censorship of particular words as a convenient guise for banning the expression of unpopular views. We have been able, as noted above, to discern little social benefit that might result from running the risk of opening the door to such grave results.

It is, in sum, our judgment that, absent a more particularized and compelling reason for its actions, the State may not, consistently with the First and Fourteenth Amendments, make the simple public display here involved of this single four-letter expletive a criminal offense. Because that is the only arguably sustainable rationale for the conviction here at issue, the judgment below must be

Reversed.

MR. JUSTICE BLACKMUN, with whom THE CHIEF JUSTICE and MR. JUSTICE BLACK join.

I dissent.

Cohen's absurd and immature antic, in my view, was mainly conduct and little speech. See *Street v. New York*, 394 U.S. 576 (1969); *Cox v. Louisiana*, 379 U.S. 536, 555 (1965); *Giboney v. Empire Storage Co.*, 336 U.S. 490, 502 (1949). The California Court of Appeal appears so to have described it, 1 Cal. App. 3d 94, 100, 81 Cal. Rptr. 503, 507, and I cannot characterize it otherwise. Further, the case appears to me to be well within the sphere of *Chaplinsky v. New Hampshire*, 315 U.S. 568 (1942), where Mr. Justice Murphy, a known champion of First Amendment freedoms, wrote for a unanimous bench. As a consequence, this Court's agonizing over First Amendment values seems misplaced and unnecessary....

Employment Division
v. Smith

494 U.S. 872 (1990)

Alfred Smith and Galen Black were counselors at a drug and alcohol treatment program in Oregon. They belonged to the Native American Church, whose members use peyote in religious ceremonies. Church members consider peyote, which has hallucinogenic properties, as "the means for communicating with the Great Spirit." Oregon law prohibited any use of peyote, and state officials defended the ban as necessary for the "war on drugs" being waged by state and federal agencies, although Congress had exempted Native American Church members from federal drug laws. Smith and Black were fired after they admitted using peyote in church ceremonies, and applied for unemployment benefits. The state appealed to the Supreme Court after the highest state court ruled that the Free Exercise clause of the First Amendment required an exception for the religious use of peyote. Ruling in 1990, the Supreme Court upheld the Oregon law and the denial of benefits to Smith and Black. Three years later, Congress passed the Religious Freedom Restoration Act, which overruled the Supreme Court decision and prohibited states from banning peyote use in religious ceremonies.

Employment Division, Department of Human Resources of Oregon v. Smith, 494
U.S. 872 (1990)

Counsel for petitioners: David B. Frohnmayer, Attorney General of Oregon,
Salem, Oregon
Counsel for respondents: Craig J. Dorsey, Portland, Oregon

Chief Justice Rehnquist: We'll hear argument next in Number 88-1213, *Employment Division of Oregon v. Alfred Smith.*

Narrator: It's November 6, 1989. We're in the chamber of the United States
Supreme Court in Washington, D.C. Chief Justice William Rehnquist has
called for argument a case that poses claims of religious freedom against the
"war on drugs" being waged by state and federal officials.

This case began when two Oregon residents, Alfred Smith and Galen Black,
were fired by the drug and alcohol treatment agency for which they worked as
counselors. The agency served many Native Americans, whose rates of substance
abuse and addiction are several times the national rate. Smith and Black belong
to the Native American Church, whose members use peyote as their central religious sacrament. Peyote is a natural substance, part of a cactus plant, and has a
psychotropic effect that produces religious "visions" for church members.

Smith and Black were fired for admitting peyote use in church ceremonies,
in violation of agency policy that made illegal drug use grounds for "immediate
termination from employment." Peyote use, for any purpose, is illegal in
Oregon, even though the federal government and more than a dozen states
have exempted Native American Church members from drug prosecution.
Oregon officials turned down Smith and Black's applications for unemployment benefits, but the Oregon Supreme Court ruled in their favor, citing a 1963
U.S. Supreme Court decision, *Sherbert v. Verner.* This case struck down the
denial of jobless benefits to a Seventh-Day Adventist who was fired for refusing
to work on Saturdays, her church's Sabbath day. State officials appealed this
ruling to the U.S. Supreme Court, which sent the case back to state judges for
clarification. After the Oregon court reaffirmed its first decision, the state
appealed a second time to the U.S. Supreme Court

Oregon officials argue that illegal drug use is not the same as honoring the
Sabbath. They claim that allowing the religious use of peyote would hinder, in
their brief's words, "a battle against dangerous drugs that in real terms…is a
war." The Native American Church countered with a claim in its brief that
"peyote is consecrated with powers to heal mind, body, and spirit" and is "the
means for communicating with the Great Spirit."

Faced with these conflicting claims, the Supreme Court hears argument first from Oregon's attorney general, Dave Frohnmayer. Chief Justice Rehnquist welcomes him to the podium.

Rehnquist: General Frohnmayer, you may proceed.

Frohnmayer: Thank you, Mr. Chief Justice, and may it please the Court. This case is before this Court a second time. The first question was whether claimants were entitled to receive unemployment compensation benefits after being fired as drug counselors. It is undisputed that they violated their employer's job-related rule that they be drug free because they ingested peyote in the ceremonies of the Native American Church. A majority of this Court held that the claimants were not entitled to unemployment benefits under the doctrine of *Sherbert* v. *Verner* if their conduct, even if religiously motivated, violated a valid Oregon criminal law. After the Oregon Supreme Court's ultimate decision on federal grounds on remand, the question is this: Does the Free Exercise Clause require every state to exempt the religious peyote use by the Native American Church, or perhaps even beyond that, other substance use by other religions, from the reach of generally applicable criminal laws regulating the use of controlled substances by all citizens?

Narrator: Frohnmayer outlined the state's position on the issues before the Court.

Frohnmayer: The Oregon Supreme Court's resolution of the federal law question, we believe, seriously compromises three compelling and intersecting state interests. The first is the state's interest in regulating all peyote and hallucinogenic drug use in order to further the health and safety interests of its citizens. The second is the state's interest in a regulatory scheme as a whole, so that law enforcement does not face a patchwork of exemptions of other drugs on a drug-by-drug, religion-by-religion, believer-by-believer basis. And the third and compelling interest is that the state constitution's heightened requirement of neutrality in our jurisdiction, requires it to avoid giving the preference of one church over another.

Narrator: Frohnmayer explains why Oregon considers peyote a dangerous drug.

Frohnmayer: Peyote, by all accounts, is a powerful and unpredictable hallucinogen. That fact is largely conceded even by respondents, at least for the public generally, and it is amply illustrated by the record. Its active ingredient is mescaline.

It stimulates respiratory changes, reflexes and pulse rates, which are physiologically measurable. The spectrum of effects experienced are similar, and in most respects identical, to those of LSD, psilocybin, and mescaline, accompanied by vivid visual and auditory hallucinations, altered perceptions of time, space, and body—emotional reactions that range from joy and exhilaration to extreme anxiety and even terror. There is no way to predict, even for the experienced user, how the user will react on a given occasion. There are effects on the central nervous system and behavior which cause inability to distinguish reality and nonreality. And it does induce psychotic reactions in a small number of users.

The record is consistent with what is known generally about this substance, and why every jurisdiction in the country regulates it intensely. It is almost universally a Schedule I drug, which means that it has a high potential for abuse. There is no currently accepted medical use, and there is lack of accepted safety for use even under medical supervision. The experiences under the influence of this substance may be good, but they are unpredictable, and they are indifferent to the motives of the user. The risk is largely unquestioned by respondents, and the risk cannot be meaningfully distinguished from the risk of using any other hallucinogen. These dangers are great enough that Oregon has chosen, with respect to any user, to have a blanket regulation without exemption.

Narrator: Frohnmayer turns to the decision of his state's Supreme Court.

Frohnmayer: In the face of these considerations, the Oregon Supreme Court has concluded, however, that the federal Constitution commands a judicially crafted exemption for sincere adult users of a single church. And this poses for us a dilemma. On the one hand, if the exemption is crafted so narrowly that it applies to one group on a de minimis basis, then that means that our state and federal constitutions have preferred one religion over another, and hopelessly compromised the constitutional requirements of neutrality.

Narrator: Frohnmayer argues that states can ban the religious use of any substance that lawmakers decide is dangerous. He faces questions about the sacramental practices of other churches.

Court: Your flat rule position would permit a state to outlaw totally the use of alcohol, including wine, in religious ceremonies?

Frohnmayer: That's a different question.

Court: Why is that different?

Frohnmayer: The issue of sacramental wine is different because, at least at the present, it is not a Schedule I substance. The—

Court: Well, but the state certainly could prohibit the use—the consumption of alcohol within its borders, or at least the sale or use of alcohol.

Frohnmayer: But there might be a religious accommodation argument of an entirely different order than is presented here.

Court: You mean, just a better-known religion?

Frohnmayer: No. It has nothing to do with—it is religion indifferent. Even during prohibition there was a statutory exemption for the use of sacramental—

Court: Yes, but what I am asking is supposing a state did not give that statutory exemption.

Frohnmayer: There, an argument for accommodation is stronger, stronger in at least two respects. First is that there—that to the extent that this Court examines or re-examines the nature of the compelling state interest and the potential danger of the ingestion of sacramental wine in small quantities, it might well question whether the state's overall interest in regulation of a very dangerous substance—

Court: So if this were a Schedule IV substance it would be a different case?

Frohnmayer: It could be a different case.

Court: I see.

Frohnmayer: The second is clearly that the use of peyote in these ceremonies is at least in part for its very hallucinogenic properties. That is to say, the religious experience, at least for some communicants, comes from the achievement of the heightened hallucinogenic effect, where this is also not true of the ingestion of sacramental wine in small quantities.

Court: You don't think there is any special spiritual feeling in taking communion?

Frohnmayer: Well, the feeling is different than the induction of an actual altered state of consciousness. What I am saying is that those two factors at least distinguish, and would presumably cause this Court or any other to say that the argument for accommodation is much stronger in the case of those religious sacraments than in the case where it is unquestionably a very dangerous substance for everyone else, acknowledged and conceded to be, and where it is taken for the purposes of inducing the very state that causes the danger, at least with respect to everyone else.

Narrator: Frohnmayer replies to the claim that exempting the religious use of peyote would "accommodate" the Native American Church and solve the First Amendment problem.

Frohnmayer: Let's make one other point. That is, we have a claim by respondent that line drawing of the kind that we find so objectionable in pursuit of our interests in religious neutrality is easy. And we point to the lower federal court cases suggesting that other persons using peyote, other persons using hashish, LSD or marijuana for sincere religious reasons, that those cases can be easily distinguished. We simply invite this Court's careful review of those cases, which are shamelessly result-driven and involve religious gerrymandering from which no consistent neutral principle emerges. And our point is that if we cannot accommodate on equal grounds, then the requirement of accommodation must fail.

Narrator: Frohnmayer wraps up his argument with an appeal for judicial restraint and caution.

Frohnmayer: And there is a final and critical point here related to our health and safety interest. That is that denominational practices, and indeed individual believers, even in long-standing religions, can and do change. They change the nature of their religious beliefs, they change the nature of their doctrine, and that is the very essence of freedom of religion and belief. So a constitutional exemption that is bound in time and place is very risky. If we exempt a practice, even if we are presently satisfied by its safety, control passes forever into private hands. And that is proper. But then we must ask, before we let that control pass in the form of a constitutional exemption, denomination specific or not, now and in the future, what are the contours of that exemption and how will it be conferred. Because if the denominational or church controls weaken or change, there are still enshrined in the Bill of Rights a permanent exemption for the practices of that religion.

Narrator: Craig Dorsay is a lawyer with the Native American Program of Oregon Legal Services. He speaks for Alfred Smith and Galen Black, and first addresses the issue of wine in religious services.

Dorsay: Mr. Chief Justice, and may it please the Court. I am compelled as an initial matter to address the subject raised by Justice Stevens relating to the use of alcohol, which I think raised one of the primary problems with this case as it comes before the Court. I think, if you looked at this situation and Indian people were in charge of the United States right now, or in charge of government, and you look at the devastating impact that alcohol has had on Indian people and Indian tribes through the history of the United States, you might find that alcohol was the Schedule I substance and peyote was not listed at all. And we are getting here to the heart of an ethnocentric view, I think, of what constitutes religion in the United States. And I think that needs to be looked at very hard before determining what is a dangerous substance and what is not.

Narrator: Justice Scalia is skeptical about the comparison of sacramental wine and peyote.

Scalia: Well, it could—couldn't it be that the exception that the Oregon court was referring to might have been an exception for the use of peyote in insignificant quantities that could not produce any hallucinogenic or other adverse physical effect? Might not that be the exception that they were referring to? And if that's the case, then your pointing to the traditional use of wine at religion services would not make any difference. I don't assume that the states would be compelled to allow excessive use of alcohol, drunken parties, under— on grounds of religion. I don't think that that is the—

Dorsay: Well, that is correct. And that interest still exists here, for instance, for people who might overuse alcohol in a religious ceremony, or for instance, if communion is administered to minors, or some other situation in which the state has a legitimate interest.

Scalia: Yeah, but, you see, I don't see a correlation between the wine and the peyote. I mean, it is acknowledged that the peyote—do you disagree with what the Attorney General said, that the whole purpose of the ingestion of the peyote is its hallucinogenic effect.

Dorsay: No, I do not disagree with that. What I disagree with is the fact that that ingestion is harmful. There is no documented evidence that the use of the peyote in these carefully circumscribed ceremonials has any harm to the individual, to society at large, or to the state's law enforcement efforts.

Court: How did it get to be a Schedule I controlled substance?

Dorsay: Well, I think it has—

Scalia:: I mean, somebody thinks it is harmful.

Dorsay: Yes. We do not know that for sure. It obviously—the drug mescaline has a high potential for abuse. That is what Schedule I says. The synthetic derivative has obviously been misused in society at large. There is, however, no evidence that peyote, as used by the Native American Church, has been misused in the sense that it has been misused in society.

Narrator: Dorsay runs into trouble with questions about First Amendment protection for acts that violate criminal laws.

Court: Why do you say that these people are entitled to workmen's compensation?

Dorsay: Because they had a right to practice their religion under the First Amendment to the Constitution.

Court: So the First Amendment issue is here, I take it?

Dorsay: It is, yes, in either form. But what is perhaps not here, and we believe it is not necessary to address the criminality, because the Oregon Supreme Court has decided that as a matter of state law.

Court: But it says that then—your court says they are entitled to compensation because the First Amendment requires it.

Dorsay: That is correct.

Court: Even though the employee breached the rules of the employer.

Dorsay: Well, we have a dispute about that. If you look at the record in this case—

Court: Well, suppose it is that there was a rule like that.

Dorsay: If that was the rule, and if the employees knew of that rule when they were hired, then the state could validly deny unemployment benefits. But—

Court: Despite the First Amendment.

Dorsay: No, not—only if the interest was criminalized. Not if—under the previous decisions of this Court, even where an employee is fired for misconduct; all the previous decisions, the employees were fired for misconduct, anyone else in their situation would have been validly denied—been denied unemployment benefits.

Narrator: Dorsay restates his argument for a religious exception to Oregon's drug laws. Once again, Justice Scalia peppers him with skeptical questions.

Dorsay: The state has failed to meet its burden under the First Amendment to justify what we believe would be the total destruction of this religion, and that is because of the test that has been established by this Court in First Amendment cases. There is a sincere religious belief, it is a bona fide religion that is conceded by the state. But once that is shown, the state must show, as Justice O'Connor summarized in the *Goldman* case, that the interest will in fact be substantially harmed by granting the type of exemption requested, and that the state interest will be undermined by granting the exemption, and there is no less restrictive alternative that can be granted in this case.

And it is our belief that the state cannot meet any of the burdens in this case. The compelling state interest is the regulation of drug abuse generally, but we do not have any evidence in this case that peyote has been abused or that it contributes to the drug abuse problem. In fact, all of the evidence is to the contrary. We have the findings, for instance, of the federal agency charged with enforcement of the drug laws in this country, which found that and concluded that the religious use of peyote by the Native American Church does not cause a law enforcement problem in this country.

Scalia: Why can't the state say we don't want Native American Church members to use it either. We think this is dangerous. It is harmful to people. We don't want children to be brought into this church and taught to use this thing, it is harmful to them. It is a Schedule I substance; we have made that determination.

Dorsay: Because the First Amendment, I believe, requires something more than a mere legislative statement that we believe it may be harmful. States can come up with all kinds of reasons to outlaw all kinds of conduct, as we have cited in our supplemental brief; for instance, that driving of Amish buggies without the reflector warning system is certainly a dangerous act. But if you allow the mere legislative proscription without an actual inquiry into whether harm has in fact occurred, then you are—

Scalia: Excuse me, what do you mean "in fact occurred?" You would not accept scientific evidence that the use of peyote is physically harmful?

Dorsay: I would not accept that.

Scalia: In general. You would require the showing in the particular context of the religious service?

Dorsay: Not in the context of the religious service. The evidence is divided. The evidence is particularly divided. In respect to this church, however, there is reliable scientific evidence that the use of peyote in the ceremony of the Native American Church contributes to rehabilitation of people who have problems with drug and alcohol abuse.

Narrator: The Supreme Court decided this case on April 17, 1990. Five members of the Court, in an opinion written by Justice Antonin Scalia, upheld Oregon's denial of unemployment benefits to Alfred Smith and Galen Black. Other justices might have limited an opinion to the narrow issue in this case: should Oregon recognize a religious exception for peyote use in Native American Church ceremonies.

Justice Scalia, however, seized on this case to cast doubt on a half-century of Supreme Court rulings in "free exercise of religion" cases. Scalia put his premise in these words: "We have never held that an individual's religious beliefs excuse him from compliance with an otherwise valid law prohibiting conduct that the State is free to regulate." Scalia brushed aside some of the Court's historic free exercise decisions. These cases, he wrote, involved "the Free Exercise Clause in conjunction with other constitutional protections, such as freedom of speech and of the press, or the right of parents to direct the education of their children." Scalia, instead, quoted from a 1940 opinion in a flag-salute case that was later overruled, and an 1879 decision upholding a ban on Mormon polygamy in Utah.

Justice Harry Blackmun wrote for the three dissenters. The majority opinion, he warned, "effectuates a wholesale overturning of settled law concerning the religious clauses of our Constitution." Blackmun argued that Oregon had not met its burden of proving a "compelling" interest in banning peyote use in religious ceremonies. Blackmun noted that Oregon had never prosecuted anyone for religious use of peyote. "The State's asserted interest," he wrote, "amounts only to the symbolic preservation of an unenforced prohibition."

Many Supreme Court decisions, like those on school prayer and abortion, affect millions of people. The decision in this case did not really affect anyone. Four years before the Court's decision, the drug and alcohol treatment program that fired Smith and Black agreed to allow the religious use of peyote by employees. Congress voted in 1993 to overturn the Court's decision, passing the Religious Freedom Restoration Act, which put into law the "compelling interest" standard that Justice Scalia had dismissed.

Most Supreme Court opinions stick to the facts and apply settled precedent. But sometimes a new majority of justices flexes its muscles and uses a case to revise constitutional doctrine, often over the protest of the minority. The decision in *Employment Division v. Smith* fits this pattern of narrow issues and sweeping opinions. And it illustrates how cases that affect only a handful of people can expose deep divisions over conflicts between individuals and state authority.

EDITED SUPREME COURT OPINIONS
Employment Division v. Smith
Argued November 6, 1989—Decided April 17, 1990

JUSTICE SCALIA delivered the opinion of the Court.

This case requires us to decide whether the Free Exercise Clause of the First Amendment permits the State of Oregon to include religiously inspired peyote use within the reach of its general criminal prohibition on use of that drug, and thus permits the State to deny unemployment benefits to persons dismissed firm their jobs because of such religiously inspired use....

The Free Exercise Clause of the First Amendments which has been made applicable to the States by incorporation into the Fourteenth Amendment, see *Cantwell v. Connecticut*, 310 U.S. 296, 303 (1940), provides that "Congress shall make no law respecting an establishment of religion, or *prohibiting the free exercise thereof....* U.S. Const., Amdt. 1 (emphasis added). The free exercise of religion means, first and foremost, the right to believe and profess whatever religious doctrine one desires. Thus, the First Amendment obviously excludes all governmental regulation of religious *beliefs* as such."...

But the "exercise of religion" often involves not only belief and profession but the performance of (or abstention from) physical acts: assembling with others for a worship service, participating in sacramental use of bread and wine, proselytizing, abstaining from certain foods or certain modes of transportation. It would be true, we think (though no case of ours has involved the point), that a State would be "prohibiting the free exercise [of religion]" if it sought to ban such acts or abstentions only when they are engaged in for religious reasons, or only because of the religious belief that they display. It would doubtless be unconstitutional, for example, to ban the casting of "statues that are to be used for worship purposes," or to prohibit bowing down before a golden calf.

Respondents in the present case, however, seek to carry the meaning of "prohibiting the free exercise [of religion]" one large step further. They contend that their religious motivation for using peyote places them beyond the reach of a criminal law that is not specifically directed at their religious practice, and that is concededly constitutional as applied to those who use the drug for other reasons. They assert, in other words, that "prohibiting the free exercise [of religion]" includes requiring any individual to observe a generally applicable law that requites (or forbids) the performance of an act that his religious belief forbids (or requires). As a textual matter, we do not think the words must be given that meaning....

We have never held that an individual's religious beliefs excuse him from compliance with an otherwise valid law prohibiting conduct that the State is free to regulate. On the contrary, the record of more than a century of our free exercise jurisprudence contradicts that proposition. As described succinctly by Justice Frankfurter in *Minersville School Dist. Bd. of Ed. v. Gobitis*, 310 U.S. 586, 594–595 (1940): "Conscientious scruples have not, in the course of the long struggle for religious toleration, relieved the individual from obedience to a general law not aimed at the promotion or restriction of religious beliefs. The mere possession of religious convictions which contradict the relevant concerns of a political society does not relieve the citizen from the discharge of political responsibilities (footnote omitted)." We first had occasion to assert that principle in *Reynolds v. United States*, 98 U.S. 145 (1879), where we rejected the claim that criminal laws against polygamy could not be constitutionally applied to those whose religion commanded the practice. "Laws," we said, "are made for the government of actions, and while they cannot interfere with mere religious belief and opinions they may with practices.... Can a man excuse his practices to the contrary because of his religious belief? To permit this would be to make the professed doctrines of religious belief superior to the law of the land, and in effect to permit every citizen to become a law unto himself."...

Subsequent decisions have consistently held that the right of free exercise does not relieve an individual of the obligation to comply with a "valid and neutral law of general applicability on the ground that the law proscribes (or prescribes) conduct that his religion prescribes (or proscribes)."

The only decisions in which we have held that the First Amendment bars application of a neutral, generally applicable law to religiously motivated action have involved not the Free Exercise Clause alone, but the Free Exercise Clause in conjunction with other constitutional protections, such as freedom of speech and of the press,...or the right of parents...to direct the education of their children...

The present case does not present such a hybrid situation, but a free exercise claim unconnected with any communicative activity or parental right. Respondents urge us to hold, quite simply, that when otherwise prohibitable conduct is accompanied by religious convictions, not only the convictions but the conduct itself must be free from governmental regulation. We have never held that, and decline to do so now. There being no contention that Oregon's drug law represents an attempt to regulate religious beliefs, the communication of religious beliefs, or the raising of one's children in those beliefs, the rule to which we have adhered ever since *Reynolds* plainly controls....

Respondents argue that even though exemption from generally applicable criminal laws need not automatically be extended to religiously motivated actors, at least the claim for a religious exemption must be evaluated under the balancing test set forth in *Sherbert v. Verner*, 374 U.S. 398 (1963). Under the *Sherbert* test, governmental actions that substantially burden a religious practice must be justified by a compelling governmental interest....

The "compelling government interest" requirement seems benign, because it is familiar from other fields. But using it as the standard that must be met before the government may accord different treatment on the basis of race,...or before the government may regulate the content of speech,... is not remotely comparable to using it for the purpose asserted here. What it produces in those other fields—equality of treatment and an unrestricted flow of contending speech—are constitutional norms; what it would produce here—a private right to ignore generally applicable laws is a constitutional anomaly.

Nor is it possible to limit the impact of respondents' proposal by requiring a "compelling state interest" only when the conduct prohibited is "central" to the individual's religion....

If the "compelling interest" test is to be applied at all, then, it must be applied across the board, to all actions thought to be religiously commanded. Moreover, if "compelling interest" really means what it says (and watering it down here would subvert its rigor in the other fields where it is applied), many laws will not meet the test. Any society adopting such a system would be courting anarchy, but that danger increases in direct proportion to the society's diversity of religious beliefs, and its determination to coerce or suppress none of them. Precisely because "we are a cosmopolitan nation made up of people of almost every conceivable religious preference,"...and precisely because we value and protect that religious divergence, we cannot afford the luxury of deeming *presumptively invalid*, as applied to the religious objector, every regulation of conduct that does not protect an interest of the highest order....

Values that are protected against government interference through enshrinement in the Bill of Rights are not thereby banished from the political process. Just as a society that believes in the negative protection accorded to the press by the First Amendment is likely to enact laws that affirmatively foster the dissemination of the printed word, so also a society that believes in the negative protection accorded to religious belief can be expected to be solicitous of that value in its legislation as well. It is therefore not surprising that a number of States have made an exception to their drug laws for sacramental peyote use....

But to say that a nondiscriminatory religious-practice exemption is permitted, or even that it is desirable, is not to say that it is constitutionally required, and that the appropriate occasions for its creation can be discerned by the courts. It may fairly be said that leaving accommodation to the political process will place at a relative disadvantage those religious practices that are not widely engaged in; but that unavoidable consequence of democratic government must be preferred to a system in which each conscience is a law unto itself or in which judges weigh the social importance of all laws against the centrality of all religious beliefs....

Because respondents' ingestion of peyote was prohibited under Oregon law, and because that prohibition is constitutional, Oregon may, consistent with the Free Exercise Clause, deny respondents unemployment compensation when their dismissal results from use of the drug. The decision of the Oregon Supreme Court is accordingly reversed.

It is so ordered.

JUSTICE BLACKMUN, with whom JUSTICE BRENNAN and JUSTICE MARSHALL join, dissenting.

This Court over the years painstakingly has developed a consistent and exacting standard to test the constitutionality of a state statute that burdens the free exercise of religion. Such a statute may stand only if the law in general, and the State's refusal to allow a religious exemption in particular, are justified by a compelling interest that cannot be served by less restrictive means....

Until today, I thought this was a settled and inviolate principle of this Court's First Amendment jurisprudence. The majority, however, perfunctorily dismisses it as a "constitutional anomaly."...

The Court views traditional free exercise analysis as somehow inapplicable to criminal prohibitions (as opposed to conditions on the receipt of benefits), and to state laws of general applicability (as opposed, presumably, to laws that expressly single out religious practices)....

The Court cites cases in which, due to various exceptional circumstances, we found strict scrutiny inapposite, to hint that the Court has repudiated that standard altogether.... In short, it effectuates a wholesale overturning of settled law concerning the Religion Clauses of our Constitution. One hopes that the Court is aware of the consequences, and that its result is not a product of over-reaction to the serious problems the country's drug crisis has generated.

This distorted view of our precedents leads the majority to conclude that strict scrutiny of a state law burdening the free exercise of religion is a "luxury" that a well-ordered society cannot afford,...and that the repression of minority religions is an "unavoidable consequence of democratic government."...I do not believe the Founders thought their dearly bought freedom from religious persecution a "luxury," but an essential element of liberty—and they could not have thought religious intolerance "unavoidable," for they drafted the Religion Clauses precisely in order to avoid that intolerance....

In weighing the clear interest of respondents Smith and Black (hereinafter respondents) in the free exercise of their religion against Oregon's asserted interest in enforcing its drug laws, it is important to articulate in precise terms the state interest involved. It is not the State's broad interest in fighting the critical "war on drugs" that must be weighed against respondents' claim, but the State's narrow interest in refusing to make an exception for the religious, ceremonial use of peyote....

The State's interest in enforcing its prohibition, in order to be sufficiently compelling to outweigh a free exercise claim, cannot be merely abstract or sym-bolic. The State cannot plausibly assert that unbending application of a crimi-nal prohibition is essential to fulfill any compelling interest. If it does not, in fact, attempt to enforce that prohibition. In this case, the State actually has not evinced any concrete interest in enforcing its drug laws against religious users of peyote. Oregon has never sought to prosecute respondents, and does not claim that it has made significant enforcement efforts against other religious users of peyote. The State's asserted interest thus amounts only to the symbolic preser-vation of an unenforced prohibition....

The State proclaims an interest in protecting the health and safety of its citizens from the dangers of unlawful drugs. It offers, however, no evidence that the religious use of peyote has ever harmed anyone....

The carefully circumscribed ritual context in which respondents used peyote is far removed from the irresponsible and unrestricted recreational use of unlawful drugs. The Native American Church's internal restrictions on, and supervision of, its members' use of peyote substantially obviate the State's health and safety concerns....

Finally, the State argues that granting an exception for religious peyote use would erode its interest in the uniform, fair, and certain enforcement of its drug laws. The State fears that, if it grants an exemption for religious peyote use, a flood of other claims to religious exemptions will follow. It would then be placed in a dilemma, it says, between allowing a patchwork of exemptions that would hinder its law enforcement efforts, and risking a violation of the Establishment Clause by arbitrarily limiting its religious exemptions....

The State's apprehension of a flood of other religious claims is purely speculative. Almost half the States, and the Federal Government, have maintained an exemption for religious peyote use for many years, and apparently have not found themselves overwhelmed by claims to other religious exemptions. Allowing an exemption for religious peyote use would not necessarily oblige the State to grant a similar exemption to other religious groups. The unusual circumstances that make the religious use of peyote compatible with the State's interests in health and safety and in preventing drug trafficking would not apply to other religious claims. Some religions, for example, might not restrict drug use to a limited ceremonial context, as does the Native American Church....

Respondents believe, and their sincerity has never been at issue, that the peyote plant embodies their deity, and eating it is an act of worship and communion. Without peyote, they could not enact the essential ritual of their religion. See Brief for Association on American Indian Affairs et al. as *Amici Curiae* 5-6 ("To the members, peyote is consecrated with powers to heal body, mind and spirit. It is a teacher; it teaches the way to spiritual life through living in harmony and balance with the forces of the Creation. The rituals are an integral part of the life process. They embody a form of worship in which the sacrament Peyote is the means for communicating with the Great Spirit")....

For these reasons, I conclude that Oregon's interest in enforcing its drug laws against religious use of peyote is not sufficiently compelling to outweigh respondents' right to the free exercise of their religion. Since the State could not constitutionally enforce its criminal prohibition against respondents, the interests underlying the State's drug laws cannot justify its denial of unemployment benefits....

I dissent.

Hazelwood
School District
v. Kuhlmeier

484 U. S. 260 (1988)

In May 1983 the editors of the *Spectrum*, the student newspaper of Hazelwood East High School in suburban St. Louis, submitted two articles to their journalism teacher. One article included quotes from several students, identified by name, who talked about the impact of their parents' divorce on them. One student related that her father "played cards with the guys" and ignored his wife and kids. The other article discussed teenage pregnancy, with quotes from three Hazelwood students—whose names were not used—who became pregnant. This article included details of the students' sex lives and birth control practices. Hazelwood's principal, Robert Reynolds, ordered the teacher to pull the articles; since time was short, the next *Spectrum* issue appeared with two blank pages. Kathy Kuhlmeier and two other student editors sued the school district and principal Reynolds. By a five-to-three vote, the Supreme Court held that Reynolds was justified in censoring the two articles because they were "unsuitable for immature audiences." The dissenters argued that the First Amendment protects student expression that "neither disrupts classwork nor invades the rights of others."

Counsel for petitioners: Robert P. Baine Jr., St. Louis, Missouri
Counsel for respondents: Leslie D. Edwards, St. Louis, Missouri

Chief Justice William Rehnquist: We will hear arguments first this afternoon in No. 86-836, *Hazelwood School District v. Cathy Kuhlmeier*.

Narrator: It's October 13, 1987. We're in the chamber of the United States Supreme Court in Washington, D.C. Chief Justice William Rehnquist has called for argument a case that examines the reach of the First Amendment into public schools. The broad question before the Court is this: Can a high school principal order the removal of articles from a school newspaper? Put another way, do student journalists have a right to publish articles about issues of concern to their fellow students without censorship by school officials?

This case began on May 10, 1983, in the principal's office at Hazelwood East High School in suburban St. Louis, Missouri. Students in a journalism class put out a weekly newspaper, the *Spectrum*, under a teacher's supervision. Class members researched and wrote two articles that dealt with issues familiar to most high school students: divorce and teenage pregnancy. The article on divorce quoted three Hazelwood students by name, and gave their accounts of why their parents divorced. The other article gave personal stories of three Hazelwood students who became pregnant, including details of their sex lives. The article stated that "all names have been changed to keep the identity of these girls a secret."

A substitute teacher, Howard Emerson, had recently been assigned to the journalism class. When he read the two articles, he took them to Hazelwood's principal, Robert Reynolds, who promptly ordered them removed from the *Spectrum*. Reynolds later testified that he felt the parents whose children discussed their divorce should have been allowed to respond in the article. He also stated that he could identify each of the three pregnant girls, and was sure many students could as well.

After the *Spectrum* appeared without the censored articles, Cathy Kuhlmeier and two other student journalists sued the Hazelwood School District for violating their First Amendment rights of free speech and press. They relied on a landmark Supreme Court decision of 1969, *Tinker v. School District of Des Moines, Iowa*, upholding the right of high school students to wear black armbands to protest the Vietnam War.

A federal district judge ruled against Cathy Kuhlmeier and her fellow students, but a federal appellate court reversed this decision, citing *Tinker* and holding that the censored articles would not "disrupt classwork, give rise to substantial disorder, or invade the rights of others." The Supreme Court granted the school district's petition for review of that decision. Robert Baine, a prominent St. Louis lawyer, argues for the district. Chief Justice Rehnquist welcomes him to the podium.

Rehnquist: Mr. Baine, you may proceed whenever you're ready.

Baine: Thank you, Mr. Chief Justice, and may it please the Court:

This case comes before the Court to resolve the issue of whether a school-sponsored high school newspaper produced and published by a journalism class as a part of the school-adopted curriculum under a teacher's supervision and subject to a principal's review is a public forum for the purpose of the First Amendment.

Narrator: Baine explains what happened when Howard Emerson took the articles on divorce and pregnancy to Principal Reynolds.

Baine: When that teacher received the articles from the students and reviewed them, he attempted to contact—as the evidence in trial court showed—he attempted to contact the principal about these stories, as he had an objection to them. He was unable to do that, so he went and put them into proof, and sent the proof to the principal, and asked the principal his opinion about it.

And the principal said that those stories, because they involved the subject matter that was in them—the story of the three young pregnant ladies who told how they got pregnant, whether they used birth control, the reaction of the father of the child, the reaction of their parents to the pregnancy, and other items; and the article on divorce where a freshman gave a story of why, or the recounting of why, she believed her parents got divorced, and her name was involved—the principal said to Mr. Emerson, who was then the substitute teacher, "What can be done about this?"

And Mr. Emerson said, "We can delete pages 4 and 5, and make page 6 into page 4, and we have got a four-page paper." The principal said, "Go ahead and do that," and that is what happened. So the articles that the principal had an objection to were the articles involving the recounting of the tales of the pregnancy of three schoolgirls and the recounting of the tale of why the parents of one of the freshmen—in fact, several parents of students, but particularly one named freshman's parents—got a divorce.

Narrator: Baine continues.

Baine: When the principal had the question placed to him by the substitute teacher, he had to make a decision, you know. And he looked at the article, and he said, "I know who these girls are." He looked at the article about the divorce, and he said, "I know who this girl is, and I know who her parents are. I do not think that the parents have had an opportunity to respond. The issue of fairness and balance is missing in that article." The trial court specifically commented on its finding of the credibility of the principal in that case.

So when you take into consideration the fact that the trial court found that there was a protectable interest, even espoused by the article, and that is the girls should remain anonymous, and the article did not protect that, we feel that the court found that it was not a public forum; that it was adopted on a curriculum basis; and that, as a curricular writing, it was subject to the control of the principal.

Narrator: Baine faces a question on the power of Principal Reynolds to censor the *Spectrum* articles.

Court: And you would fix the limits at that point, I take it, the limits of what the school and its principal can do? What I am trying to find out is what your standard is.

Baine: In this case, whether or not to involve students in a public telling of their life and to put it in a semi-official publication of the school district, I think that is not a hard decision for the principal to make. And certainly, discussing their family life, the private lives of the family members who make up the patrons of the district, is not appropriate fare for the school newspaper. It would give an opinion to the students that there was some bridge or bar between the school and the community that really does not exist.

Narrator: Chief Justice Rehnquist presses Baine on the censorship issue.

Rehnquist: Mr. Baine, supposing, in this particular journalism class, the faculty and the school board said, "We are going to let you put out a student newspaper, and it is a little bit devoted to journalism. But one thing that we want you to understand above everything else is that the faculty advisor has the absolute authority to censor anything if he or she wants to. It may be arbitrary, but if you come into the class, that is what you are going to come up with."

Baine: Well, as a matter of fact—

Rehnquist: Do you think that would violate the First Amendment if the faculty advisor goes ahead and says, "Look, I just do not think much of this article; it does not suit me"?

Baine: Well, Mr. Chief Justice, I think that—

Rehnquist: Can you answer the question?

Baine: I think that they could do that, yes.

Narrator: Justice Antonin Scalia takes over the questioning.

Scalia: Mr. Baine, may I just interrupt. I just wanted to ask you if you really meant what you said in answer to Chief Justice Rehnquist's question. You said that the teacher could have just total power or censorship. That would mean that he could exclude all political articles that favored the Republicans and print only those that favored the Democrats. I do not think that you mean that, do you?

Baine: Well, first of all, again, I would beg that the word censorship—in the classroom—be eliminated.

Scalia: Well, forget the label. Could they do that? Could you give the authority to the teacher?

Baine: I would say that that is not the fact that we have in this case.

Scalia: I understand that it is not the fact.

Baine: And that is a tough hypothetical.

Scalia: But what is your answer to it? I mean, you gave one answer to the Chief Justice, and I wonder if that is the answer.

Baine: The answer is, if you can establish clearly on the part of the school a viewpoint of discrimination, that that would abridge fundamental First Amendment rights.

Scalia: So then the school could not give total power to the teacher to exclude anything that he wanted to? You cannot have it both ways.

Baine: I mean, there is no evidence in this case that that is a fact.

Scalia: That does not help us much.

Narrator: Scalia presses on.

Scalia: Let us talk about viewpoint discrimination. The principal could not exclude an article that discussed teenage sexuality and pregnancy of some of his students, and portrayed the whole thing in a favorable light—in effect, sanctioning promiscuity by the students—but permit an article that discussed the same topic, but seemed to frown upon that kind of activity. The principal could not take a position on a subject like that. If he allows sexuality to be talked about, he has to allow both the pros and the cons of adolescent sex to be set forth. Is that right?

Baine: I guess the answer is, if it is reasonable in light of the circumstance, reasonable in light of the age of the people, reasonable in light of the audience that they are trying to reach, you know—

Scalia: Well, he says, "We are trying to form some moral attitudes in the kids in this school. It is one of the things that this school does, and I do not want an article that condones this sort of thing." Is he going to be able to do that or not?

Baine: I think that what we have in this case is an article that says that, if we are going to talk about it, we are not going to involve individuals.

Scalia: I understand this case. I just want to know your position. Are you categorical that the principal or whoever has the last word cannot exercise that last word on the basis of some value judgments that discriminate between various positions on particular issues?

Baine: I am saying that he can.

Scalia: He can?

Baine: Yes.

Narrator: Baine ends with a sweeping claim of the principal's censorship powers. When he concludes, Chief Justice Rehnquist welcomes Leslie Edwards to the podium. She argues for Cathy Kuhlmeier and her fellow student journalists. Edwards faces a round of skeptical questions.

Chief Justice Rehnquist: Thank you, Mr. Baine. We will hear now from you, Ms. Edwards.

Edwards: Mr. Chief Justice, and may it please the Court:

The essence of their ability to put out a student newspaper was their right to communicate with each other, with other students, as well as with other members of the school community. It was an institution that existed before the First Amendment, and I think that the fact—and Mr. Baine did not mention this at all—that this is a newspaper has to have some effect upon how the Court looks at the issues.

One thing that Mr. Baine did not mention in addition is the concept that has been recognized of local control over curriculum. And I think that an important inherent aspect to that principle is that it means ideas—that, when you are talking about local control, you are talking about local control over ideas.

Court: When you say local control, Ms. Edwards, does that mean student control?

Edwards: No, sir. I am talking about the school district—the school board that is elected by the people, the principal, and the superintendent. I think that is an established interest that they have which is valid.

Court: And how does that help you in this case?

Edwards: Well, I think that, when you balance or confront the First Amendment with that interest, it is very dangerous because it assumes ideas and viewpoint control. So I think that just means that we have to look at it a little more carefully.

Court: Than if what were otherwise?

Edwards: Than if you had a situation of an Army facility where the Army's interest is in security, order, and maintaining a certain discipline. We are not talking about suppression. The government's interest in that situation is not speech-related; it is not content-related. It is related to order, security, or another government interest. That is a little bit separate sort of issue.

Court: Let me ask you one other question. In your view, does this case depend on some sort of representations that were made to the students putting out the newspaper, by either the faculty or the school board, or would it be totally the same no matter what the faculty or school board had tried to establish in the way of a system?

Edwards: I certainly think that it does depend. Because they could have set up a newspaper, call it that, which is mimeographed, which is used in class, which is handed out in homerooms, in which they are told to discuss only school issues, be a bulletin board—and, in fact, "We are going to give you a weekly interview with the principal." Fine, they set the limits; that is within their power.

Court: Supposing they set them a little bit differently and said that this is going to be printed the way that ordinary newspapers are. "It does not come out during class, you are going to work on it as an extracurricular activity, but here are the rules. You are going to be subject to review on your subject of topics, and," to take Justice Scalia's example, "we want to promote morality as we see it. So, if you are touching subjects such as high school sex, we will encourage and insist on one point of view rather than another."

Edwards: I think that they can do that, but I think that there would be trouble doing it with an extracurricular activity.

Court: Why?

Edwards: Well, because I assume that extracurricular means that they are only putting in the money and do not have a journalism instructor there.

Court: Well, supposing that there is an instructor.

Edwards: Then I think that it sort of falls similarly where we do—in the middle. We are not extracurricular, and we are not a laboratory experience only in the classroom.

Court: But what does that distinction contribute to the First Amendment argument, the difference between the curricular and extracurricular?

Edwards: Access. The harm that the First Amendment is designed to prevent is that a viewpoint that the government does not like for any reason is excluded. And when you have students allowed to make certain editorial control decisions or allowed to have certain access to their expression in the written columns, then the First Amendment applies, and that is protected.

Court: Supposing it said, "The students are to write these pieces, and we are not going to write anything ourselves, but the faculty advisor reserves the right to say no to anything that involves taking a position that is morally undesirable for high school students."

Edwards: I think that the school board, the principal and superintendent, superiors, can delegate the editorial function to an advisor, and he can exercise that in whichever way he thinks—as long as it is not viewpoint-based. Now, if he says that it is viewpoint-based, then I do not think that would be protected.

Court: So the advisor cannot say, "I reject this article, which encourages what I think is immorality on the part of high school students, but I will accept this article, which I think encourages morality"?

Edwards: It does not serve an editorial function, and it does not serve an educational interest. I do not think that would be constitutional.

Narrator: Justice Scalia presses Edwards on whether school officials are advisors or censors.

Edwards: I do not think that it only has to be one or the other. I mean, I think that the school can—

Scalia: I could set up a newspaper then and say, "You are not going to have any articles in it that encourage the smoking of pot." I can do that?

Edwards: If it is viewpoint-based, I do not think that they can.

Scalia: They cannot. So I either have to have no newspaper, or I have to have a newspaper that has articles encouraging the kids who go to that school to smoke pot.

Edwards: Along with other viewpoints, yes. They have to allow that viewpoint, if that is what you are asking.

Narrator: Leslie Edwards gave up ground in her effort to limit the censorship powers of school officials to "viewpoint discrimination." Justice Scalia pushes harder on this point.

Scalia: Once again, you leave us with a terrible choice: either no newspapers at all or newspapers that have to be offensive as no private newspapers need be.

Edwards: Well, why would a student newspaper need to be either? I mean, I think that—

Scalia: Because nobody can stop them. Well, all right, you have to get very responsible adolescents who have very good judgment as to what is offensive to the whole community or not—and care.

Edwards: I think that private newspapers print offensive things all of the time to some portions of the population.

Scalia: They do not try to, I do not think.

Edwards: Well, you have this advisor, this instructor, supposedly monitoring it a little. I mean, there may be some restraint because you have a teacher, you have an advisor, you have a curriculum developed to try and learn how to do it according to ethical and journalistic standards that are better than the private. I mean, the private aim at that also, but you have a little bit more control because you have an advisor there who hopefully has some background in journalism, some experience perhaps as a reporter.

Scalia: You let him do it?

Edwards: Yes, I think he could.

Scalia: He could exclude it because he thinks this will offend the community?

Edwards: As long as it is not only because of a viewpoint discrimination, yes.

Scalia: Well, but it is. I mean, he thinks this viewpoint will offend the community.

Edwards: It seems to me that offending the community would not have—

Scalia: The students want to print something—*Hitler was right*. And the advisor says, "Gee, this community will not like that piece." And there is a school bond issue coming up, he thinks. There is just no solution for that problem.

Edwards: Well, I think that the advisor can exercise editorial control.

Scalia: But the principal?

Edwards: Not viewpoint. Well, to say that he cannot—what I am saying is that it requires strict scrutiny if he does. And there may be a compelling state interest. That is fine. It may be inflammatory. Then he can constitutionally.

Scalia: Well, so can the principal then?

Edwards: Yes, if it is inflammatory, libel, obscenity, and disrupting school, and invading rights of privacy of others.

Narrator: Questions from the justices put both lawyers on the defensive in this spirited argument. Robert Baine wound up with a claim for complete editorial control by the school principal. Leslie Edwards would limit that censorship power to material that could subject the school to legal liability. Neither was able to draw a "bright line" that separated the First Amendment rights of student journalists from the censorship powers of school officials.

The Supreme Court backed away from a judicial effort to draw a "bright line" standard when it decided this case on January 13, 1988. The bottom line was that Cathy Kuhlmeier and her fellow students lost their case. Five justices joined the majority opinion of Justice Byron White, who stuck closely to the facts of the case. The most that White would say on the broader free speech issue was that "educators do not offend the First Amendment by exercising editorial control over the style and content of student speech in school-sponsored expressive activities so long as their actions are reasonably related to legitimate pedagogical concerns. "

Justice White concluded that Principal Reynolds had acted "reasonably" in removing the divorce and pregnancy articles from the *Spectrum*. Reynolds was properly concerned, White wrote, about "the treatment of controversial issues" in the student paper, and "the need to protect the privacy" of persons who were named or could be identified from the censored articles.

Speaking for three dissenters, Justice William Brennan wrote that the Hazelwood students "expected a civics lesson" in putting out a newspaper. What they got instead, Brennan wrote scornfully, was an "Orwellian" lesson in "thought control" by school officials. Brennan accused the majority of allowing viewpoint discrimination in the guise of protecting students from "sensitive topics" like divorce and pregnancy. The "civics lesson" the students expected, Brennan concluded, was "not the one the Court teaches them today."

Cathy Kuhlmeier graduated from Hazelwood East High School before the Supreme Court ruled against her, but the *Spectrum* is still published by journalism students. And the principal still retains final editorial control. That was the "civics lesson" from the Supreme Court to students across the country.

EDITED SUPREME COURT OPINIONS
Hazelwood School District v. Kuhlmeier
Argued October 13, 1987—Decided January 13, 1988

JUSTICE WHITE delivered the opinion of the Court.

This case concerns the extent to which educators may exercise editorial control over the contents of a high school newspaper produced as part of the school's journalism curriculum.

Petitioners are the Hazelwood School District in St. Louis County, Missouri; various school officials; Robert Eugene Reynolds, the principal of Hazelwood East High School; and Howard Emerson, a teacher in the school district. Respondents are three former Hazelwood East students who were staff members of *Spectrum*, the school newspaper. They contend that school officials violated their First Amendment rights by deleting two pages of articles from the May 13, 1983, issue of *Spectrum*.

Spectrum was written and edited by the Journalism II class at Hazelwood East. The newspaper was published every three weeks or so during the 1982-1983 school year. More than 4,500 copies of the newspaper were distributed during that year to students, school personnel, and members of the community....

The Journalism II course was taught by Robert Stergos for most of the 1982–1983 academic year. Stergos left Hazelwood East to take a job in private industry on April 29, 1983, when the May 13 edition of *Spectrum* was nearing completion, and petitioner Emerson took his place as newspaper adviser for the remaining weeks of the term.

The practice at Hazelwood East during the spring 1983 semester was for the journalism teacher to submit page proofs of each *Spectrum* issue to Principal Reynolds for his review prior to publication. On May 10, Emerson delivered the proofs of the May 13 edition to Reynolds, who objected to two of the articles scheduled to appear in that edition. One of the stories described three Hazelwood East students' experiences with pregnancy; the other discussed the impact of divorce on students at the school.

Reynolds was concerned that, although the pregnancy story used false names "to keep the identity of these girls a secret," the pregnant students still might be identifiable from the text. He also believed that the article's references to sexual activity and birth control were inappropriate for some of the younger students at the school. In addition, Reynolds was concerned that a student identified by name in the divorce story had complained that her father "wasn't spending enough time with my mom, my sister and I" prior to the divorce, "was always out of town on business or out late playing cards with the guys," and "always argued about everything" with her mother.... Reynolds believed that the student's parents should have been given an opportunity to respond to these remarks or to consent to their publication. He was unaware that Emerson had deleted the student's name from the final version of the article.

Reynolds believed that there was no time to make the necessary changes in the stories before the scheduled press run and that the newspaper would not appear before the end of the school year if printing were delayed to any significant extent. He concluded that his only options under the circumstances were to publish a four-page newspaper instead of the planned six-page newspaper, eliminating the two pages on which the offending stories appeared, or to publish no newspaper at all. Accordingly, he directed Emerson to withhold from publication the two pages containing the stories on pregnancy and divorce. He informed his superiors of the decision, and they concurred.

Respondents subsequently commenced this action in the United States District Court for the Eastern District of Missouri seeking a declaration that their First Amendment rights had been violated, injunctive relief, and monetary damages. After a bench trial, the District Court denied an injunction, holding that no First Amendment violation had occurred. 607 F. Supp. 1450 (1985)....

The Court of Appeals for the Eighth Circuit reversed. 795 F. 2d 1368 (1986). The court held at the outset that *Spectrum* was not only "a part of the school adopted curriculum," *id.*, at 1373, but also a public forum, because the newspaper was "intended to be and operated as a conduit for student viewpoint." *Id.*, at 1372. The court then concluded that *Spectrum*'s status as a public forum precluded school officials from censoring its contents except when " 'necessary to avoid material and substantial interference with school work or discipline...or the rights of others.'" *Id.*, at 1374 (quoting *Tinker v. Des Moines Independent Community School Dist.*, 393 U.S. 503, 511 (1969)).

The Court of Appeals found "no evidence in the record that the principal could have reasonably forecast that the censored articles or any materials in the censored articles would have materially disrupted classwork or given rise to substantial disorder in the school." 795 F. 2d, at 1375. School officials were entitled to censor the articles on the ground that they invaded the rights of others, according to the court, only if publication of the articles could have resulted in tort liability to the school. The court concluded that no tort action for libel or invasion of privacy could have been maintained against the school by the subjects of the two articles or by their families. Accordingly, the court held that school officials had violated respondents' First Amendment rights by deleting the two pages of the newspaper.

We granted certiorari, 479 U.S. 1053 (1987), and we now reverse.

Students in the public schools do not "shed their constitutional rights to freedom of speech or expression at the schoolhouse gate." *Tinker, supra*, at 506.

They cannot be punished merely for expressing their personal views on the school premises—whether "in the cafeteria, or on the playing field, or on the campus during the authorized hours," 393 U.S., at 512–513—unless school authorities have reason to believe that such expression will "substantially interfere with the work of the school or impinge upon the rights of other students." Id., at 509.

We have nonetheless recognized that the First Amendment rights of students in the public schools "are not automatically coextensive with the rights of adults in other settings," Bethel School District No. 403 v. Fraser, 478 U.S. 675, 682 (1986), and must be "applied in light of the special characteristics of the school environment." Tinker, supra, at 506; cf. New Jersey v. T. L. O., 469 U.S. 325, 341–343 (1985). A school need not tolerate student speech that is inconsistent with its "basic educational mission," Fraser, supra, at 685, even though the government could not censor similar speech outside the school.

The question whether the First Amendment requires a school to tolerate particular student speech—the question that we addressed in Tinker—is different from the question whether the First Amendment requires a school affirmatively to promote particular student speech. The former question addresses educators' ability to silence a student's personal expression that happens to occur on the school premises. The latter question concerns educators' authority over school-sponsored publications, theatrical productions, and other expressive activities that students, parents, and members of the public might reasonably perceive to bear the imprimatur of the school. These activities may fairly be characterized as part of the school curriculum, whether or not they occur in a traditional classroom setting, so long as they are supervised by faculty members and designed to impart particular knowledge or skills to student participants and audiences.

Educators are entitled to exercise greater control over this second form of student expression to assure that participants learn whatever lessons the activity is designed to teach, that readers or listeners are not exposed to material that may be inappropriate for their level of maturity, and that the views of the individual speaker are not erroneously attributed to the school. Hence, a school may in its capacity as publisher of a school newspaper or producer of a school play "disassociate itself," Fraser, 478 U.S., at 685, not only from speech that would "substantially interfere with [its] work…or impinge upon the rights of other students," Tinker, 393 U.S., at 509, but also from speech that is, for example, ungrammatical, poorly written, inadequately researched, biased or prejudiced, vulgar or profane, or unsuitable for immature audiences. A school must be able to set high standards for the student speech that is disseminated under its auspices, standards that may be higher than those demanded by some newspaper

publishers or theatrical producers in the "real" world and may refuse to disseminate student speech that does not meet those standards. In addition, a school
must be able to take into account the emotional maturity of the intended
audience in determining whether to disseminate student speech on potentially
sensitive topics, which might range from the existence of Santa Claus in an ele-
mentary school setting to the particulars of teenage sexual activity in a high
school setting. A school must also retain the authority to refuse to sponsor student speech that might reasonably be perceived to advocate drug or alcohol use,
irresponsible sex, or conduct otherwise inconsistent with "the shared values of a
civilized social order," *Fraser, supra,* at 683, or to associate the school with any
position other than neutrality on matters of political controversy. Otherwise,
the schools would be unduly constrained from fulfilling their role as "a principal
instrument in awakening the child to cultural values, in preparing him for later
professional training, and in helping him to adjust normally to his environment." *Brown v. Board of Education,* 347 U.S. 483, 493 (1954).

Accordingly, we conclude that the standard articulated in Tinker for determining when a school may punish student expression need not also be the standard for determining when a school may refuse to lend its name and resources
to the dissemination of student expression. Instead, we hold that educators do
not offend the First Amendment by exercising editorial control over the style
and content of student speech in school-sponsored expressive activities so long
as their actions are reasonably related to legitimate pedagogical concerns.

We also conclude that Principal Reynolds acted reasonably in requiring
the deletion from the May 13 issue of *Spectrum* of the pregnancy article, the
divorce article, and the remaining articles that were to appear on the same
pages of the newspaper.

The initial paragraph of the pregnancy article declared that "[a]ll names
have been changed to keep the identity of these girls a secret." The principal
concluded that the students' anonymity was not adequately protected, however, given the other identifying information in the article and the small
number of pregnant students at the school. Indeed, a teacher at the school cred-
ibly testified that she could positively identify at least one of the girls and possibly all three. It is likely that many students at Hazelwood East would have been
at least as successful in identifying the girls. Reynolds therefore could reasonably have feared that the article violated whatever pledge of anonymity had
been given to the pregnant students. In addition, he could reasonably have
been concerned that the article was not sufficiently sensitive to the privacy
interests of the students' boyfriends and parents, who were discussed in the article but who were given no opportunity to consent to its publication or to offer a
response. The article did not contain graphic accounts of sexual activity. The

girls did comment in the article, however, concerning their sexual histories and their use or nonuse of birth control. It was not unreasonable for the principal to have concluded that such frank talk was inappropriate in a school-sponsored publication distributed to 14-year-old freshmen and presumably taken home to be read by students' even younger brothers and sisters....

In sum, we cannot reject as unreasonable Principal Reynolds' conclusion that neither the pregnancy article nor the divorce article was suitable for publication in *Spectrum*. Reynolds could reasonably have concluded that the students who had written and edited these articles had not sufficiently mastered those portions of the Journalism II curriculum that pertained to the treatment of controversial issues and personal attacks, the need to protect the privacy of individuals whose most intimate concerns are to be revealed in the newspaper, and "the legal, moral, and ethical restrictions imposed upon journalists within [a] school community" that includes adolescent subjects and readers. Finally, we conclude that the principal's decision to delete two pages of *Spectrum*, rather than to delete only the offending articles or to require that they be modified, was reasonable under the circumstances as he understood them. Accordingly, no violation of First Amendment rights occurred.

The judgment of the Court of Appeals for the Eighth Circuit is therefore

Reversed.

JUSTICE BRENNAN, with whom JUSTICE MARSHALL and JUSTICE BLACKMUN join, dissenting.

When the young men and women of Hazelwood East High School registered for Journalism II, they expected a civics lesson. *Spectrum*, the newspaper they were to publish, "was not just a class exercise in which students learned to prepare papers and hone writing skills, it was a...forum established to give students an opportunity to express their views while gaining an appreciation of their rights and responsibilities under the First Amendment to the United States Constitution...." 795 F. 2d 1368, 1373 (CA8 1986). "[At the beginning of each school year," *id.*, at 1372, the student journalists published a Statement of Policy—tacitly approved each year by school authorities—announcing their expectation that "*Spectrum*, as a student-press publication, accepts all rights implied by the First Amendment.... Only speech that 'materially and substantially interferes with the requirements of appropriate discipline' can be found unacceptable and therefore prohibited."...

The school board itself affirmatively guaranteed the students of Journalism II an atmosphere conducive to fostering such an appreciation and exercising the full panoply of rights associated with a free student press. "School sponsored student publications," it vowed, "will not restrict free expression or diverse view-points within the rules of responsible journalism."...

This case arose when the Hazelwood East administration breached its own promise, dashing its students' expectations. The school principal, without prior consultation or explanation, excised six articles—comprising two full pages—of the May 13, 1983, issue of *Spectrum*. He did so not because any of the articles would "materially and substantially interfere with the requirements of appropriate discipline," but simply because he considered two of the six "inappropriate, personal, sensitive, and unsuitable" for student consumption.

In my view the principal broke more than just a promise. He violated the First Amendment's prohibitions against censorship of any student expression that neither disrupts classwork nor invades the rights of others, and against any censorship that is not narrowly tailored to serve its purpose.

Free student expression undoubtedly sometimes interferes with the effectiveness of the school's pedagogical functions. Some brands of student expression do so by directly preventing the school from pursuing its pedagogical mission: The young polemic who stands on a soapbox during calculus class to deliver an eloquent political diatribe interferes with the legitimate teaching of calculus. And the student who delivers a lewd endorsement of a student-government candidate might so extremely distract an impressionable high school audience as to interfere with the orderly operation of the school. See *Bethel School Dist. No. 403 v. Fraser*, 478 U.S. 675 (1986). Other student speech, however, frustrates the school's legitimate pedagogical purposes merely by expressing a message that conflicts with the school's, without directly interfering with the school's expression of its message: A student who responds to a political science teacher's question with the retort, "socialism is good," subverts the school's inculcation of the message that capitalism is better.

Even the maverick who sits in class passively sporting a symbol of protest against a government policy, cf. *Tinker v. Des Moines Independent Community School Dist.*, 393 U.S. 503 (1969), or the gossip who sits in the student commons swapping stories of sexual escapades could readily muddle a clear official message condoning the government policy or condemning teenage sex. Likewise, the student newspaper that, like *Spectrum*, conveys a moral position at odds with the school's official stance might subvert the administration's legitimate inculcation of its own perception of community values.

Even if we were writing on a clean slate, I would reject the Court's rationale for abandoning *Tinker* in this case. The Court offers no more than an obscure tangle of three excuses to afford educators "greater control" over school-sponsored speech than the Tinker test would permit: the public educator's prerogative to control curriculum; the pedagogical interest in shielding the high school audience from objectionable viewpoints and sensitive topics; and the school's need to dissociate itself from student expression....

None of the excuses, once disentangled, supports the distinction that the Court draws. Tinker fully addresses the first concern; the second is illegitimate; and the third is readily achievable through less oppressive means.

The Court is certainly correct that the First Amendment permits educators "to assure that participants learn whatever lessons the activity is designed to teach...."

That is, however, the essence of the *Tinker* test, not an excuse to abandon it. Under *Tinker*, school officials may censor only such student speech as would "materially disrup[t]" a legitimate curricular function. Manifestly, student speech is more likely to disrupt a curricular function when it arises in the context of a curricular activity—one that "is designed to teach" something—than when it arises in the context of a noncurricular activity. Thus, under *Tinker*, the school may constitutionally punish the budding political orator if he disrupts calculus class but not if he holds his tongue for the cafeteria....

The Court's second excuse for deviating from precedent is the school's interest in shielding an impressionable high school audience from material whose substance is "unsuitable for immature audiences."...

Tinker teaches us that the state educator's undeniable, and undeniably vital, mandate to inculcate moral and political values is not a general warrant to act as "thought police" stifling discussion of all but state-approved topics and advocacy of all but the official position.

Finally, even if the majority were correct that the principal could constitutionally have censored the objectionable material, I would emphatically object to the brutal manner in which he did so. Where "[t]he separation of legitimate from illegitimate speech calls for more sensitive tools"...the principal used a paper shredder.

He objected to some material in two articles, but excised six entire articles. He did not so much as inquire into obvious alternatives, such as precise deletions or additions (one of which had already been made), rearranging the layout, or delaying publication. Such unthinking contempt for individual rights is intolerable from any state official. It is particularly insidious from one to whom the public entrusts the task of inculcating in its youth an appreciation for the cherished democratic liberties that our Constitution guarantees....

The young men and women of Hazelwood East expected a civics lesson, but not the one the Court teaches them today.

I dissent.

Hustler Magazine, Inc. v. Falwell

485 U.S. 46 (1988)

Larry Flynt and Jerry Falwell are two of the most colorful—and controversial—figures in the United States. Both are outspoken and eager to reach and influence the American public. Flynt publishes a raunchy magazine called *Hustler*, which features graphic pictures of nude women and sex acts. Falwell is a Baptist minister, television evangelist, and founder of the Moral Majority, an influential political group in the 1980s. In 1983, *Hustler* ran a full-page ad for Campari, an Italian liqueur, which sponsored an ad series in which celebrities discussed their "first time" with Campari, full of sexual innuendo. The *Hustler* ad included Falwell's picture and his description of his first sexual encounter, with his mother, in an outhouse. In small print at the bottom were the words: "Ad parody—not to be taken seriously." Falwell took it seriously and persuaded a jury to award him $200,000 for emotional distress. The Supreme Court unanimously reversed the award, ruling that parody, no matter how vulgar, is protected by the First Amendment. The legal battle between Flynt and Falwell has recently been portrayed in the award-winning film, *The People* v. *Larry Flynt*, with the First Amendment in a featured role.

TRANSCRIPT OF EDITED AND NARRATED ARGUMENTS IN
Hustler Magazine, Inc. v. Falwell, 485 U.S. 46 (1988)

Counsel for petitioners: Alan Isaacman, Beverly Hills, California
Counsel for respondents: Norman Roy Grutman, New York City

Chief Justice William Rehnquist: We'll hear arguments first this morning in No. 86-1278, *Hustler Magazine and Larry C. Flynt v. Jerry Falwell*.

Narrator: It's December 2, 1987. We're in the chamber of the United States Supreme Court in Washington, D.C. Chief Justice William Rehnquist has called for argument a case that involves two of the most colorful—and controversial—figures in America today.

Larry Flynt, the defendant in this case, began his career in commercial sex with a string of strip-tease clubs in Ohio. He plowed the profits from live strippers into a show-all magazine called *Hustler*, whose nude pictures went far beyond those in competitors like *Playboy* and *Penthouse*. Flynt made a fortune from *Hustler*, which had a circulation in 1983 of two million and profits of $13 million.

Jerry Falwell, the plaintiff in this case, had an alcoholic father and became a lifelong "teetotaler" who never touched alcohol. Jerry was devoted to his mother, and followed her Baptist faith into the ministry. By 1983, Falwell led a church with 28,000 members, preached to millions over a national radio and television network, and headed a politically potent organization called the Moral Majority.

The legal battle between Larry Flynt and Jerry Falwell began in November 1983. The inside cover of *Hustler* looked just like an advertisement for an Italian liqueur called Campari. Presented as an interview with Falwell, the ad stated that his first sexual encounter was with his mother in an outhouse, and that Falwell got drunk before he preached. At the bottom, in small print, were the words, "Ad parody—not to be taken seriously."

Falwell took the *Hustler* ad seriously and sued Flynt for invasion of privacy, libel, and intentional infliction of emotional distress. The first two claims were denied, but a jury awarded Falwell damages of $200,000 on the emotional distress claim, although jurors also ruled that *Hustler* readers would not believe that Falwell had sex with his mother or preached in a drunken state.

After a federal appellate court upheld the jury's award, the Supreme Court granted Flynt's request for review. In their briefs to the Court, both sides discussed the landmark case of *New York Times v. Sullivan*. The justices ruled in 1964 that the First Amendment requires that "debate on public issues should be uninhibited, robust, and wide-open." Does this decision protect Flynt, or did the parody ad cross the constitutional line? Alan Isaacman, an experienced First

Amendment lawyer, argues for Larry Flynt and poses the legal question before the Court. Chief Justice Rehnquist welcomes him to the podium.

Chief Justice Rehnquist: Mr. Isaacman, you may proceed whenever you're ready.

Isaacman: Mr. Chief Justice, and may it please the Court:

This case raises as a general question the question of whether the Court should expand the areas left unprotected by the First Amendment and create another exception to protected speech. And in this situation, the new area that is sought to be protected is satiric or critical commentary of a public figure which does not contain any assertions of fact.

In a specific way, the question becomes, is rhetorical hyperbole, satire, parody, or opinion protected by the First Amendment when it doesn't contain assertions of fact and when the subject of the rhetorical hyperbole is a public figure? Another way of putting this case is, can the First Amendment limitations which have been set out in *New York Times* v. *Sullivan* and its progeny be evaded by a public figure who, instead of alleging libel or instead of alleging invasion of privacy, seeks recovery for an allegedly injurious falsehood by labeling his cause of action intentional infliction of emotional distress?

Narrator: Isaacman explains the history of mutual conflict and contempt between Larry Flynt and Jerry Falwell.

Mr. Isaacman: In judging the publication that's at issue here, I think it's important to look at the context in which it appeared. The speaker, of course, was *Hustler* magazine, and *Hustler* magazine is known by its readers as a magazine that contains sexually explicit pictures and irreverent humor. As an editorial policy, it takes on the sacred cows and the sanctimonious in our society. It focuses on three subject areas primarily. It focuses on sex, it focuses on politics, and it focuses on religion.

Hustler magazine has been the target of attacks and critical commentary by Jerry Falwell for years and for years prior to this ad publication. *Hustler* magazine is at the other end of the political spectrum from Jerry Falwell. On the other hand, Jerry Falwell—filling out the context of this speech—is the quintessential public figure. It's hard to imagine a person in this country who doesn't hold political office who can—has more publicity associated with his name than Jerry Falwell.

Jerry Falwell is the head of the Moral Majority. The Moral Majority, he testified at the trial, numbers some 6 million people. It's a political organization, he indicates. It was set up to advance certain political views. One of the foremost views is to attack what he considers to be pornography and to attack "kings of porn," in his words. And foremost among those kings of porn in his mind is Larry Flynt.

Narrator: Justice John Paul Stevens asks Isaacman to explain why *Hustler* printed such a vulgar parody of Reverend Falwell.

Isaacman: It is a parody of a Campari ad, number one, if it does that.

Stevens: I understand.

Isaacman: And that's a legitimate view for it to express. And we all can understand how it parodied the ad. It is also a satire of Jerry Falwell, and he is in many respects the perfect candidate to put in this Campari ad because he's such a ridiculous figure to be in this ad—somebody who has campaigned against alcohol, campaigned against sex, and that kind J of thing.

Stevens: Well, is the public interest that you're describing—you're building up here that there's some interest in making him look ludicrous, or is it just there's public interest in doing something that people might think is funny? What is the public interest?

Isaacman: There are two public interests. With respect to Jerry Falwell alone, there are two public interests. One is there is a public interest in having *Hustler* express its view that what Jerry Falwell says, as the rhetorical question at the end of the ad parody indicates, is B.S. And *Hustler* has every right to say that somebody who's out there campaigning against it, saying don't read our magazine, and we're poison on the minds of America, and don't engage in sex outside of wedlock, and don't drink alcohol—*Hustler* has every right to say that man is full of B.S. And that's what this ad parody says.

And the first part of the ad parody does—it puts him in a ridiculous setting. Instead of Jerry Falwell speaking from the television with a beatific look on his face and the warmth that comes out of him, and the sincerity in his voice—and he's a terrific communicator—and he's standing on a pulpit, and he may have a Bible in his hand—instead of that situation, *Hustler* is saying, "Let's deflate this stuffed shirt, let's bring him down to our level, or at least to the level where he will listen to what we have to say." [Laughter.]

Isaacman: I was told not to joke in the Supreme Court really didn't mean to do that.

Narrator: This round of laughter in the Supreme Court chamber prompts questions from Justice Antonin Scalia that are both humorous and serious.

Scalia: Mr. Isaacman, to contradict Vince Lombardi, the First Amendment is not everything. It's a very important value, but it's not the only value in our society certainly. You're giving us no help in trying to balance it, it seems to me, against another value, which is that good people should be able to enter public life and public service.

   The rule you give us says that, if you stand for public office or become a public figure in any way, you cannot protect yourself or, indeed, your mother, against a parody of your committing incest with your mother in an outhouse. Now, is that not a value that ought to be protected? Do you think George Washington would have stood for public office if that was the consequence? And there's no way to protect the values of the First Amendment and yet attract people into public service? Can't you give us some line that would balance the two?

Isaacman: Well, one of the lines was suggested by a question earlier, and that is in the private figure or public figure area, if the Court really wants to balance. But somebody who's going into public life, George Washington as an example— there's a cartoon in, I think it's the cartoonists' society brief—that has George Washington being led on a donkey, and underneath there's a caption that so and so who's leading the donkey is leading this ass, or something to that effect.

Scalia: I can handle that. I think George could handle that. But that's a far cry from committing incest with your mother in an outhouse. I mean, there's no line between the two? We can't protect that kind of parody and not protect this?

Isaacman: There's no line in terms of the meaning because *Hustler* wasn't saying that he was committing incest with his mother. Nobody could understand it to be saying that as a matter of fact. And what you're talking about, Justice Scalia, is a matter of taste. And as, Justice Scalia, you said in *Pope v. Illinois*, just as it's useless to argue about taste, it's useless to litigate about it. And what we're talking about here is, well, is this tasteful or not tasteful. That's really what we're talking about, because nobody believed that Jerry Falwell was being accused of committing incest.

Narrator: Alan Isaacman concludes his argument on a serious note.

Isaacman: In summing up, what I would like to do is say this is not just a dispute between *Hustler* and Jerry Falwell, and a rule that's applied in this case is not just that *Hustler* magazine can no longer perform what it does for its readers— and that is produce this type of irreverent humor or other types of irreverent humor. It affects everything that goes on in our national life. And we have a long tradition, as Judge Wilkinson said, of satiric commentary. You can't pick up a newspaper in this country without seeing cartoons or editorials that have critical comments about people.

If Jerry Falwell can sue because he suffered emotional distress, anybody else who's in public life should be able to sue because they suffered emotional distress. And the standard that was used in this case—does it offend generally accepted standards of decency and morality—is no standard at all. All it does is allow the punishment of unpopular speech.

Narrator: Norman Roy Grutman takes the podium for Jerry Falwell. Ironically, Grutman had successfully defended another adult magazine publisher, Bob Guccioni of *Penthouse*, in an earlier lawsuit by Falwell. But Grutman is known for his forceful advocacy for every client, and he argues Falwell's case with passion.

Grutman: Mr. Chief Justice, and may it please the Court:

Deliberate, malicious character assassination is what was proven in this case. By the defendant's own explicit admission, the publication before this Court was the product of a deliberate plan to assassinate, to assault the character and integrity of the plaintiff, and to cause him severe emotional disturbance— with total indifference then and now to the severity of the injury caused.

When the publication was protested by the bringing of this lawsuit, the unregenerate defendant published it again. Justice Scalia, I'd like to answer a question that you raised with my adversary: How often are you going to be able to get proof like this? I dare say, very infrequently, and I dare say that the kind of behavior with which the Court is confronted is aberrational. This is not a responsible publisher. This is a wanton, reckless, deliberately malicious publisher who sets out—for the sheer, perverse joy of simply causing injury—to abuse the power that he has as a publisher.

Narrator: The Association of American Editorial Cartoonists filed a brief supporting Larry Flynt that included many satiric and hostile cartoons of political leaders. Justices Sandra O'Connor and Byron White turn to this form of parody.

O'Connor: Well, do you think a vicious cartoon should subject the drawer of that cartoon to potential liability?

Grutman: Only in the event that the cartoon constitutes that kind of depiction which would be regarded by the average member of the community as so intolerable that no civilized person should have to bear it. That's the definition of the Court.

White: Well, Mr. Grutman, you're certainly posing a much broader proposition than is necessary for you to win this case.

Grutman: Indeed, but I was answering the question of Justice O'Connor.

White: Well, the way you put it from the very outset—you put it the same way. We're judging this case on the basis that the jury found that no one could reasonably have believed that this was a statement of fact. That's the way we judge this case.

Grutman: No. I'd like to address that point, Justice White, because I think a kind of semantic conundrum has been presented here when counsel says that there was no statement of fact. There was a statement of fact. Just as we argued in our brief, you could state gravity causes things to fly upward. That is a statement of fact. It's just a false statement of fact.

Narrator: Chief Justice Rehnquist hangs political cartoons—including caricatures of himself—in his office. He takes over the grilling of Norman Grutman.

Rehnquist: What about a cartoonist who sits down at his easel, or whatever cartoonists sit down at, and thinks to himself, "A candidate for the presidency acts as just a big windbag, a pompous turkey, and I'm going to draw this cartoon showing him as such." You know part of his intent—he enjoys cartooning and just likes to make people look less than they are, to show up the dark side of people. But he knows perfectly well that's going to create emotional distress in this particular person. Now, does that meet your test?

Grutman: No. It does not, unless what he depicts is something like showing the man committing incest with his mother when that's not true, or molesting children, or running a bordello, or selling narcotics.

Rehnquist: What about the state of mind required from the defendant?

Grutman: Well, the state of mind is precisely what we're concerned with.

Rehnquist: What about the state of mind I've hypothesized to you. Does that satisfy your test for the constitutional, or not?

Grutman: No, it would not. If the man sets out with the purpose of simply making a legitimate aesthetic, political, or some other kind of comment about the person about whom he was writing or drawing, and that is not an outrageous comment, then there's no liability.

Rehnquist: Even though he knows it will inflict emotional distress?

Grutman: It has to be—correct, because you cannot have emotional distress for mere slights, for the kinds of things which people in an imperfect world have got to put up with—calling somebody some of the epithets that were mentioned in the opposing argument, blackmailer, or some other conclusory and highly pejorative terms—an epithet.

Narrator: Justices Scalia and O'Connor press Grutman on the limits of satire and parody.

Scalia: Mr. Grutman, you've given us a lot of words to describe this: outrageous, heinous—

Grutman: Repulsive and loathsome.

Scalia: Repulsive and loathsome. I don't know, maybe you haven't looked at the same political cartoons that I have, but some of them—and a long tradition of this, not just in this country, but back into English history—I mean, politicians depicted as horrible-looking beasts, and you talk about portraying someone as committing some immoral act. I would be very surprised if there were not a number of cartoons depicting one or another political figure as at least the piano player in a bordello.

Grutman: Justice Scalia, we don't shoot the piano player. I understand that.

Scalia: But can you give us something that the cartoonist or the political figure can adhere to other than such general words as heinous and what not? I mean, does it depend on how ugly the beast is, or what?

Grutman: No, it's not the amount of hair the beast has or how long his claws may be. I believe that this is a marker of an evolving social sensibility. Between the 1700s and today, I would suggest, people have become more acclimatized to the use of the kinds of language or the kinds of things that, had they been depicted at an earlier age, would have been regarded as socially unacceptable. And while that evolutionary change is taking place, and it's a salutary thing, there are certain kinds of things—it's difficult to describe them. This Court struggled for years to put a legal definition on obscenity, and Justice Stewart could say no more than "I know what it is when I see it."

Well, this kind of rare aberrational and anomalous behavior, whatever it is, whatever the verbal formulation that the nine of you may come upon—clearly, it can be condensed in the formal words that I used, which are not mine—they belong to the oracles of the restatement, who have tried to say that it is for the jury to decide whether or not what is being depicted is done in so offensive, so awful, and so horrible a way that it constitutes the kind of behavior that nobody should have to put up with.

O'Connor: Well, Mr. Grutman, in today's world, people don't want to have to take these things to a jury. They want to have some kind of a rule to follow so that, when they utter it, or write it, or draw it in the first place, they're comfortable in the knowledge that it isn't going to subject them to a suit.

Grutman: I frankly think that it isn't too much to expect, Justice O'Connor, that a responsible author, artist, or anyone would understand that attempting to falsely depict as a representational fact that someone is committing incest with his mother in an outhouse, saying that she's a whore, and saying, when the person involved is an abstemious Baptist minister, that he always gets drunk before he goes into the pulpit—it isn't too much to say that anybody who would do that ought to take the consequences for casting that into the stream.

Narrator: The arguments in *Hustler Magazine* v. *Falwell* concluded with Norman Grutman's complaint that the parody ad was a "worthless kind of verbal assault" that inflicted emotional harm on Jerry Falwell. But the jury's finding that the ad could not "reasonably be understood as describing actual facts" about Falwell's sex life or drinking habits faced Grutman with an uphill battle.

The justices decided this case on February 24, 1988. The questioning from the bench forecast the Court's unanimous opinion. Chief Justice Rehnquist and Justice Scalia, the Court's hard-line conservatives, agreed with its long-time liberals, Justices William Brennan and Thurgood Marshall, that the First Amendment protects Larry Flynt as much as the most prestigious journalist.

Chief Justice Rehnquist assigned the opinion to himself. The question before the Court, he wrote, was "whether a public figure may recover damages for emotional harm caused by the publication of an ad parody offensive to him, and doubtless gross and repugnant in the eyes of most." Rehnquist displayed his interest and knowledge of political cartooning in recounting what he called "slashing and one-sided" cartoons of presidents George Washington, Abe Lincoln, and Teddy and Franklin Roosevelt. Rehnquist concluded that "our political discourse would have been considerably poorer" without this form of satire and ridicule.

Between the lines of the Court's opinion was this advice to Jerry Falwell: "Grin and bear it." Falwell did not grin at the outcome. "The Supreme Court has given the green light to Larry Flynt and his ilk," he responded. *Hustler* magazine still provokes outrage in many people. But, as Chief Justice Rehnquist wrote, outrage as a basis for damages "would allow a jury to impose liability on the basis of the jurors' tastes or views...." This is not, he cautioned, the purpose of the First Amendment.

EDITED SUPREME COURT OPINIONS
Hustler Magazine v. Falwell
Argued December 2, 1987—Decided February 24, 1988

CHIEF JUSTICE REHNQUIST delivered the opinion of the Court.

Petitioner *Hustler Magazine*, Inc., is a magazine of nationwide circulation. Respondent Jerry Falwell, a nationally known minister who has been active as a commentator on politics and public affairs, sued petitioner and its publisher, petitioner Larry Flynt, to recover damages for invasion of privacy, libel, and intentional infliction of emotional distress. The District Court directed a verdict against respondent on the privacy claim, and submitted the other two claims to a jury. The jury found for petitioners on the defamation claim, but found for respondent on the claim for intentional infliction of emotional distress and awarded damages. We now consider whether this award is consistent with the First and Fourteenth Amendments of the United States Constitution.

The inside front cover of the November 1983 issue of *Hustler Magazine* featured a "parody" of an advertisement for Campari Liqueur that contained the name and picture of respondent and was entitled "Jerry Falwell talks about his first time." This parody was modeled after actual Campari ads that included interviews with various celebrities about their "first times." Although it was apparent by the end of each interview that this meant the first time they sampled Campari, the ads clearly played on the sexual double entendre of the general subject of "first times." Copying the form and layout of these Campari ads, *Hustler*'s editors chose respondent as the featured celebrity and drafted an alleged "interview" with him in which he states that his "first time" was during a drunken incestuous rendezvous with his mother in an outhouse. The *Hustler* parody portrays respondent and his mother as drunk and immoral, and suggests that respondent is a hypocrite who preaches only when he is drunk. In small print at the bottom of the page, the ad contains the disclaimer, "Ad parody— not to be taken seriously." The magazine's table of contents also lists the ad as "Fiction; Ad and Personality Parody."

Soon after the November issue of *Hustler* became available to the public, respondent brought this diversity action in the *United States District Court for the Western District of Virginia against Hustler Magazine, Inc., Larry C. Flynt, and Flynt Distributing Co., Inc.* Respondent stated in his complaint that publication of the ad parody in *Hustler* entitled him to recover damages for libel, invasion of privacy, and intentional infliction of emotional distress. The case proceeded to trial. At the close of the evidence, the District Court granted a directed verdict for petitioners on the invasion of privacy claim. The jury then found against respondent on the libel claim, specifically finding that the ad parody could not "reasonably be understood as describing actual facts about [respondent or actual events in which [he] participated."...The jury ruled for respondent on the intentional infliction of emotional distress claim, however, and stated that he should be awarded $100,000 in compensatory damages, as well as $50,000 each in punitive damages from petitioners. Petitioners' motion for judgment notwithstanding the verdict was denied.

On appeal, the United States Court of Appeals for the Fourth Circuit affirmed the judgment against petitioners. *Falwell v. Flint,* 797 F. 2d 1270 (1986). The court rejected petitioners' argument that the "actual malice" standard of *New York Times Co. v. Sullivan,* 376 U.S. 254 (1964), must be met before respondent can recover for emotional distress. The count agreed that because respondent is concededly a public figure, petitioners are "entitled to the same level of First Amendment protection in the claim for intentional infliction of emotional distress that they received in [respondent's] claim for libel." 797 F. 2d, at 1274. But this does not mean that a literal application of the actual malice rule is appropriate in the context of an emotional distress claim. In the court's view, the *New York Times* decision emphasized the constitutional importance not of the falsity of the statement or the defendant's disregard for the truth; but of the heightened level of culpability embodied in the requirement of "knowing...or reckless" conduct. Here, the *New York Times* standard is satisfied by the state-law requirement, and the jury's finding, that the defendants have acted intentionally or recklessly. The Court of Appeals then went on to reject the contention that because the jury found that the ad parody did not describe actual facts about respondent, the ad was an opinion that is protected by the First

Amendment. As the court put it, this was "irrelevant," as the issue is "whether [the ad's] publication was sufficiently outrageous to constitute intentional infliction of emotional distress."...

Petitioners then filed a petition for rehearing en banc but this was denied by a divided court. Given the importance of the constitutional issues involved, we granted certiorari.

This case presents us with a novel question involving First Amendment limitations upon a State's authority to protect its citizens from the intentional infliction of emotional distress. We must decide whether a public figure may recover damages for emotional harm caused by the publication of an ad parody offensive to him, and doubtless gross and repugnant in the eyes of most. Respondent would have us find that a State's interest in protecting public figures from emotional distress is sufficient to deny First Amendment protection to speech that is patently offensive and is intended to inflict emotional injury, even when that speech could not reasonably have been interpreted as stating actual facts about the public figure involved. This we decline to do.

At the heart of the First Amendment is the recognition of the fundamental importance of the free flow of ideas and opinions on matters of public interest and concern. "[T]he freedom to speak one's mind is not only an aspect of individual liberty—and thus a good unto itself—but also is essential to the common quest for truth and the vitality of society as a whole." *Bose Corp. v. Consumers Union of United States, Inc.*, 466 U.S. 486, 503-604 (1984). We have therefore been particularly vigilant to ensure that individual expressions of ideas remain free from governmentally-imposed sanctions. The First Amendment recognizes no such thing as a "false" idea. *Gertz v. Robert Welch, Inc.*, 418 U.S. 323, 339 (1974). As Justice Holmes wrote, "when men have realized that time has upset many fighting faiths, they may come to believe even more than they believe the very foundations of their own conduct that the ultimate good desired is better reached by free trade in ideas—that the best test of truth is the power of the thought to get itself accepted in the competition of the market...." *Abrams v. United States*, 250 U.S. 616, 630 (1919) (dissenting opinion).

The sort of robust political debate encouraged by the First Amendment is bound to produce speech that is critical of those who hold public office or those public figures who are "intimately involved in the resolution of important public questions or, by reason of their fame, shape events in areas of concern to society at large."...

Such criticism, inevitably, will not always be reasoned or moderate; public figures as well as public officials will be subject to "vehement, caustic, and sometimes unpleasantly sharp attacks," *New York Times, supra*, at 270.

Of course, this does not mean that any speech about a public figure is immune from sanction in the form of damages. Since *New York Times Co. v. Sullivan*, 376 U.S. 254 (1964), we have consistently ruled that a public figure may hold a speaker liable for the damage to reputation caused by publication of a defamatory falsehood, but only if the statement was made "with knowledge that it was false or with reckless disregard of whether it was false or not." *Id.*, at 279-280. False statements of fact are particularly valueless; they interfere with the truth-seeking function of the marketplace of ideas, and they cause damage to an individual's reputation that cannot easily be repaired by counterspeech, however persuasive or effective. See *Gertz*, 418 U.S., at 340, 344, n. 9. But even though falsehoods have little value in and of themselves, they are "nevertheless inevitable in free debate," *id.*, at 340, and a rule that would impose strict liability on a publisher for false factual assertions would have an undoubted "chilling" effect on speech relating to public figures that does have constitutional value. "Freedoms of expression require 'breathing space.'"…

This breathing space is provided by a constitutional rule that allows public figures to recover for libel or defamation only when they can prove both that the statement was false and that the statement was made with the requisite level of culpability.

Respondent argues, however, that a different standard should apply in this case because here the State seeks to prevent not reputational damage, but the severe emotional distress suffered by the person who is the subject of an offensive publication.…

In respondent's view, and in the view of the Court of Appeals, so long as the utterance was intended to inflict emotional distress, was outrageous, and did in fact inflict serious emotional distress, it is of no constitutional import whether the statement was a fact or an opinion, or whether it was true or false. It is the intent to cause injury that is the gravamen of the tort, and the State's interest in preventing emotional harm simply outweighs whatever interest a speaker may have in speech of this type.

Generally speaking the law does not regard the intent to inflict emotional distress as one which should receive much solicitude, and it is quite understandable that most if not all jurisdictions have chosen to make it civilly culpable where the conduct in question is sufficiently "outrageous." But in the world of debate about public affairs, many things done with motives that are less than admirable are protected by the First Amendment.

Thus while such a bad motive may be deemed controlling for purposes of tort liability in other areas of the law, we think the First Amendment prohibits such a result in the area of public debate about public figures.

Were we to hold otherwise, there can be little doubt that political cartoonists and satirists would be subjected to damages awards without any showing that their work falsely defamed its subject. Webster's defines a caricature as "the deliberately distorted picturing or imitating of a person, literary style, etc. by exaggerating features or mannerisms for satirical effect." Webster's New Unabridged Twentieth Century Dictionary of the English Language 275 (2d ed. 1979). The appeal of the political cartoon or caricature is often based on exploitation of unfortunate physical traits or politically embarrassing events— an exploitation often calculated to injure the feelings of the subject of the portrayal. The art of the cartoonist is often not reasoned or evenhanded, but slashing and one-sided. One cartoonist expressed the nature of the art in these words:

"The political cartoon is a weapon of attack, of scorn and ridicule and satire; it is least effective when it tries to pat some politician on the back. It is usually as welcome as a bee sting and is always controversial in some quarters." Long, The Political Cartoon: Journalism's Strongest Weapon, The Quill 56, 57 (Nov. 1962).

Several famous examples of this type of intentionally injurious speech were drawn by Thomas Nast, probably the greatest American cartoonist to date, who was associated for many years during the post-Civil War era with Harper's Weekly. In the pages of that publication Nast conducted a graphic vendetta against William M. "Boss" Tweed and his corrupt associates in New York City's "Tweed Ring." It has been described by one historian of the subject as "a sustained attack which in its passion and effectiveness stands alone in the history of American graphic art." M. Keller, The Art and Politics of Thomas Nast 177 (1968). Another writer explains that the success of the Nast cartoon was achieved "because of the emotional impact of its presentation. It continuously goes beyond the bounds of good taste and conventional manners." C. Press, The Political Cartoon 251 (1981).

Despite their sometimes caustic nature, from the early cartoon portraying George Washington as an ass down to the present day, graphic depictions and satirical cartoons have played a prominent role in public and political debate. Nast's castigation of the Tweed Ring, Walt McDougall's characterization of Presidential candidate James G. Blaine's banquet with the millionaires at Delmonico's as "The Royal Feast of Belshazzar," and numerous other efforts have undoubtedly had an effect on the course and outcome of contemporaneous debate. Lincoln's tall, gangling posture, Teddy Roosevelt's glasses and teeth, and Franklin D. Roosevelt's jutting jaw and cigarette holder have been memorialized by political cartoons with an effect that could not have been obtained by the photographer or the portrait artist. From the viewpoint of history it is clear that our political discourse would have been considerably poorer without them.

Respondent contends, however, that the caricature in question here was so "outrageous" as to distinguish it from more traditional political cartoons. There is no doubt that the caricature of respondent and his mother published in Hustler is at best a distant cousin of the political cartoons described above, and a rather poor relation at that. If it were possible by laying down a principled standard to separate the one from the other, public discourse would probably suffer little or no harm. But we doubt that there is any such standard, and we are quite sure that the pejorative description "outrageous" does not supply one. "Outrageousness" in the area of political and social discourse has an inherent subjectiveness about it which would allow a judge to impose liability on the basis of the jurors' tastes or views, or perhaps on the basis of their dislike of a particular expression. An "outrageousness" standard thus runs afoul of our long-standing refusal to allow damages to be awarded because the speech in question may have an adverse emotional impact on the audience....

We conclude that public figures and public officials may not recover for the tort of intentional infliction of emotional distress by reason of publications such as the one here at issue without showing in addition that the publication contains a false statement of fact which was made with "actual malice," i. e., with knowledge that the statement was false or with reckless disregard as to whether or not it was true. This is not merely a "blind application" of the *New York Times* standard, see *Time, Inc. v. Hill*, 385 U.S. 374, 390 (1967), it reflects our considered judgment that such a standard is necessary to give adequate "breathing space" to the freedoms protected by the First Amendment.

Here it is clear that respondent Falwell is a "public figure" for purposes of First Amendment laws. The jury found against respondent on his libel claim when it decided that the Hustler ad parody could not "reasonably be understood as describing actual facts about [respondent] or actual events in which [he] participated."...

The Court of Appeals interpreted the jury's finding to be that the ad parody "was not reasonably believable," 797 F. 2d, at 1278, and in accordance with our custom we accept this finding. Respondent is thus relegated to his claim for damages awarded by the jury for the intentional infliction of emotional distress by "outrageous" conduct. But for reasons heretofore stated this claim cannot, consistently with the First Amendment, form a basis for the award of damages when the conduct in question is the publication of a caricature such as the ad parody involved here. The judgment of the Court of Appeals is accordingly

Reversed.

JUSTICE KENNEDY took no part in the consideration or decision of this case.

JUSTICE WHITE, concurring in the judgment.

As I see it, the decision in *New York Times Co. v. Sullivan*, 376 U.S. 254 (1964), has little to do with this case, for here the jury found that the ad contained no assertion of fact. But I agree with the Court that the judgment below, which penalized the publication of the parody, cannot be squared with the First Amendment.

Hurley *v.* Irish-American Gay, Lesbian and Bisexual Group of Boston

515 U.S.—(1995)

Every year on March 17, the Irish community in Boston celebrates St. Patrick's Day with a parade through the Irish stronghold of South Boston. The parade also commemorates Evacuation Day, when British troops and their "loyalist" supporters departed the city in 1776. The parade committee is headed by John J. Hurley, known to all as "Wacko." In 1992, a small group applied to join the parade and to march under the banner of the Irish-American Gay, Lesbian and Bisexual Group. Hurley turned them down, but a state judge ordered the parade committee to let them march. The next year, the two groups clashed again, and the state's highest court ruled that excluding groups for the "sexual orientation" of its members violated the state public accommodations law. Hurley appealed to the Supreme Court, which ruled unanimously in 1995 that forcing Hurley and the parade committee to include groups which did not share the "traditional religious and social values" of the parade's Catholic sponsors violated their First Amendment right to "choose the content of [their] own message."

TRANSCRIPT OF EDITED AND NARRATED ARGUMENTS IN
Hurley v. Irish-American Gay, Lesbian and Bisexual Group of Boston, 515 U.S.—
(1995)

Counsel for petitioners: Chester Darling, Boston, Massachusetts
Counsel for respondents: John Ward, Boston, Massachusetts

Chief Justice William Rehnquist: We'll hear argument first this morning in
Number 94-749, John J. Hurley and the South Boston Allied War Veterans
Council v. the Irish-American Gay, Lesbian and Bisexual Group of Boston.

Narrator: It's April 25, 1995. We're in the chamber of the United States Supreme
Court in Washington, D.C. Chief Justice William Rehnquist has called for
argument a case that questions one of our most venerated slogans: "Everyone
loves a parade!" The parade in question is the annual St. Patrick's and Evacuation Day parade in South Boston, a heavily and proudly Irish neighborhood in
Boston, Massachusetts.

   March 17 is the occasion for two celebrations in Boston. The Irish community celebrates St. Patrick's Day, and Evacuation Day commemorates the departure of British troops and their "loyalist" supporters in 1776. The South Boston
parade, with marching bands and fireworks, draws up to 20,000 marchers and a
million spectators. The parade is organized by the South Boston Allied War Veterans Council, headed by John J. Hurley, a colorful character known to all as
"Wacko" Hurley.

   This case began in 1992, when a small group applied to join the parade
under the long title of the Irish-American Gay, Lesbian and Bisexual Group of
Boston. Hurley and the Veterans Council turned them down, but a state judge
ordered the parade committee to let them march, which a small contingent did
without disruption. The two groups clashed again in 1993, when the Council's
refusal to approve a permit led to this lawsuit.

   The Massachusetts Supreme Judicial Court ruled that the exclusion violated the state' s public accommodations law, which prohibits discrimination
based on sexual orientation. The state judges held the parade was recreational
in nature and should be open to all. "Wacko" Hurley and the Council asked the
Supreme Court to reverse the state court ruling. The parade organizers claim
the First Amendment protects their right to exclude groups that do not share
their "traditional religious and social values." The gay, lesbian and bisexual
group looks to state civil rights law for protection against discrimination. Argument begins today with Chester Darling, who speaks for Hurley and the Veterans Council. Chief Justice Rehnquist welcomes Darling to the podium.

Chief Justice Rehnquist: Mr. Darling.

Darling: Mr. Chief Justice, and may it please the Court:

The central issue in this case is whether government can mandate the expression of messages and viewpoints in a privately organized parade over the objections of the private organizers.

After ordering the respondent, the Irish-American Lesbian, Bisexual, and Gay Group of Boston, into the 1992 and 1993 parades, and after a hearing before a trial court, a judgment issued and was affirmed by the supreme judicial court of Massachusetts, and in that judgment the supreme judicial court upheld a statement and declaration by the trial court that a proper celebration of St. Patrick's and Evacuation Day requires diversity and inclusiveness.

This pronouncement reflects only one of the plain errors and misapplications of well-settled law that requires reversal and a vacation in this action.

The Veterans Council clearly stated what the expressive purpose of their parades were. They announced during the trial and prior to their application, filing their application itself, that they wished to celebrate their traditional religious and social values.

Narrator: Justice Ruth Ginsburg presses Darling on his claim that parade organizers could exclude any group whose message they disliked. Justice Antonin Scalia has a follow-up question.

Ginsburg: Mr. Darling, I understood your brief to say this is your parade and you can do with it what you will, somebody else can do what they will with their parade. That's the essence of your argument. It's your parade to make it do whatever you want it to do.

Darling: That's correct, Justice. My clients define the scope and content of the parade. They vote to include and exclude people and groups with messages that they approve of in their parade that are consistent with the overall theme, a celebration of the patron saint of the Archdiocese of Boston, St. Patrick.

Scalia: Are there any limitations on that?

Darling: Yes, the limitations are adjudged on a case-by-case and a group-by-group manner by the veterans. They vote to include and exclude groups, and they vote on the basis of their own personal feelings. Not just Mr. Hurley but the vote of sixty people made the determination to exclude the respondent in this case.

Scalia: Mr. Darling, I thought you said you couldn't do whatever you wanted with a parade. I thought you conceded that you could not exclude gays, lesbians, and bisexuals from marching in the parade if they want to march, so long as they are not trying to convey a message which you do not want conveyed.

You don't contest that the Massachusetts law is applicable to the parade insofar as the exclusion of someone simply for being a homosexual or lesbian or a bisexual is concerned, right?

Darling: No, that's correct, Justice Scalia. The fact that my clients do not have a litmus test so far as sexual orientation is concerned for participation in the parade is very clear from the record. My clients have excluded messages, not the people.

Narrator: One reason the gay, lesbian and bisexual group asked to march in Boston was to protest the exclusion of gays from New York's parade. Darling's effort to explain their purpose hits the funny bone of Justice David Souter.

Darling: They sought to demonstrate and proclaim their diversity on the basis of their sexual orientation in the parade. They also had a political message to support the people that were excluded from the St. Patrick's Day parade in New York, and my clients have messages that they really don't have to explain. They merely have to display them. They—

Souter: The message is, it's great to be Irish.

Darling: That's one of them, Justice Souter.

Souter: That's enough, isn't it? [General laughter]

Narrator: When the laughter ends, questions turn to religion. Chief Justice Rehnquist notes the parade's Catholic sponsors, and Justice John Paul Stevens asks why a Baptist group was invited to march with them.

Rehnquist: Well, what you're saying, I gather, Mr. Darling, is it isn't just a message it's great to be Irish, but that it's great to be Roman Catholic, too—

Darling: Your Honor, Mr. Chief Justice, the messages contained in my client's parade are numerous and powerful messages. They include an antiabortion group. Now, that group had been excluded for several years because they wished to display signs and pictures, and shout to the crowd, the spectators, and hand out literature as they passed down the street.

Rehnquist: Well, could you answer my question more directly? Is the Roman Catholic religion a part of your message?

Darling: It certainly is, Mr. Chief Justice. The Ancient Order of Hibernians have been an integral part of the veterans parade for many years. They declined to participate in the parade because of the forced inclusion of the respondent in the '92 and 1993 parades. My clients wanted that religious component in their parade, the Ancient Order of Hibernians. Because of the forced inclusion of the viewpoint by the courts, the Hibernians did not participate. My client's speech was diminished.

Stevens: Why do they let the Baptists join the parade if it's a Catholic parade?

Darling: Well, it's part of their cultural expression, Justice Stevens. They're ecumenical in their Irish—

Stevens: Up to a point. [General laughter.]

Narrator: Darling explains how the Veterans Council responded to the gay group's parade application. He ends on an uncompromising note.

Darling: After they found out what the messages of the group were, they took a vote, and they voted to exclude any group with any sexual theme from their parade. They're entitled to do that. They're entitled to define the parade in any form and shape that they wish. That was not pretextual.

The court found, as being discriminatory, the very fact that my clients voted to exclude any groups with sexual themes to be discriminatory in itself. Therefore, I think the focus is correct on that area. I sincerely think that values and messages do not necessarily mean sexual orientation. They mean a viewpoint, and it's the viewpoint that was imposed on the parade that brought us here today.

If my clients were marching with a group of people that did not have the signs and the messages that are reflected in this record, then there would be no dispute. The fact that the sign, the proclamations on the sign, and their announced messages that were determined to be as I read to the court by the trial judge, my clients can reject. They can include and exclude any messages they wish to.

Narrator: John Ward takes the podium to argue for the gay, lesbian and bisexual group, whose long title he shortens to GLIB.

Ward: Mr. Chief Justice, and may it please the Court:

This is a case about discrimination. The finding of the trial judge in this case was that the council excluded the members of GLIB on the basis of their sexual orientation....

Narrator: Ward conceded in his brief that parade organizers could exclude groups whose "message" they disliked. Justice Anthony Kennedy presses Ward on this issue.

Kennedy: Well, do you contest—I assume you concede that your clients wanted to be in the parade because they wanted to proclaim a message.

Ward: Well, I think the term "message" as it's been used in this case really is more confusing than illuminating, Justice Kennedy. My clients wanted to be included in the parade. They—the trial—they wanted to be included in what the trial judge found to be an open recreational event. The trial judge found that they had been discriminated against. He ordered that they be included on the same basis as everybody else. Everybody else self-identified.

Kennedy: Do you think it's a fair conclusion from this record that the plaintiffs had no interest in proclaiming their message in this event?

Ward: I think that there is a difference between who someone is and what their message is. They did not come in with a sign saying "Gay is Good."

Kennedy: Precisely, but the First Amendment is concerned with the latter.

Ward: I'm sorry.

Kennedy: The First Amendment is concerned with the latter, and if messages are the grounds for the exclusion from the parade, it would seem to me that that is the end of it.

Ward: The council has the right to exclude on the basis of viewpoint. What the trial judge found was that they excluded on the basis of sexual orientation. That's discrimination under state law.

Narrator: Justice Scalia sees a message behind the gay group's parade banner. Ward's answer mixes up geography, moving Linda Brown in the famous school integration case from Topeka, Kansas, to Little Rock, Arkansas.

Scalia: To get back to the question of why GLIB wanted to be in the parade, they didn't want to be there to recreate, as was found by the Massachusetts supreme court. GLIB's purposes are to express its members' pride in their dual identities as Irish or Irish-American, to demonstrate to the Irish-American community and to the gay, lesbian, and bisexual community the diversity within those—and to show support. All of those are expressive activities. They were there to express something, weren't they?

Ward: Justice Scalia, I think that when Linda Brown went to school in Little Rock her going in there was expressing something. For purposes of the discrimination statute, the expression is incidental.

Narrator: Ward's effort to distance his clients from their message prompts a serious question from Chief Justice Rehnquist and humor from Justice Sandra O'Connor.

Ward: This group, the order of the trial court simply said, let them in on the same basis as everybody else. If they wanted to—if the council wanted to exclude all signs, they could have done so. They were certainly entirely free to do that. There was nothing in the order of the court that said that GLIB, unlike any other group, can come in with some sort of message.

Rehnquist: That may be the rule for the Massachusetts antidiscrimination law, but if Massachusetts antidiscrimination law results in forcing parade organizers to allow people with signs and placards that are inconsistent with what the parade says its message is, then it's a problem under the First Amendment, isn't it?

Ward: That is correct, but what I—I think I—

Rehnquist: You're saying that didn't happen.

Ward: I'm saying that didn't happen, and I'm saying it for two reasons, Mr. Chief Justice. First of all, there was a state finding also that this was an open recreational event, that there really was—

O'Connor: Well, let's pose it in a different context. Suppose there's a Ringling Brothers Barnum and Bailey Circus in town and they have a parade, and an animal rights group wants to join the parade with their signs that say, animals shouldn't be used as they are in circuses. Now, do you think they have a right under a public accommodation law to join that parade?

Ward: Justice O'Connor, I see a very clear distinction between viewpoint discrimination and discrimination against people simply for being who they are.

Question: Yes, but a Barnum and Bailey parade doesn't have any viewpoint other than just, gee, the circus is in town and everybody come. [General laughter.]

Narrator: Justice Kennedy pushes Ward into a corner, from: which he tries to escape.

Kennedy: You would agree that if the reason for the exclusion of your clients was solely because of their message—solely because of their message—that the exclusion would be within the First Amendment rights of the organizers of a private parade?

Ward: However, there was no message in that sense.

Kennedy: Would you agree with that proposition?

Ward: I would agree that the council is free to discriminate on the basis of viewpoint. It is not free—

Kennedy: Including your client's viewpoint.

Ward: Correct. In other words—yes. If my clients came in with a sign saying, "Gay is Good," they could keep it out. However, that's not what happened here.

Narrator: Chief Justice Rehnquist asks Ward a fact question, and Justice Scalia pounces on his answer.

Rehnquist: Well, what did your group's sign say?

Ward: It said simply, Mr. Chief Justice, it said "Irish-American, Gay, Lesbian and Bisexual Group of Boston," which is the identity of who these people were. It did not say, repeal the sodomy laws. It did not say, we question your traditional values It did not say anything of that kind.

Scalia: That is enough to show that you are proud of that fact, which is what their object is to express their pride in those dual identities. That's all you need to show that pride, is to hang it up in a sign. How else does one show pride in a certain thing?

Ward: In the same sense that a black person marching in the parade, I take it, would be proud of his or her identity.

Scalia: That's right, and if that person held up a sign and said, black unity, that would be an expression of pride in blackness.

Ward: Except that generally speaking, lesbians, gay men, and bisexual people are not immediately evident to the—

Scalia: Exactly. I mean, the point at issue is whether there's an expression of anything in their mere marching with a sign saying what they are, and it seems to me you must acknowledge that it is—there is an expression of pride in what they are.

Ward: I would call it self-identifying, just as a Star of David, just as—

Scalia: So long as you mean, by self-identifying, pride. I'll accept that. [General laughter.]

Narrator. Justice Stevens is puzzled by the arguments of both sides in this case. He asks Ward to enlighten him.

Stevens: It's really remarkable in this case, it seems to me, both of you seem to agree on the applicable law. They agree they can't exclude you because of who you are, and you agree they can exclude you if you're sending a message.

So the real question is, how do you decide which it is, and the point, the question is, for me at least, do you answer that question by looking at your motive, their interpretation of what you look like, or the reasonable neutral person's interpretation of the sign? What is the standard?

Ward: I think it's objective facts. I think that's what's illustrative here, are the tests that the court has used in the club cases. It's an objective question. It's an objective question.

You look at two things. You look at what kind of event the council has created, what the court found that it was an open recreational event, and then you look at the impact of the inclusion of the unwanted group on that event.

Narrator: Justice Stevens is still puzzled. He and Ward debate the "message" issue with no resolution. Ward ends on a modest note: just let his clients hold a banner with their group's name but no message.

Stevens: Mr. Ward, can I ask another question, following up on my preceding question? If it's an objective test, and say objectively the neutral observer would say yes, there's an expression going on here, but nevertheless the evidence was very clear that the real motive was that they didn't want you to march with them, which is what that found, that real motive would really not be controlling under the objective test, would it?

Ward: Well, it controls as to the finding of discrimination. It controls as to the finding.

Stevens: Yes, but it would be permissible discrimination if the objective observer—

Ward: Oh—

Stevens:—would think that there's a message there they don 't like. Now, maybe they would have excluded you whether or not there was a message, but maybe they can get away with it if there's a message. That's the—

Ward: I think what that really means, Justice Stevens, is there are some circumstances under which discrimination is incidental. That's the Ku Klux Klan case, for example, where the Ku Klux Klan, which we both cite, the Ku Klux Klan wanted to march through a town of Maryland with members only, and the NAACP wanted to march alongside of them.

The trial judge said the mere inclusion of this unwanted group would destroy the message. That's a far cry from this case, where the trial court and the supreme judicial court both found an open recreational event in which the parade organizers, despite what they later said, which was found to be basically pretextual, stood more or less indifferent to the messages.

Upon the arrival of the hated group, or the unwanted group, let's say, they immediately assert that we have always organized around a specific expressive purpose that excludes the mere presence of this group.

The trial judge didn't buy it. Frankly, I don't blame him. And the remedy that he ordered was, treat them like everybody else. It was not, give them special rights to come in with some sign saying whatever they wanted to say. It would say simply to exclude them. You let everybody else self-identify. Let them self-identify.

Narrator: After oral argument ended, the justices took less than two months to decide this case. The Court's opinion, issued on April 25, 1995, was unanimous.

Every justice voted to reverse the Massachusetts Supreme Court and uphold the right of the South Boston parade organizers to exclude the gay, lesbian and bisexual group from future parades.

John Ward had trouble during his argument in separating his clients as persons with distinctive sexual orientations from the "message" on their parade banner. Justice David Souter made this point in his opinion for the Court. "GLIB was formed for the very purpose of marching" in the St. Patrick's Day parade, he wrote, "in order to celebrate its members' identity as openly gay, lesbian, and bisexual descendants of the Irish immigrants...." Marching under a banner with the group's name, even without any other words, communicates a message that conflicts with the "traditional religious and social values" of the parade's Catholic sponsors.

Souter placed more weight on the First Amendment rights of the Veterans Council than the Massachusetts public accommodations law. Allowing GLIB to march against the Council's wishes would open the way for any group to march, even descendants of British loyalists who object to Irish independence. Such a ruling, Souter wrote, "violates the fundamental rule of protection under the First Amendment, that a speaker has the autonomy to choose the content of his own message."

This decision in this case keeps Irish-Americans with nontraditional sexual orientations out of an Irish-American parade. But it also keeps the Ku Klux Klan out of Martin Luther King Day parades, and homophobic groups from marching in gay pride parades. The Court's decision allows parades with just one message, but we may have more parades with more messages, more bands and more balloons.

EDITED SUPREME COURT OPINION
Hurley v. Irish-American Gay, Lesbian and Bisexual Group of Boston
Argued April 25, 1995—Decided June 17, 1995

JUSTICE SOUTER delivered the opinion of the Court.

The issue in this case is whether Massachusetts may require private citizens who organize a parade to include among the marchers a group imparting a message the organizers do not wish to convey. We hold that such a mandate violates the First Amendment.

March 17 is set aside for two celebrations in South Boston. As early as 1737, some people in Boston observed the feast of the apostle to Ireland, and since 1776 the day has marked the evacuation of royal troops and Loyalists from the city, prompted by the guns captured at Ticonderoga and set up on Dorchester Heights under General Washington's command. Washington himself reportedly drew on the earlier tradition in choosing St. Patrick "as the response to Boston," the password used in the colonial lines on evacuation day.

Although the General Court of Massachusetts did not officially designate March 17 as Evacuation Day until 1938,…the City Council of Boston had previously sponsored public celebrations of Evacuation Day, including notable commemorations on the centennial in 1876, and on the 125th anniversary in 1901, with its parade, salute, concert, and fireworks display….

The tradition of formal sponsorship by the city came to an end in 1947, however, when Mayor James Michael Curley himself granted authority to organize and conduct the St. Patrick's Day-Evacuation Day Parade to the petitioner South Boston Allied War Veterans Council, an unincorporated association of individuals elected from various South Boston veterans groups. Every year since that time, the Council has applied for and received a permit for the parade, which at times has included as many as 20,000 marchers and drawn up to 1 million watchers. No other applicant has ever applied for that permit….Through 1992, the city allowed the Council to use the city's official seal, and provided printing services as well as direct funding.

1992 was the year that a number of gay, lesbian, and bisexual descendants of the Irish immigrants joined together with other supporters to form the respondent organization, GLIB, to march in the parade as a way to express pride in their Irish heritage as openly gay, lesbian, and bisexual individuals, to demonstrate that there are such men and women among those so descended, and to express their solidarity with like individuals who sought to march in New York's St. Patrick's Day Parade…. Although the Council denied GLIB's application to take part in the 1992 parade, GLIB obtained a state-court order to include its contingent, which marched uneventfully among that year's 10,000 participants and 750,000 spectators….

In 1993, after the Council had again refused to admit GLIB to the upcoming parade, the organization and some of its members filed this suit against the Council, the individual petitioner John J. "Wacko" Hurley, and the City of Boston, alleging violations of the State and Federal Constitutions and of the state public accommodations law, which prohibits any distinction, discrimination or restriction on account of…sexual orientation…relative to the admission of any person to, or treatment in any place of public accommodation, resort or amusement." Mass. Gen. Laws §272:98. After finding that "[f]or at least the past 47 years, the Parade has traveled the same basic route along the public streets of South Boston, providing entertainment, amusement, and recreation to participants and spectators alike,"…the state trial court ruled that the parade fell within the statutory definition of a public accommodation, which includes "any place"…which is open to and accepts or solicits the patronage of the general public and, without limiting the generality of this definition, whether or not it be…(6) a boardwalk or other public highway [or]…(8) a place of public amusement, recreation, sport, exercise or entertainment," Mass. Gen. Laws § 272:92A. The court found that the Council had no written criteria and employed no particular procedures for admission, voted on new applications in batches, had occasionally admitted groups who simply showed up at the parade without having submitted an application, and did "not generally inquire into the specific messages or views of each applicant."…The court consequently rejected the Council's contention that the parade was private" (in the sense of being exclusive), holding instead that the "lack of genuine selectivity in choosing participants and sponsors demonstrates that the Parade is a public event."…It found the parade to be "eclectic," containing a wide variety of "patriotic, commercial, political, moral, artistic, religious, athletic, public service, trade union, and eleemosynary themes," as well as conflicting messages.

The court rejected the Council's assertion that the exclusion of "groups with sexual themes merely formalized [the fact] that the Parade expresses traditional religious and social values,"…and found the Council's "final position [to be] that GLIB would be excluded because of its values and its message, *i.e.*, its members' sexual orientation,"…

This position, in the court's view, was not only violative of the public accommodations law but "paradoxical" as well, since "a proper celebration of St. Patrick's and Evacuation Day requires diversity and inclusiveness."…

The court rejected the notion that GLIB's admission would trample on the Council's First Amendment rights since the court understood that constitutional protection of any interest in expressive association would "requir[e] focus on a specific message, theme, or group" absent from the parade.…

If there were no reason for a group of people to march from here to there except to reach a destination, they could make the trip without expressing any message beyond the fact of the march itself. Some people might call such a procession a parade, but it would not be much of one. Real "[p]arades are public dramas of social relations, and in them performers define who can be a social actor and what subjects and ideas are available for communication and consideration." S. Davis, Parades and Power: Street Theatre in Nineteenth-Century Philadelphia 6 (1986). Hence, we use the word "parade" to indicate marchers who are making some sort of collective point, not just to each other but to bystanders along the way. Indeed a parade's dependence on watchers is so extreme that nowadays, as with Bishop Berkeley's celebrated tree, "if a parade or demonstration receives no media coverage, it may as well not have happened."…Parades are thus a form of expression, not just motion, and the inherent expressiveness of marching to make a point explains our cases involving protest marches.

Not many marches, then, are beyond the realm of expressive parades, and the South Boston celebration is not one of them. Spectators line the streets; people march in costumes and uniforms, carrying flags and banners with all sorts of messages (*e.g.*, "England get out of Ireland," "Say no to drugs"); marching bands and pipers play, floats are pulled along, and the whole show is broadcast over Boston television...

To be sure, we agree with the state courts that in spite of excluding some applicants, the Council is rather lenient in admitting participants. But a private speaker does not forfeit constitutional protection simply by combining multifarious voices, or by failing to edit their themes to isolate an exact message as the exclusive subject matter of the speech. Nor, under our precedent, does First Amendment protection require a speaker to generate, as an original matter, each item featured in the communication....

Respondents' participation as a unit in the parade was...expressive. GLIB was formed for the very purpose of marching in it, as the trial court found, in order to celebrate its members' identity as openly gay, lesbian, and bisexual descendants of the Irish immigrants, to show that there are such individuals in the community, and to support the like men and women who sought to march in the New York parade.

The Massachusetts public accommodations law under which respondents brought suit has a venerable history. At common law, innkeepers, smiths, and others who "made profession of a public employment," were prohibited from refusing, without good reason, to serve a customer....

As with many public accommodations statutes across the Nation, the legislature continued to broaden the scope of legislation, to the point that the law today prohibits discrimination on the basis of "race, color, religious creed, national origin, sex, sexual orientation..., deafness, blindness or any physical or mental disability or ancestry" in "the admission of any person to, or treatment in any place of public accommodation, resort or amusement." Mass. Gen. Laws § 272:98. Provisions like these are well within the State's usual power to enact when a legislature has reason to believe that a given group is the target of discrimination, and they do not, as a general matter, violate the First or Fourteenth Amendments....

In the case before us, however, the Massachusetts law has been applied in a peculiar way. Its enforcement does not address any dispute about the participation of openly gay, lesbian, or bisexual individuals in various units admitted to the parade. The petitioners disclaim any intent to exclude homosexuals as such, and no individual member of GLIB claims to have been excluded from parading as a member of any group that the Council has approved to march. Instead, the disagreement goes to the admission of GLIB as its own parade unit carrying its own banner....

Since every participating unit affects the message conveyed by the private organizers, the state court's application of the statute produced an order essentially requiring petitioners to alter the expressive content of their parade. Although the state courts spoke of the parade as a place of public accommodation,...once the expressive character of both the parade and the marching GLIB contingent is understood, it becomes apparent that the state court's application of the statute had the effect of declaring the sponsors' speech itself to be the public accommodation. Under this approach any contingent of protected individuals with a message would have the right to participate in petitioners' speech, so that the communication produced by the private organizers would be shaped by all those protected by the law who wished to join in with some expressive demonstration of their own. But this use of the State's power violates the fundamental rule of protection under the First Amendment, that a speaker has the autonomy to choose the content of his own message.

Petitioners' claim to the benefit of this principle of autonomy to control one's own speech is as sound as the South Boston parade is expressive. Rather like a composer, the Council selects the expressive units of the parade from potential participants, and though the score may not produce a particularized message, each contingent's expression in the Council's eyes comports with what merits celebration on that day. Even if this view gives the Council credit for a more considered judgment than it actively made, the Council clearly decided to exclude a message it did not like from the communication it chose to make, and that is enough to invoke its right as a private speaker to shape its expression by speaking on one subject while remaining silent on another. The message it disfavored is not difficult to identify. Although GLIB's point (like the Council's) is not wholly articulate, a contingent marching behind the organization's banner would at least bear witness to the fact that some Irish are gay, lesbian, or bisexual, and the presence of the organized marchers would suggest their view that people of their sexual orientations have as much claim to unqualified social acceptance as heterosexuals and indeed as members of parade units organized around other identifying characteristics. The parade's organizers may not believe these facts about Irish sexuality to be so or they may object to unqualified social acceptance of gays and lesbians or have some other reason for wishing to keep GLIB's message out of the parade. But whatever the reason, it boils down to the choice of a speaker not to propound a particular point of view, and that choice is presumed to lie beyond the government's power to control.

Parades and demonstrations...are not...neutrally presented or selectively viewed. Unlike the programming offered on various channels by a cable network, the parade does not consist of individual, unrelated segments that happen to be transmitted together for individual selection by members of the audience. Although each parade unit generally identifies itself, each is understood to contribute something to a common theme, and accordingly there is no customary practice whereby private sponsors disavow "any identity of viewpoint" between themselves and the selected participants. Practice follows practicability here, for such disclaimers would be quite curious in a moving parade....

Without deciding on the precise significance of the likelihood of misattribution, it nonetheless becomes clear that in the context of an expressive parade, as with a protest march, the parade's overall message is distilled from the individual presentations along the way, and each unit's expression is perceived by spectators as part of the whole.

The statute, Mass. Gen. Laws § 272:98, is a piece of protective legislation that announces no purpose beyond the object both expressed and apparent in its provisions, which is to prevent any denial of access to (or discriminatory treatment in) public accommodations on proscribed grounds, including sexual orientation. On its face, the object of the law is to ensure by statute for gays and lesbians desiring to make use of public accommodations what the old common law promised to any member of the public wanting a meal at the inn, that accepting the usual terms of service, they will not be turned away merely on the proprietor's exercise of personal preference. When the law is applied to expressive activity in the way it was done here, its apparent object is simply to require speakers to modify the content of their expression to whatever extent beneficiaries of the law choose to alter it with messages of their own. But in the absence of some further, legitimate end, this object is merely to allow exactly what the general rule of speaker's autonomy forbids.

It might, of course, have been argued that a broader objective is apparent: that the ultimate point of forbidding acts of discrimination toward certain classes is to produce a society free of the corresponding biases. Requiring access to a speaker's message would thus be not an end in itself, but a means to produce speakers free of the biases, whose expressive conduct would be at least neutral toward the particular classes, obviating any future need for correction. But if this indeed is the point of applying the state law to expressive conduct, it is a decidedly fatal objective. Having availed itself of the public thoroughfares "for purposes of assembly [and] communicating thoughts between citizens," the Council is engaged in a use of the streets that has "from ancient times, been a part of the privileges, immunities, rights, and liberties of citizens." *Hague* v. *Committee for Industrial Organization*, 307 U.S. 496, 515 (1939) (opinion of

Roberts, J.). Our tradition of free speech commands that a speaker who takes to the street corner to express his views in this way should be free from interference by the State based on the content of what he says....

The very idea that a noncommercial speech restriction be used to produce thoughts and statements acceptable to some groups or, indeed, all people, grates on the First Amendment, for it amounts to nothing less than a proposal to limit speech in the service of orthodox expression. The Speech Clause has no more certain antithesis....

While the law is free to promote all sorts of conduct in place of harmful behavior, it is not free to interfere with speech for no better reason than promoting an approved message or discouraging a disfavored one, however enlightened either purpose may strike the government....

Our holding today rests not on any particular view about the Council's message but on the Nation's commitment to protect freedom of speech. Disapproval of a private speaker's statement does not legitimize use of the Commonwealth's power to compel the speaker to alter the message by including one more acceptable to others. Accordingly, the judgment of the Supreme Judicial Court is reversed and the case remanded for proceedings not inconsistent with this opinion.

It is so ordered.

Miller *v.* California

413 U.S. 15 (1973)

Marvin Miller got into legal trouble for mailing brochures that advertised books with titles like *Sex Orgies Illustrated*. Some of Miller's brochures included pictures of "men and women in groups of two or more engaging in a variety of sexual activities, with genitals often prominently displayed." One brochure arrived in the mail of a resident of conservative Orange County, California, whose elderly mother opened it and was highly offended. Miller was arrested and convicted under a state obscenity law. His appeal to the Supreme Court argued that pictures in the brochures—which included Oriental frescoes and paintings—had artistic value and did not meet the Court's requirement that sexual material "cannot be proscribed unless it is found to be utterly without redeeming social value." Miller's lawyers also argued that a "national standard" in obscenity cases would protect publishers from local Comstockery. By a five-to-four vote, the Court upheld Miller's conviction, allowed jurors to apply a "community standard" for obscenity, and revised its prior test to allow prosecution of material that "lacks serious literary, artistic, political, or scientific value." Miller failed the new test and went to jail for offending the Orange County residents.

TRANSCRIPT OF EDITED AND NARRATED ARGUMENTS IN
Miller v. California, 413 U.S. 15 (1973)

Counsel for appellant: Burton Marks, Los Angeles, California
Counsel for appellee: Michael Capizzi, Assistant District Attorney, Orange County, California

Chief Justice Warren Burger: We will hear arguments next in No. 70-73, Miller against California.

Narrator: It's January 18, 1972. We're in the chamber of the United States Supreme Court in Washington, D.C. Chief Justice Warren Burger has called for argument a case that confronts the justices with an unpleasant and unenviable task: deciding which books, magazines, and films meet the legal definition of obscenity.

The Supreme Court has struggled for some forty years to define obscenity. It began in 1957 in the case of *Roth v. United States*, upholding the conviction of a bookseller for sending "obscene, indecent, and filthy matter" through the mail. The justices adopted this test for obscenity: "whether to the average person, applying contemporary community standards, the dominant theme of the material taken as a whole appeals to prurient interest." Webster defines "prurient" as "an unwholesome interest" in sex.

The Court's obscenity test in Roth quickly proved unworkable. Who is the "average" person? What are "contemporary community standards" on sex? Who decides what are "wholesome" and "unwholesome" interests in sex? Many people chuckled when Justice Potter Stewart offered his personal obscenity test in 1964: "I know it when I see it."

Today's argument stems from the criminal conviction of Marvin Miller in conservative Orange County, California, for sending ads through the mail for books like *Sex Orgies Illustrated*. Miller's lawyers argue that applying the "community standards" test would subject booksellers to prosecution in areas where many people think sex itself is unwholesome. They ask the Court to require a "national test" in obscenity cases. The state's lawyers urge the Court to retain the "community standards" test, fearing that a "national" standard would allow residents of New York City and San Francisco to set the standard for all cities and towns.

Burton Marks, who specializes in defending obscenity cases, argues for Marvin Miller. Chief Justice Burger welcomes him to the podium.

Burger: Mr. Marks, you may proceed.

Marks: Mr. Chief Justice, and may it please the Court:

The purpose of my argument, which eventually, I hope, will tie in with the questions which were raised on certiorari—I am going to make some statements which may sound as if they are perjurative or demeaning; they are not so intended. I express them merely as a statement of what I have experienced in the defense of obscenity cases.

My first observation is that, as far as I can tell, probably no member of this Court has engaged in either the prosecution or the defense of an obscenity case where you are required to deal with the various rules of law and procedure which have been set forth by this Court concerning the handling of such a case. And therefore it's somewhat equivalent, as my wife used to say, "You can understand that I have a lot of pain when I have a child, but you'll never experience it." There is a lot of pain in the trial and trying to work out the rules which have been established by this Court.

The second proposition is that this Court has expressed, or perhaps not expressed but sub-vocalized, the assumption that lower courts and lower judges, both State and Federal, will obey the mandates of this Court when it comes to deciding an obscenity case.

This case is an illustration of the fact that such an assumption is totally false, and is an illustration of what, in my opinion, is an immutable position on dealing with pornography, that, for the most part, it is a visceral turn-off to the majority of the courts in which you go in front of.

Narrator: Marks asks the justices for a clearer standard in obscenity cases.

Marks: Now, the first proposition that I have with respect to the rules laid down by this Court is that there is an irreconcilable conflict between the decisions of this Court; irreconcilable in the sense that they are logically inconsistent. However, one court pointed out, and I have not been able to find the case, that logic is the minion and not the master of the law. So we can avoid that little proposition that perhaps this Court has been logically inconsistent, because it really doesn't matter if we can fashion some rules where we can handle what we're doing.

Narrator: The books that Marvin Miller offered for sale include pictures of sex acts. Burton Marks suggests that jurors and expert witnesses have little guidance in deciding if these books are obscene.

Marks: The fact that these particular pictures are drawings—artistic—seems to be irrelevant. The fact that some of them are copies of frescoes which come from Indian art and Japanese art also seems to be irrelevant, since it now becomes the job of the jury to determine, under certain rules laid down, whether or not they are obscene or not obscene. And also the job, apparently, of some experts to determine whether the average person looking at the pictures, as they come to him through the mail, the average non-consenting adult—let's assume that that's the class we're talking about—that the average non-consenting adult, upon seeing these pictures, will have an immediate appeal to his prurient interest because of this exhibition.

Narrator: Right after this statement, the Court adjourns for the day. The next morning, Marks resumes his argument.

Marks: I think that in taking the history of this case, if you please, it illustrates the futility of making a decision by this Court in the ordinary manner as to whether or not, for instance, contemporary standards are national or local, because it really doesn't matter. The judges below simply will not pay any attention to the cases. They do not rule, as a matter of law, in obscenity cases. It is a very visceral reaction. You get a shock value on obscenity in no other cases. They, in my experience, do not function.

And I suggest to the Court that the answer to the dilemma which is posed—that the paradox, the irreconcilable conflict between the cases—is that this Court set up a series of rules by which courts must act in obscenity cases.

Narrator: Marks restates his argument for a "national test" in obscenity cases.

Marks: There should be rules whereby they are compelled to either state that it is protected or not protected, so that somewhere along the line, before the criminal process starts, the person who is going to be involved in a criminal prosecution will at least have the vaguest idea that what he is trying to purvey or sell is not, or is, within the marketplace.

And I give you the following example, and I say this is why I believe it comes within the context of the certiorari questions, because we have here the question—national standards or State standards? If we do not have national standards, I think our brief pointed out that in the area of film, in the area of books which cross State lines, there must be a common standard, because otherwise State A can impose unreasonable burdens upon what kinds of films are shown in the motion picture theaters in their neighborhoods. Perhaps one community, local or State, doesn't like R films, because R-rated films have sex portrayed in them. X films sometimes have more violence than an R film and less sex. It depends upon the individual idea of the censor himself.

Narrator: Chief Justice Burger has a question.

Burger: Let me ask you about this administrative process you were just suggesting to be interposed before a criminal proceeding starts. Are you suggesting something like the old-fashioned board of censorship, to take a look at it first and advise the publisher?

Marks: I'm am suggesting the process whereby, if there is cause to believe, probable cause to believe, that material which is being sent out or is being sold on the stands is or may be violative of the penal statute, or may be obscene within the area of the State statue—but the judge issues a show-cause order, and perhaps even a seizure warrant. The material is seized. It's brought into court. One-day hearing. Expert testimony. Two days to make a decision.

The decision should be in writing, stating the judge's reasons for believing that the material is or is not protected.

Narrator: The Court laid out its obscenity standard in the *Roth* case in 1957. Marks faces a final question about *Roth*.

Court: Well, do you think that *Roth* should be overruled?

Marks: I think it should be overruled. I think that the First Amendment should bar criminal prosecutions in the absence of direct knowledge—I can't; I don't know.

Court: In the absence of what?

Marks: In the absence of direct knowledge—a prior knowing hearing that the matter is probably within the context or framework or prohibited speech.

And then set up a set of rules so that the judges know exactly what to do when they get an obscenity case. And I say bar the criminal prosecution, take it out of the criminal area, until you have a prior hearing as to the obscenity or non-obscenity of the material.

Narrator: Michael Capizzi takes the podium for the state of California. He sprinkles his argument with legal terms: *de novo* means "from the beginning" and *vel non* means "or not."

Capizzi: Honorable Chief Justice, may it please the Court:

Now, the appellant contends that this Court, at least members of this

Court should continue to conduct *de novo* hearings to determine obscenity *vel non*. He further suggests that in reaching that determination of constitutional fact, a mixed question of fact and law, the judge, when applying contemporary standards for customary limits of candor, should adopt a national community standard.

What appellant requests may be easier for this Court than for other courts, because the scope of this Court's judicial inquiry is nationwide. However, I suggest that, even for this Court, it's not an easy task and is, in fact, an impossible task.

Appellant also suggests that each judge, from the trial level through each level of review, should redetermine the issue of *de novo* using the same test, the national test. And I would submit that this is practically impossible. Local, trial, appellate, and State Supreme Court justices just don't have the sufficient scope of judicial inquiry to apply a national standard. With respect to their contact with national standards or customary limits of candor, I would suggest that it is no broader than the average potential juror.

Narrator: Justice William Douglas has a question.

Douglas: I suppose if that's true, what you're saying, and I gather it is, it would be also very difficult for a publisher, an author, to know when he had crossed the line.

Capizzi: I don't think it's that difficult for a publisher to know when he's crossed the line. In fact, the reporter's transcript in this particular case, I believe it's volume 2, around page 50, give or take a few pages, indicates that Mr. Miller indicated to the person who was sending the material itself, that what they were advertising, he considered to be pornography. And the brochures are nothing but the graphic depictions of sexual activity that are contained in what he, himself, described as pornography.

Narrator: Capizzi argues that the books Marvin Miller offered for sale would meet any obscenity test.

Capizzi: I would suggest, however, that if we do apply the approach in the instant case, that each level of court must determine a constitutional fact-law question that's readily apparent, that in this case, as far as that constitutional fact is concerned, that this material is obscene, no matter what test is used, whether we use a local, State, or national community. It exceeds candor of any community; it predominantly appeals to the prurient interest; and is utterly without redeeming social importance. That is the California test.

Having concluded that i's not constitutionally protected, it's submitted that this material should fall into the same category as any other conduct that the State can regulate by police power, any other conduct which is not itself constitutionally protected. And the States, in regulating that other, nonconstitutional conduct, can define it in any manner they wish.

Narrator: Capizzi restates his argument against a "national" obscenity standard.

Capizzi: Reason also requires that a local or State standard be adopted. Obviously one local area will accept material another local area will not. A national standard could very likely prevent a local community that had liberal attitudes and would accept material from receiving that material, because of the restrictive influence of a conservative community some 2,500 miles away. And the opposite is also true. The conservative community would be forced to accept material because of a nationwide standard that is diluted by a more liberal standard of a community, again 2,500 miles away.

Thus, adoption of a national standard would have just the effect that the appellant in this case and the *amici* are suggesting is undesirable. It would have the result of making us all one, making us all little tin soldiers out of a mold, and all receiving the same material, the same standard, and would not provide for differences from one community to another.

Narrator: The Roth case required that jurors apply "contemporary" standards of obscenity. Chief Justice Burger has a question about this term.

Burger: Well, are you suggesting that a standard would become outdated and therefore not contemporary after the lapse of two or three years; is that what you think contemporary means?

Capizzi: I think it must be a standard, yes, Mr. Chief Justice, that exists at the same time as the distribution or the time of the crime. I think it has to exist in tune with our particular times; it's not a community standard that existed in, say, 1850 or 1791, because of the term "contemporary." Thus we have—

Burger: Well, there's quite a difference between saying that we aren't bound by the standards of 1791 than saying that the standard is outdated if it's based on some sort of survey made in 1965. I get it that you're suggesting that this has to be kept up to date on a month-by-month basis, to see what people are thinking just lately.

Capizzi: I think that is true, Mr. Chief Justice, that because of—

Burger: Then you've set out an impossible task for yourself, haven't you?

Narrator: Justice William Rehnquist opens the way for Capizzi to restate his argument for a "local" obscenity test.

Rehnquist: Mr. Capizzi, if, in fact, the Court were to adopt a local or community standard as opposed to a Federal standard, wouldn't the guarantee of jury trial in each case be itself some way of evidencing the jury's reaction, would be some evidence of the local community's standard, without the necessity of expert testimony.

Capizzi: Yes, Mr. Justice Rehnquist, I believe that it would. It would relieve this Court and appellate courts from determining that which they are not really capable of determining on their own, the constitutional fact-law would permit us to rely on the jury verdict, and, assuming there was a conviction, a sufficient-evidence test to determine whether or not it complied with due process.

And I think the changing standard from one geographical location to another again has constitutional background, simply because we do have the one variable, as I was suggesting, the contemporary community standards. It's a changing standard, and it must be a standard that's contemporary with out times. So why is it so inconsistent to say we have another variable? A geographical difference, a variable, a variation, that would differ from one geographical location to another.

We have procedure for punishing utterances in one location and not in another; "Fire!" in a crowded theater is punishable, and in an open field it's not. The words are the same; it's the location that constitutes a clear and present danger, and maybe that's what we're saying in this case: if one community can consider a matter which violates its particular standard for limits of candor, dangerous and within its police power, and yet another community really wouldn't so consider it.

Narrator: The case of Miller v. California was argued in January 1972. Both sides expected a decision before the Supreme Court's term ended in June. However, the justices ordered the lawyers to return in November 1972 for reargument. They gave no reason. But the Court had recently added several obscenity cases to its docket, and most likely wanted to consider them together.

The second time around, Burton Marks and Michael Capizzi covered the same ground and restated their original arguments. The Court finally decided the case on June 21, 1973. By a five-to-four vote, the justices upheld Marvin

Miller's conviction. Chief Justice Burger wrote for the majority, explaining that "a re-examination of standards enunciated in earlier cases" led the Court to adopt a new obscenity test.

The new test defined obscenity in these words: "works which, taken as a whole, appeal to the prurient interest in sex, which portray sexual conduct in a patently offensive way, and which, taken as a whole, do not have serious literary, artistic, political, or scientific value."

Burger also adopted the "contemporary community standards" test of obscenity. The Constitution does not require, he wrote, "that the people of Maine or Mississippi accept public depiction of conduct found tolerable in Las Vegas, or New York City."

Burger denied any intent to impose "the harsh hand of censorship" on sexual materials. But the dissenters were not impressed. Justice William Douglas dismissed the new obscenity test as an unworkable "hodge-podge." Marvin Miller was going to prison, Douglas wrote, "under freshly written standards…which until today's decision were never the part of any law." Even Justice Potter Stewart, who said of obscenity that "I know it when I see it," did not see it in Miller's books and joined the dissenters.

Justice Douglas correctly observed that "obscenity cases usually generate tremendous emotional outbursts." Was he also correct in writing that "they have no business being in the courts"? Polls show that Americans have become more tolerant of sex-oriented materials over the past two decades. Prosecutors bring fewer obscenity charges, jurors make fewer guilty findings, and the courts uphold fewer convictions. But Maine and Mississippi are still not Las Vegas or New York, and we still see local outbursts over obscenity.

EDITED SUPREME COURT OPINIONS
Miller v. California
Argued January 18–19, 1972—Reargued November 7, 1972
—Decided June 21, 1973

MR. CHIEF JUSTICE BURGER delivered the opinion of the Court.

This is one of a group of "obscenity-pornography" cases being reviewed by the Court in a re-examination of standards enunciated in earlier cases involving what Mr. Justice Harlan called "the intractable obscenity problem."

Appellant conducted a mass mailing campaign to advertise the sale of illustrated books, euphemistically called "adult" material. After a jury trial, he was convicted of violating California Penal Code § 311.2 (a), a misdemeanor, by knowingly distributing obscene matter….

Appellant's conviction was specifically based on his conduct in causing five unsolicited advertising brochures to be sent through the mail in an envelope addressed to a restaurant in Newport Beach, California. The envelope was opened by the manager of the restaurant and his mother. They had not requested the brochures; they complained to the police.

The brochures advertise four books entitled *Intercourse, Man-Woman, Sex Orgies Illustrated,* and *An Illustrated History of Pornography,* and a film entitled *Marital Intercourse.* While the brochures contain some descriptive printed material, primarily they consist of pictures and drawings very explicitly depicting men and women in groups of two or more engaging in a variety of sexual activities, with genitals often prominently displayed.

This case involves the application of a State's criminal obscenity statute to a situation in which sexually explicit materials have been thrust by aggressive sales action upon unwilling recipients who had in no way indicated any desire to receive such materials. This Court has recognized that the States have a legitimate interest in prohibiting dissemination or exhibition of obscene material when the mode of dissemination carries with it a significant danger of offending the sensibilities of unwilling recipients or of exposure to juveniles....

It is in this context that we are called on to define the standards which must be used to identify obscene material that a State may regulate without infringing on the First Amendment as applicable to the States through the Fourteenth Amendment.... This much has been categorically settled by the Court, that obscene material is unprotected by the First Amendment....

We acknowledge, however, the inherent dangers of undertaking to regulate any form of expression. State statutes designed to regulate obscene materials must be carefully limited....

As a result, we now confine the permissible scope of such regulation to works which depict or describe sexual conduct. That conduct must be specifically defined by the applicable state law, as written or authoritatively construed. A state offense must also be limited to works which, taken as a whole, appeal to the prurient interest in sex, which portray sexual conduct in a patently offensive way, and which, taken as a whole, do not have serious literary, artistic, political, or scientific value....

We emphasize that it is not our function to propose regulatory schemes for the States. That must await their concrete legislative efforts. It is possible, however, to give a few plain examples of what a state statute could define for regulation....

(a) Patently offensive representations or descriptions of ultimate sexual acts, normal or perverted, actual or simulated.

(b) Patently offensive representations or descriptions of masturbation, excretory functions, and lewd exhibition of the genitals.

Sex and nudity may not be exploited without limit by films or pictures exhibited or sold in places of public accommodation any more than live sex and nudity can be exhibited or sold without limit in such public places. At a minimum, prurient, patently offensive depiction or description of sexual conduct must have serious literary, artistic, political, or scientific value to merit First Amendment protection....

Under the holdings announced today, no one will be subject to prosecution for the sale or exposure of obscene materials unless these materials depict or describe patently offensive "hard core" sexual conduct specifically defined by the regulating state law, as written or construed and are satisfied that these specific prerequisites will provide fair notice to a dealer in such materials that his public and commercial activities may bring prosecution....

It is certainly true that the absence, since *Roth*, of a single majority view of this Court as to proper standards for testing obscenity has placed a strain on both state and federal courts. But today, for the first time since *Roth* was decided in 1957, a majority of this Court has agreed on concrete guidelines to isolate "hard core" pornography from expression protected by the First Amendment....

This may not be an easy road, free from difficulty. But no amount of "fatigue" should lead us to adopt a convenient "institutional" rationale—an absolutist, "anything goes" view of the First Amendment—because it will lighten our burdens. "Such an abnegation of judicial supervision in this field would be inconsistent with our duty to uphold the constitutional guarantees."...

Under a National Constitution, fundamental First Amendment limitations on the powers of the States do not vary from community to community, but this does not mean that there are, or should or can be, fixed, uniform national standards of precisely what appeals to the "prurient interest" or is "patently offensive " These are essentially questions of fact, and our Nation is simply too big and too diverse for this Court to reasonably expect that such standards could be articulated for all 50 States in a single formulation, even assuming the prerequisite consensus exists. When triers of fact are asked to decide whether "the average person, applying contemporary community standards" would consider certain materials "prurient," it would be unrealistic to require that the answer be based on some abstract formulation The adversary system, with lay jurors as the usual ultimate fact finders in criminal prosecutions, has historically permitted triers of fact to draw on the standards of their community, guided always by limiting instructions on the law. To require a State to structure obscenity proceedings around evidence of a national "community standard" would be an exercise in futility....

During the trial, both the prosecution and the defense assumed that the relevant "community standards" in making the factual determination of obscenity were those of the State of California, not some hypothetical standard of the entire United States of America. Defense counsel at trial never objected to the testimony of the state's expert on community standards or to the instructions of the trial judge on "statewide" standards....

We conclude that neither the State's alleged failure to offer evidence of "national standards," nor the trial court's charge that the jury consider state community standards, were constitutional errors. Nothing in the First Amendment requires that a jury must consider hypothetical and unascertainable "national standards" when attempting to determine whether certain materials are obscene as a matter of fact....

It is neither realistic nor constitutionally sound to read the First Amendment as requiring that the people of Maine or Mississippi accept public depiction of conduct found tolerable in Las Vegas, or New York City....

People in different States vary in their tastes and attitudes, and this diversity is not to be strangled by the absolutism of imposed uniformity....

We hold that the requirement that the jury evaluate the materials with reference to "contemporary standards of the State of California" serves this protective purpose and is constitutionally adequate.

The dissenting Justices sound the alarm of repression. But, in our views to equate the free and robust exchange of ideas and political debate with commercial exploitation of obscene material demeans the grand conception of the First Amendment and its high purposes in the historic struggle for freedom....

The First Amendment protects works which, taken as a whole, have serious literary, artistic, political, or scientific value, regardless of whether the government or a majority of the people approve of the ideas these works represent....

One can concede that the "sexual revolution" of recent years may have had useful by-products in striking layers of prudery from a subject long irrationally kept from needed ventilation. But it does not follow that no regulation of patently offensive "hard core" materials is needed or permissible; civilized people do not allow unregulated access to heroin because it is a derivative of medicinal morphine.

In sum, we (a) reaffirm the *Roth* holding that obscene material is not protected by the First Amendment; (b) hold that such material can be regulated by the States, subject to the specific safeguards enunciated above, without a showing that the material is "*utterly* without redeeming social value"; and (c) hold that obscenity is to be determined by applying "contemporary community standards."...

The judgment of the Appellate Department of the Superior Court, Orange County, California, is vacated and the case remanded to that court for further proceedings not inconsistent with the First Amendment standards established by this opinion.

MR. JUSTICE DOUGLAS, dissenting.

Today we leave open the way for California to send a man to prison for distributing brochures that advertise books and a movie under freshly written standards defining obscenity which until today's decision were never the part of any law.

The Court has worked hard to define obscenity and concededly has failed in *Roth v. United States*, 354 U.S. 476, it ruled that "[o]bscene material is material which deals with sex in a manner appealing to prurient interest *Id.*, at 487. Obscenity, it was said, as rejected by the First Amendment because it is "utterly without redeeming social importance."…The presence of a "prurient interest" was to be determined by "contemporary community standards."…That test, it has been said could lot be determined by one standard here and another standard there, *Jacobellis v. Ohio*, 378 U.S. 184, 194, but "on the basis of a national standard."…

My Brother STEWART in *Jacobellis* commented that the difficulty of the Court in giving content to obscenity was that it was "faced with the task of trying to define what may be indefinable."…

But even those members of this Court who had created the new and changing standards of "obscenity" could not agree on their application. And so we adopted a *per curiam* treatment of so-called obscene publications that seem to pass constitutional muster under the several constitutional tests which had been formulated…. Those are the standards we ourselves have written into the Constitution. Yet how under these vague tests can we sustain convictions for the sale of an article prior to the time when some court has declared it to be obscene?

Today the Court retreats from the earlier formulations of the constitutional test and undertakes to make new definitions. This effort, like the earlier ones, is earnest and well intentioned. The difficulty is that we do not deal with constitutional terms, since "obscenity" is not mentioned in the Constitution or Bill of Rights and the First Amendment makes no such exception from "the press" which it undertakes to protect nor, as I have said on other occasions, is an exception necessarily implied, for there was no recognized exception to the free press at the time the Bill of Rights was adopted which treated "obscene" publications differently from other types of papers, magazines, and books. So there are no constitutional guidelines for deciding what is and what is not "obscene." The Court is at large because we deal with tastes and standards of literature. What shocks me may be sustenance for my neighbor. What causes one person to boil up in rage over one pamphlet or movie may reflect only his neurosis, not shared by others. We deal here with a regime of censorship which, if adopted, should be done by constitutional amendment after full debate by the people.

Obscenity cases usually generate tremendous emotional outbursts. They have no business being in the courts. If a constitutional amendment authorized censorship, the censor would probably be an administrative agency. Then criminal prosecutions could follow, as, if, and when publishers defied the censor and sold their literature. Under that regime a publisher would know when he was on dangerous ground. Under the present regime—whether the old standards or the new ones are used—the criminal law becomes a trap. A brand-new test would put a publisher behind bars under a new law improvised by the courts after the publication....

If a specific book, play, paper, or motion picture has in a civil proceeding been condemned as obscene and review of that finding has been completed, and thereafter a person publishes, shows, or displays that particular book or film, then a vague law has been made specific. There would remain the underlying question whether the First Amendment allows an implied exception in the case of obscenity. I do not think it does and my views on the issue have been stated over and over again. But at least a criminal prosecution brought at that juncture would not violate the time-honored void-for-vagueness test.

No such protective procedure has been designed by California in this case. Obscenity—which even we cannot define with precision—is a hodge-podge. To send men to jail for violating standards they cannot understand, construe, and apply is a monstrous thing to do in a Nation dedicated to fair trials and due process.

The idea that the First Amendment permits government to ban publications that are "offensive" to some people puts an ominous gloss on freedom of the press. That test would make it possible to ban any paper or any journal or magazine in some benighted place. The First Amendment was designed to induce "a condition of unrest," to "create dissatisfaction with conditions as they are," and even to stir "people to anger"...

The idea that the First Amendment permits punishment for ideas that are "offensive" to the particular judge or jury sitting in judgment is astounding. No greater leveler of speech or literature has ever been designed. To give the power to the censor, as we do today, is to make a sharp and radical break with the traditions of a free society. The First Amendment was not fashioned as a vehicle for dispensing tranquilizers to the people. Its prime function was to keep debate open to "offensive" as well as to "staid" people. The tendency throughout history has been to subdue the individual and to exalt the power of government. The use of the standard "offensive" gives authority to government that cuts the very vitals out of the First Amendment. As is intimated by the Court's opinion, the materials before us may be garbage. But so is much of what is said in political campaigns, in the daily press, on TV, or over the radio. By reason of the First

Amendment—and solely because of it—speakers and publishers have not been threatened or subdued because their thoughts and ideas may be "offensive" to some....

If there are to be restraints on what is obscene, then a constitutional amendment should be the way of achieving the end. There are societies where religion and mathematics are the only free segments. It would be a dark day for America if that were our destiny. But the people can make it such if they choose to write obscenity into the Constitution and define it.

We deal with highly emotional, not rational, questions. To many the Song of Solomon is obscene. I do not think we, the judges, were ever given the constitutional power to make definitions of obscenity. If it is to be defined, let the people debate and decide by a constitutional amendment what they want to ban as obscene and what standards they want the legislatures and the courts to apply. Perhaps the people will decide that the path towards a mature, integrated society requires that all ideas competing for acceptance must have no censor. Perhaps they will decide otherwise. Whatever the choice, the courts will have some guidelines. Now we have none except our own predilections.

New York Times Co.
v. Sullivan

376 U. S. 254 (1964)

T he "sit-in" movement against lunch-counter segregation began in February 1960 in Greensboro, North Carolina, and quickly spread across the South. Thousands of protesters, most of them college students, were arrested for challenging Jim Crow laws. On March 29, 1960, the New York Times published a full-page advertisement that solicited funds to pay the legal expenses of jailed students and their most noted supporter, Dr. Martin Luther King, Jr. The ad described police attacks on "sit-in" demonstrators in several cities, including Montgomery, Alabama, where students from Alabama State College gathered at the state capitol to protest the expulsion of their leaders. The ad contained several minor factual errors, prompting the Montgomery police commissioner, L. B. Sullivan, to sue the Times for libel. An all-white jury awarded Sullivan $500,000, but the Supreme Court reversed this judgment in a unanimous decision that proclaimed "a profound national commitment to the principle that debate on public issues should be uninhibited, robust, and wide-open."

TRANSCRIPT OF EDITED AND NARRATED ARGUMENTS IN
The New York Times Co. v. Sullivan, 376 U.S. 254 (1964)

Counsel for petitioner: Herbert Wechsler, New York City
Counsel for respondent: M. Roland Nachman, Jr., Montgomery, Alabama

Chief Justice Earl Warren: No. 39, New York Times Company, petitioner, versus L. B. Sullivan.

Narrator: It's January 6, 1964. We're in the chamber of the United States Supreme Court in Washington, D.C. Chief Justice Earl Warren has called for argument a case that raises a central issue under the First Amendment: Does the constitutional guarantee of "freedom of the press" allow the publication of false statements about public officials? Put another way, should minor errors by the press expose the media to costly and crippling libel suits?

This case began on March 29, 1960, when the *New York Times* published a full-page advertisement under the caption, "Heed Their Rising Voices." These were the voices of sit-in demonstrators against Jim Crow segregation in southern states. The sit-ins began on February 1, 1960, at a Woolworth's store in Greensboro, North Carolina. Blacks could shop in the store, but they couldn't sit down at the lunch counter. Four black college students sat down and were arrested when they refused to leave. Their example spurred thousands of young people to join sit-ins across the South, and to go to jail in acts of civil disobedience.

The sit-in movement strained the resources of civil rights groups, which launched a fund-raising campaign to meet the costs of bail, fines, and lawyers' fees. Dr. Martin Luther King, Jr., backed the students and loaned his prestigious name to raise money. The *New York Times* ad also carried the names of celebrities like Harry Belafonte, Marlon Brando, Nat King Cole, and Jackie Robinson.

One paragraph in the ad claimed that city officials in Montgomery, Alabama, had responded to demonstrations by students at Alabama State College by ringing the campus with police and padlocking the dining hall to starve the students into submission. The first claim was exaggerated and the second was untrue. L. B. Sullivan, the Montgomery police commissioner, was not mentioned in the ad. But he sued the *Times* for libel and won a half-million dollar verdict from an all-white jury. After the Alabama Supreme Court upheld the award, the *Times* appealed to the Supreme Court.

Chief Justice Warren welcomes the *Times'* lawyer, Herbert Wechsler, to the podium. Wechsler is a respected Columbia law school professor and is well-known to the justices.

Warren: Mr. Wechsler?

Wechsler: Mr. Chief Justice, may it please the Court. The writ calls for review of a judgment of the Supreme Court of Alabama which, in our submission, poses hazards for the freedom of the press not confronted since the early days of the Republic. The questions presented are, in general: first, how far the civil law of libel may be used by state officials to punish the publication of statements critical of their official conduct or of the conduct of the agencies of which they are in charge; and second, how far a state may force a newspaper which publishes a thousand miles away to defend libel actions instituted in its forum because its correspondents go there on occasion to cover news of national importance, a very small amount of advertising emanates from sources within the state, and a very small circulation of the paper—in this instance, 394 copies of a total daily circulation of 650,000-found its way into the state.

Narrator: Wechsler outlined the facts of the case. Commissioner Sullivan had sued not only the *Times*, but also four black ministers who led the civil rights struggle in Alabama.

Wechsler: The problems arise in this context: The action was instituted by the respondent, Mr. L. B. Sullivan, one of the three elected Commissioners of the City of Montgomery, Alabama. It was brought against the *Times* and four co-defendants who were then residents of Alabama—four clergymen, the Reverends Abernathy, Shuttlesworth, Seay and Lowery. These are the petitioners in No. 40. The complaint demands damages of half a million dollars for libel allegedly contained in two paragraphs of a full page advertisement that was published in the *Times* on March 29, 1960.

The object of the publication was to obtain financial support for the three needs—and I am now quoting—which were stated in the last paragraph, the paragraph beginning, "We urge you to join hands." And those needs are put as the defense of Martin Luther King, who, I should add, was then facing trial for perjury in Montgomery, Alabama. The funds were for the defense of Martin Luther King, the support of the embattled students, and the struggle for the right to vote. These are the stated goals of the solicitation.

The recitation in the text, these ten paragraphs of small type, is, of course, a statement designed to support this cause.

The lead caption, "Heed Their Rising Voices," is a phrase that was taken from a *New York Times* editorial of some days earlier, as is indicated in the top right-hand corner, where there's a quotation from the editorial which indicates accurately the sympathy with which this newspaper has viewed the Negro mass demonstrations in the South.

Now, the succeeding paragraphs recite a series of alleged abuses visited on student demonstrators in some dozen southern cities, including Montgomery, Alabama. Then the paragraphs go on to praise Dr. Martin Luther King, Jr., as a symbol and the inspiration of the movement, to allege that his peaceful protests have been answered by what the ad calls "the southern violators" with intimidation and violence designed to remove him as a leader. They urge the importance of defending Dr. King, and the need of material help by those who, in the language of the advertisement, "are taking the risk, facing jail and even death in glorious reaffirmation of our Constitution and its Bill of Rights."

I suggest, therefore, that the text was thus a statement of protest, an encomium, interwoven, to be sure, with a recitation of events. But it names no names but Dr. King's, and plainly makes no personal attack on any individual.

Narrator: Wechsler conceded that the *Times* ad was not fully accurate.

Wechsler: Now, the respondent claimed in the complaint, and the court and jury found, that he was libeled by the third paragraph of the advertisement, the paragraph that begins, "In Montgomery, Alabama," and by the first eight lines of the sixth paragraph, at the bottom of the middle column, the words that begin, "Again and again the southern violators." These were the portions of the advertisement set forth in the complaint on which the action was based.

Turning from the complaint to the record, the respondent's evidence showed that this third paragraph beginning "In Montgomery, Alabama" was indeed inaccurate in some particulars.

Narrator: Wechsler stressed the fact that the *Times* ad did not mention Commissioner Sullivan. He also attacked the ruling of the Alabama courts that *any* false statement that harmed someone's reputation was libel per se, a Latin term that means "by itself," without any proof of damages required.

Wechsler: Now, Commissioner Sullivan testified, and what he said was, quite simply, that he felt that the statements in the advertisement that referred to events in Montgomery reflected on him, on the other commissioners, and on the whole community. And he added that when they described police action or police activities, they were associated particularly with himself as the Commissioner who had jurisdiction over the police department. And this really is the basic claim of the respondent and the case on which he won, that references to the police brought this publication home to him because he was the Commissioner who had jurisdiction over the police. And the witnesses who testified for him, people in Montgomery, some of them friends of his, testified to just about that.

Now, we urged below, and we argue here, that such a reference as that to the police cannot be read as an allusion to the respondent, as Commissioner in charge, in the context of a prosecution of an action for libel. But even if it could, what I have said I think makes clear that any evidential basis for the claim of falsity must rest on very small discrepancies indeed between what was said and what the record shows to have been the case.

Now, the courts below denied our contention that this publication was protected by the First Amendment. All they said about it was that the First Amendment did not protect libelous statements. Then, on the libel part of the case they ruled that these paragraphs in suit were libelous per se, testing that by the general test, whether they tended to injure reputation. And that was the ruling made by the court. No jury ever passed on whether these statements were libelous.

Narrator: Wechsler summarized his legal arguments.

Wechsler: Now I come to my legal submissions. We have, on the libel part of the case, essentially two, perhaps three, really. Our first proposition is that this action was judged in Alabama by an unconstitutional rule of law, a rule of law offensive to the First Amendment, and offensive on its face to the First Amendment. Taking that rule, what it amounts to is that a public official is entitled to recover presumed and punitive damages, subject to no legal limit in amount, for the publication of a statement critical of his official action or even of the official action of an agency under his general supervision, if the court finds that the statement tends to injure reputation—which the court did find here—and the jury finds that the statement makes a reference to him. And the only defense available is that the statement is true in all its factual and material particulars.

Narrator: Under Alabama law, defendants in libel cases must prove that every statement in an article or ad is completely true. Wechsler pointed out the heavy burden this rule placed on the press. After he sat down, Commissioner Sullivan's lawyer, Roland Nachman, took the podium and hammered on the admitted errors in the ad.

Nachman: May it please the Court. I would like to address myself at the outset to what I consider to be a sharp difference between Mr. Wechsler's analysis of the facts and the facts as I see them. And I would like to do that in the context that this case is here, obviously, after a jury verdict, after the case has been before a trial court on a motion for a new trial, after it has been before the highest state appellate court. And we do not rely on there being something in the record to support it. We say there was ample and, indeed, overwhelming evidence to support the jury verdict.

Narrator: Alabama libel law also requires that plaintiffs demand a retraction of untrue statements. At the demand of Alabama's governor, John Patterson, the *Times* published a retraction of statements in the ad that he claimed libeled him, although the ad did not mention Patterson by name or office. But the *Times* refused to issue a retraction to Commissioner Sullivan. Roland Nachman pressed this point to the justices.

Nachman: Now, on the issue of falsity, which is where Mr. Wechsler began, I would like to take this step by step as this lawsuit progressed. A demand for retraction was filed, as it had to be filed under Alabama law, before the lawsuit began. An answer was received, and this is in the record.

The answer to the demand for retraction admitted at the outset that one of the serious charges contained in the ad was false, namely, that the dining halls had been padlocked, but there was a refusal to retract. This refusal to retract came, the evidence shows, after an investigation made by a string correspondent in Montgomery in which he outlined the falsity of these charges. There was still a refusal to retract. Then the lawsuit was filed, and after certain procedural matters were out of the way, motions to quash and a demurrer, the *Times* filed six separate pleas to the complaint. Not one of these pleas, not one of the six, had the slightest suggestion in it that this ad was true in any particular.

There was no difficulty in pleading truth in this case, we submit. If the *Times* had felt this ad was true or any part of it was true, it could have set that out in its plea. But it did not do so. It did not suggest in any one of its pleas that any part of this publication was true.

Narrator: Nachman moved on to argue that Alabama courts had the sole power to decide if statements were libelous. He faced critical questions on this issue, and quickly returned to his main point, that the *Times* had not defended the ad as completely true.

Nachman: So we say that we come then to the question of the retraction. Now, as Mr. Wechsler said, the *Times* retracted the same ad on the basis of the same demand from the Governor of Alabama. It refused to do so for this plaintiff, and this, may we remind the Court, was approximately six months before the trial, and it was, the evidence shows, after a second investigation had been made, this time by Mr. Sitton, who was a regular full-time regional correspondent of the *Times*, who was stationed in Atlanta.

He advised the *Times* that the first paragraph, to use his words, was virtually without foundation. As to the second paragraph, he noted the four arrests of Dr. King for speeding and loitering and the bombing and the fact that he was under indictment for perjury, a charge on which he was later acquitted.

The *Times* in its retraction stated that there were errors and misstatements in the ad, and accordingly it was retracted. it didn't specify that any part of it was true. It retracted the whole ad, and it didn't simply apologize. As I say, it stated that there were errors and misstatements in the ad.

Then, six months later, almost, when this case came to trial, the *Times*, with no plea of truth, with these investigations in the record, with live oral testimony from witnesses, including the respondent, that the matters were false, with the judicial admission, we submit, of a failure to plead truth, which is an absolute defense regardless of motive under Alabama law, this matter went to the jury and the jury found that it was false.

Narrator: Nachman argued that Alabama jurors could infer "malice" toward Commission Sullivan from the conceded errors in the ad. This prompted a string of questions from Justice Byron White.

Nachman: On the question of malice and deliberateness, to get to a matter that Mr. Justice White raised earlier in the argument, we submit, sir, that there was plenty from which the jury could find deliberateness. We think that the inconsistent treatment of Governor Patterson and this plaintiff, the treatment of this plaintiff after investigations showed falsity, the treatment of this plaintiff by the testimony of the Secretary telling the jury it was not substantially incorrect, after his own lawyers couldn't even plead truth, the failure of the *Times* to apply a very rigorous set of advertising acceptability standards, as they call them—

White: So you are saying this case unavoidably presents the question of whether or not a person may tell a deliberate lie about a public official. Is that the issue?

Nachman: No, sir, that is not the issue.

White: Doesn't it present that question under the First Amendment, whether you may publish a deliberate lie—

Nachman: Yes, Your Honor.

White:—about a public official?

Nachman: We think that the defendant, in order to succeed, must convince this Court that a newspaper corporation has an absolute immunity from anything it publishes. And, in answer to one, I believe, of Mr. Justice Stewart's questions, as I understand their contention and as I understand what they said it to be, if a newspaper charges, say, a mayor or police commissioner with taking a bribe, that there is absolute immunity against a libel suit in that regard. And we think that's something brand new in our jurisprudence. We think that it would have a devastating effect on this nation.

White: But if it were held here that a newspaper could publish a falsehood which it thought to be true, that would still not save the *Times* here?

Nachman: You mean a reasonable belief in truth?

White: Yes.

Nachman: No, sir, not under Alabama law. It would have to be true.

White: But on the facts of this case you say they knew it was false or essentially false?

Nachman: Yes, sir, we say that on the facts of this case there was ample evidence from which a jury could find that there was the kind of recklessness and abandon and inability to look at facts at the beginning before publication, which could be the equivalent of intent.

Narrator: Every justice on the bench asked questions during this argument, which rarely happens in the Supreme Court. Most observers in the chamber, which was packed with spectators and reporters, felt the justices were leaning toward the *Times* in their questions to Herbert Wechsler and Roland Nachman. Two months later, on March 9, 1964, Wechsler was teaching a class when his secretary came in and handed him a note. It read: "Judgment reversed. Decision unanimous." Wechsler's students burst into applause, shortly followed by newspaper editorialists across the country.

Justice William Brennan spoke for the Supreme Court in an opinion that broke new ground in protecting the press from libel claims by public officials. Brennan canvassed the record of the case and conceded that several statements in the *Times* ad "were not accurate descriptions of events which occurred in Montgomery." Students who demonstrated at the state capitol sang the National Anthem and not "My Country, 'Tis of Thee." Students protested the expulsion of their leaders by boycotting classes, not by refusing to register for them. The college dining hall was never padlocked, and the campus was not "ringed" by police.

Justice Brennan did not consider these minor errors significant. "Erroneous statement is inevitable in free debate," he wrote, and "must be protected if the freedoms of expression are to have the 'breathing space'" they need to survive. Brennan put the heart of his opinion in a sentence that has often been quoted: "We consider this case against a background of a profound national commitment to the principle that debate on public issues should be uninhibited, robust, and wide-open, and that it may well include vehement, caustic, and sometimes unpleasantly sharp attacks on government and public officials."

Three justices felt that Brennan had opened the door a crack by allowing libel suits based on proof of "actual malice" by the press. Justice Hugo Black, an Alabama native and "absolutist" defender of press freedom, wrote that "an unconditional right to say what one pleases about public affairs is what I consider to be the minimum guarantee of the First Amendment." Justices William Douglas and Arthur Goldberg agreed with Black on this principle.

At the time Justice Brennan wrote his opinion, critics of the Vietnam war were heaping abuse on President Lyndon Johnson. Later presidents, from Richard Nixon to Bill Clinton, have endured vehement and caustic attacks on their policies and character. But the Supreme Court has not backed down from its commitment in *New York Times versus Sullivan* that public debate must remain robust and uninhibited.

EDITED SUPREME COURT OPINIONS
New York Times Co. v. Sullivan
Argued January 6, 1994—Decided March 9, 1964

MR. JUSTICE BRENNAN delivered the opinion of the Court.

We are required in this case to determine for the first time the extent to which the constitutional protections for speech and press limit a state's power to award damages in a libel action brought by a public official against critics of his official conduct.

Respondent L. B. Sullivan is one of the three elected Commissioners of the city of Montgomery, Alabama. He testified that he was "Commissioner of Public Affairs and the duties are supervision of the Police Department, Fire Department, Department of Cemetery and Department of Scales." He brought this civil libel action against the four individual petitioners, who are Negroes and Alabama clergymen, and against petitioner the New York Times Company, a New York corporation which publishes the *New York Times*, a daily newspaper. A jury in the circuit Court of Montgomery County awarded him damages of $500,000, the full amount claimed, against all the petitioners, and the Supreme Court of Alabama affirmed....

Respondent's complaint alleged that he had been libeled by statements in a full-page advertisement that was carried in the *New York Times* on March 29, 1960. Entitled "Heed Their Rising Voices," the advertisement began by stating that "As the whole world knows by now, thousands of Southern Negro students are engaged in widespread non-violent demonstrations in positive affirmation of the right to live in human dignity as guaranteed by the U.S. Constitution and the Bill of Rights." It went on to charge that "in their efforts to uphold these guarantees, they are being met by an unprecedented wave of terror by those who would deny and negate that document which the whole world looks upon as setting the pattern for modern freedom...." Succeeding paragraphs purported to illustrate the "wave of terror" by describing certain alleged events. The text concluded with an appeal for funds for three purposes: support of the student movement, "the struggle for the right-to-vote," and the legal defense of Dr. Martin Luther King, Jr., leader of the movement, against a perjury indictment then pending in Montgomery.

The text appeared over the names of 64 persons, many widely known for their activities in public affairs, religion, trade unions, and the performing arts. Below these names, and under a line reading "We in the South who are struggling daily for dignity and freedom warmly endorse this appeal," appeared the names of the four individual petitioners and of 16 other persons, all but two of whom were identified as clergymen in various Southern cities. The advertisement was signed at the bottom of the page by the "Committee to Defend Martin Luther King and the Struggle for Freedom in the South," and the officers of the Committee were listed.

Of the 10 paragraphs of text in the advertisement, the third and a portion of the sixth were the basis of respondent's claim of libel. They read as follows:

Third paragraph:

"In Montgomery, Alabama, after students sang "My Country, 'Tis of Thee"on the State Capitol steps, their leaders were expelled from school, and truckloads of police armed with shotguns and tear-gas ringed the Alabama State College Campus. When the entire student body protested to state authorities by refusing to re-register, their dining hall was padlocked in an attempt to starve them into submission."

Sixth paragraph:

"Again and again the Southern violators have answered Dr. King's peaceful protests with intimidation and violence. They have bombed his home almost killing his wife and child. They have assaulted his person. They have arrested him seven times—for 'speeding,' 'loitering' and similar 'offenses.' And now they have charged him with 'perjury'—a *felony* under which they could imprison him for *ten years*...."

Although neither of these statements mentions respondent by name, he contended that the word "police" in the third paragraph referred to him as the Montgomery Commissioner who supervised the Police Department, so that he was being accused of "ringing" the campus with police. He further claimed that the paragraph would be read as imputing to the police, and hence to him, the padlocking of the dining hall in order to starve the students into submission. As to the sixth paragraph, he contended that since arrests are ordinarily made by the police, the statement "They have arrested [Dr. King] seven times" would be read as referring to him; he further contended that the "They" who did the arresting would be equated with the "They" who committed the other described acts and with the "Southern violators." Thus, he argued, the paragraph would be read as accusing the Montgomery police, and hence him, of "answering Dr. King's protests with intimidation and violence," bombing his home, assaulting his person, and charging him with perjury. Respondent and six other Montgomery residents testified that they read some or all of the statements as referring to him in his capacity as Commissioner.

It is uncontroverted that some of the statements contained in the two paragraphs were not accurate descriptions of events which occurred in Montgomery. Although Negro students staged a demonstration on the State Capitol steps, they sang the National Anthem and not "My Country, 'Tis of Thee." Although nine students were expelled by the State Board of Education, this was not for leading the demonstration at the Capitol, but for demanding service at a lunch counter in the Montgomery County Courthouse on another day. Not the entire student body, but most of it, had protested the expulsion, not by refusing to register, but by boycotting classes on a single day; virtually all the students did register for the ensuing semester. The campus dining hall was not padlocked on any occasion, and the only students who may have been barred from eating there were the few who had neither signed a preregistration application nor requested temporary meal tickets. Although the police were deployed near the campus in large numbers on three occasions, they did not at any time "ring" the campus, and they were not called to the campus in connection with the demonstration on the State Capitol steps, as the third paragraph implied. Dr. King had not been arrested seven times, but only four; and although he claimed to have been assaulted some years earlier in connection with his arrest for loitering outside a courtroom, one of the officers who made the arrest denied that there was such an assault....

The trial judge submitted the case to the jury under instructions that the statements in the advertisement were "libelous *per se*" and were not privileged, so that petitioners might be held liable if the jury found that they had published the advertisement and that the statements were made "of and concerning" respondent. The jury was instructed that, because the statements were libelous *per se*, "the law…implies legal injury froth the bare fact of publication itself," "falsity and malice are presumed," "general damages need not be alleged be proved but are presumed," and "punitive damages may be awarded by the jury even though the amount of actual damages is neither found nor shown." An award of punitive damages—as distinguished from "general" damages, which are compensatory in nature apparently requires proof of actual malice under Alabama laws and the judge charged that "mere negligence or carelessness is not evidence of actual malice or malice in fact, and does not justify an award of exemplary or punitive damages." He refused to charge, however, that the jury must be "convinced" of malice, in the sense of "actual intent" to harm or "gross negligence and recklessness," to make such an award, and he also refused to require that a verdict for respondent differentiate between compensatory and punitive damages. The judge rejected petitioners' contention that his rulings abridged the freedoms of speech and of the press that are guaranteed by the First and Fourteenth Amendments….

Under Alabama law as applied in this case, a publication is "libelous per se" if the words "tend to injure a person…in his reputation" or to "bring [him] into public contempt"; the trial court stated that the standard was met if the words are such as to "injure him in his public office, or impute misconduct to him in his office, of want of official integrity, or want of fidelity to a public trust…." The jury must find that the words were published "of and concerning" the plaintiff, but where the plaintiff is a public official his place in the governmental hierarchy is sufficient evidence to support a finding that his reputation has been affected by statements that reflect upon the agency of which he is in charge. Once "libel per se" has been established, the defendant has no defense as to stated facts unless he can persuade the jury that they were true in all their particulars….

Unless he can discharge the burden of proving truth, general damages are presumed, and may be awarded without proof of pecuniary injury. A showing of actual malice is apparently a prerequisite to recovery of punitive damages, and the defendant may in any event forestall a punitive award by a retraction meeting the statutory requirements. Good motives and belief in truth do not negate an inference of malice, but are relevant only in mitigation of punitive damages if the jury chooses to accord them weight.

The question before us is whether this rule of liability, as applied to an action brought by a public official against critics of his official conduct, abridges the freedom of speech and of the press that is guaranteed by the First and Fourteenth Amendments….

The general proposition that freedom of expression upon public questions is secured by the First Amendment has long been settled by our decisions. The constitutional safeguard, we have said, "was fashioned to assure unfettered interchange of ideas for the bringing about of political and social changes desired by the people." *Roth v. United States*, 354 U.S. 476, 484. "The maintenance of the opportunity for free political discussion to the end that government may be responsive to the will of the people and that changes may be obtained by lawful means, an opportunity essential to the security of the Republic, is a fundamental principle of our "constitutional system." *Stromberg v. California*, 283 U.S. 359, 369. "[I]t is a prized American privilege to speak one's mind, although not always with perfect good taste, on all public institutions," *Bridges v. California*, 314 U.S. 252, 270, and this opportunity is to be afforded for "vigorous advocacy" no less than "abstract discussion." *N.A.A.C.P. v. Button*, 371 U.S. 415, 429....

Thus we consider this case against the background of a profound national commitment to the principle that debate on public issues should be uninhibited, robust, and wide-open, and that it may well include vehement, caustic, and sometimes unpleasantly sharp attacks on government and publie officials. See *Terminiello v. Chicago*, 337 U.S. 1, 4; *De Jonge v. Oregon*, 299 U.S. 353, 365. The present advertisement, as an expression of grievance and protest on one of the major public issues of our time, would seem clearly to qualify for the constitutional protection. The question is whether it forfeits that protection by the falsity of some of its factual statements and by its alleged defamation of respondent.

Authoritative interpretations of the First Amendment guarantees have consistently refused to recognize an exception for any test of truth—whether administered by judges, juries, or administrative officials—and especially one that puts the burden of proving truth on the speaker. Cf. *Speiser v. Randall*, 357 U.S. 513, 525-526. The constitutional protection does not turn upon "the truth, popularity, or social utility of the ideas and beliefs which are offered." *N.A.A.C.P. v. Button*, 371 U.S. 415, 445. As Madison said, "Some degree of abuse is inseparable from the proper use of every thing; and in no instance is this more true than in that of the press."

MR. JUSTICE BLACK, with whom MR. JUSTICE DOUGLAS joins, concurring.

I concur in reversing this half-million-dollar judgment against the New York Times Company and the four individual defendants. In reversing the Court holds that "the Constitution delimits a states power to award damages for libel in actions brought by public officials against critics of their official conduct."...I base my vote to reverse on the belief that the First and Fourteenth Amendments not merely "delimit" a state's power to award damages to "public officials against critics of their official conduct" but completely prohibit state from exercising such a power.

The half-million-dollar verdict does give dramatic proof, however, that state libel laws threaten the very existence of an American press virile enough to publish unpopular views on public affairs and bold enough to criticize the conduct of public officials. The factual background of this case emphasizes the imminence and enormity of that threat. One of the acute and highly emotional issues in this country arises out of efforts of many people, even including some public officials, to continue state-commanded segregation of races in the public schools and other public places, despite our several holdings that such a state practice is forbidden by the Fourteenth Amendment. Montgomery is one of the localities in which widespread hostility to desegregation has been manifested. This hostility has sometimes extended itself to persons who favor desegregation, particularly to so-called "outside agitators," a term which can be made to fit papers like the *Times*, which is published in New York. The scarcity of testimony to show that Commissioner Sullivan suffered any actual damages at all suggests that these feelings of hostility had at least as much to do with rendition of this half-million-dollar verdict as did an appraisal of damages. Viewed realistically, this record lends support to an inference that instead of being damaged Commissioner Sullivan's political, social, had financial prestige has likely been enhanced by the *Times'* publication. Moreover, a second half-million-dollar libel verdict against the *Times* based on the same advertisement has already been awarded to another Commissioner. There a jury again gave the full amount claimed. There is no reason to believe that there are not more such huge verdicts lurking just around the corner for the *Times* or any other newspaper or broadcaster which states to do that is, in my judgment, precisely nil. Such was the general view held when the First Amendment was adopted and ever since Congress never has sought to challenge this viewpoint by passing any civil libel law. It did pass the Sedition Act in 1798, which made it a crime—"seditious libel"—to criticize federal officials or the Federal Government. As the Court's opinion correctly points out, however, that Act came to an ignominious end and by common consent has generally been treated as having been a wholly unjustifiable and much to be regretted violation of the First Amendment. Since the First Amendment is now made applicable to the States by the Fourteenth, it no more permits the States to impose damages for libel than if does the Federal Government.

We would, I think, more faithfully interpret the First Amendment by holding that at the very least it leaves the people and the press free to criticize officials and discuss public affairs with impunity. This Nation of ours elects many of its important officials; so do the States, the municipalities, the counties, and even many precincts. These officials are responsible to the people for the way they perform their duties. While our Court has held that some kinds of speech and writings, such as "obscenity," *Roth v. United States*, 354 U.S. 476, and "fighting words," *Chaplinsky v. New Hampshire*, 315 U.S. 568, are not expression within the protection of the First Amendment, freedom to discuss public affairs and public officials is unquestionably, as the Court today holds, the kind of speech the First Amendment was primarily designed to keep within the area of free discussion. To punish the exercise of this right to discuss public affairs or to penalize it through libel judgments is to abridge or shut off discussion of the very kind most needed. This Nation, I suspect, can live in peace without libel suits based on public discussions of public affairs and public officials. But I doubt that a country can live in freedom where its people can be made to suffer physically or financially for criticizing their government, its actions, or its officials.

An unconditional right to say what one pleases about public affairs is what I consider to be the minimum guarantee of the First Amendment.

I regret that the Court has stopped short of this holding indispensable to preserve our free press from destruction.

New York Times *v.* United States

403 U.S. 713 (1971)

The Pentagon Papers case began on June 13, 1971, when the *New York Times* published six pages of articles and documents from a top-secret Defense Department history of the Vietnam War. The *Washington Post* soon followed the *Times*. Government lawyers quickly asked federal judges to bar the two newspapers from printing further excerpts from the Pentagon Papers. This unprecedented case raised the issue of prior restraint of the press, the primary target of the First Amendment. Solicitor General Griswold argued to the Supreme Court that publication of the Pentagon Papers would "materially affect the security of the United States." Two weeks after the case began, the Supreme Court rejected his argument and ruled that the government had not met the "heavy burden" of proving that national security claims outweighed the First Amendment.

Counsel for petitioners: Alexander Bickel, Yale Law School (*New York Times*);
William Glendon, Washington, D.C. (*Washington Post*)
Counsel for respondent: Solicitor General Erwin Griswold, Washington, D.C.

Narrator: It's June 26th, 1971. The Court's regular term has ended. Chief Justice Warren Burger presides at this special session. It normally takes at least two years for a case to reach the Supreme Court. These cases started only two weeks ago. On Sunday, June 13th, the *New York Times* printed articles and documents from a top-secret Defense Department history of the Vietnam War. And the *Washington Post* soon printed other documents from the forty-seven volumes known as the Pentagon Papers.

Daniel Ellsberg initiated this unprecedented confrontation. Ellsberg graduated from Harvard during the Korean War and served in the Marine Corps. He worked for the Defense Department in Vietnam as a military analyst and helped prepare the Pentagon Papers. Ellsberg's Vietnam experience, and his exposure to secret documents, turned him from a hawk to a dove. He felt Americans should learn how their country was sucked into a war it could not win. But his speeches and articles against the war failed to change policy. So Ellsberg gave the Pentagon Papers to the *New York Times* and *Washington Post*. He wanted to stir up debate on the war, and he succeeded.

After the first article, government lawyers asked federal judges in New York and Washington for injunctions to block further publication. Judges in both cities held emergency hearings and issued conflicting rulings. Confronted with legal confusion, the Supreme Court voted to hear both cases.

The Pentagon Papers case tests the limits of the Constitution's First Amendment, which protects freedom of the press. It also involves the issue of prior restraint, the doctrine that bars government censorship *before* publication. More narrowly, it raises the government's claim for an exception to prior restraint, when publication might endanger "national security."

Solicitor General Erwin Griswold will argue for the government in both cases. A former dean of Harvard Law School, he speaks first for *all* the lawyers on the pressures they faced in preparing for this argument. Chief Justice Burger welcomes him.

Chief Justice Burger: Mr. Solicitor General, you may proceed.

Griswold: Mr. Chief Justice, and may it please the Court.
I am told that the law students of today are indignantly opposed to final

examinations because they say that no lawyer ever has to work under such pressure that he has to get things out in three or four hours. I can only say that I think it's perhaps fortunate that Mr. Glendon and Mr. Bickel and I went to law school under an earlier dispensation.

Narrator: Griswold outlined the government's position.

Griswold: It is important, I think, to get this case in perspective. The case, of course, raises important and difficult problems about the constitutional right of free speech and of the free press, and we've heard much about that from the press in the last two weeks. But it also raises important questions of the equally fundamental and important right of the Government to function.

Great emphasis has been put on the First Amendment, and rightly so. But there is also involved here a fundamental question of separation of powers in the sense of the power and authority which the Constitution allocates to the president, as chief executive and as commander-in-chief of the Army and Navy. And, involved in that, there is also the question of the integrity of the institution of the presidency: whether that institution—one of the three great powers under the separation of powers—can function effectively.

Narrator: Griswold addressed the prior restraint issue.

Griswold: The problem lies on a wide spectrum and, like all questions of constitutional law, involves the resolution of competing principles. In the first place, it seems to me that it will be helpful to make some preliminary observations. If we start out with the assumption that never—under any circumstances—can the press be subjected to prior restraints, never—under any circumstances—can the press be enjoined from publication, of course we come out with the conclusion that there can be no injunction here. But I suggest, not as necessarily conclusive in this case, but I suggest that there is no such constitutional rule, and never has been such a constitutional rule.

Narrator: Griswold claimed that "top secret" stamps on ten items in the Pentagon Papers justified injunctions against their publication. Justice Potter Stewart was skeptical.

Stewart: Mr. Solicitor General, I don't want to bring in a red herring in this case—or which might be—but do you also say that the ten items you have talked about fully justify the classification that has been given them and still remains on them?

Griswold: My position would be that as to those ten items—it's more than ten documents—as to those ten items, that they are properly classified "top secret."

Stewart: Thank you. As I understand…

Griswold: One of the items, I should make plain, is four volumes of the forty-seven volumes. Four related volumes, all dealing with one specific subject, the broaching of which to the entire world at this time would be of extraordinary seriousness to the security of the United States.

Narrator: Four volumes of the Pentagon Papers dealt with diplomatic efforts to negotiate between North Vietnam and the United States. Griswold did not know that Ellsberg withheld these volumes from the press, to protect the diplomats. He faced more questions on judicial standards for injunctions.

Court: As I understand it, Mr. Solicitor General—and you tell me, please, if I misunderstand it—your case doesn't really depend upon the classification of this material, whether it's classified or how it's classified?

Griswold: Well I think, Mr. Justice, that is true. But I also think the heart of our case is that the publication of the material specified in my closed brief will, as I have tried to argue there, materially affect the security of the United States. It will affect lives. It will affect the process of the termination of the war. It will affect the process of recovering prisoners of war. I cannot say that the termination of the war, or recovering prisoners of war, is something which has an "immediate" effect on the security of the United States. I say that it has such an effect on the security of the United States that it ought to be the basis of an injunction in this case.

Narrator: Griswold offered a concession.

Griswold: If this material had never been classified, I think we would have a considerably greater difficulty in coming in and saying—well, for example, suppose the material had been included in a public speech made by the president of the United States.

Court: Well, then it would be in the public domain already. That's something else.

Griswold: All right. But we come in and say, "You can't print this because it will gravely affect the security of the United States." I think we would plainly be out.

Court: And a very shaky case on the facts. And that's…

Griswold: Or suppose it had been…[*laughter*]

Court: And this, therefore, is a fact case, isn't it? Until we can decide this case, we have to look at the facts, the evidence in this case that's been submitted under seal.

Griswold: In large part, yes, Mr. Justice.

Narrator: Griswold criticized Judge Gerhard Gesell, who ruled in the *Washington Post* case that the government must prove "immediate harm" to the United States to justify prior restraint.

Griswold: If the standard is that we cannot prevent the publication of improperly acquired material unless we can show in substance and effect—because that's what he really meant—that there will be a break in diplomatic relations, or that there will be an armed attack on the United States, I suggest that the standard which Judge Gesell used is far too narrow. And, as I've said, that the standard should be "great and irreparable harm to the security of the United States."

Narrator: Griswold raised an alarm about diplomatic efforts to end the war.

Griswold: In the whole diplomatic area the things don't happen at 8:15 tomorrow morning. It may be weeks, or months. People tell me that already channels of communication on which great hope had been placed have dried up. I haven't the slightest doubt, myself, that the material which has already been published, and the publication of the other materials, affects American lives, and is a thoroughly serious matter. And I think that to say that it can only be enjoined if there will be a war tomorrow morning, when there's a war now going on, is much too narrow.

Narrator: Chief Justice Burger.

Burger: Thank you, Mr. Solicitor General. Mr. Bickel.

Narrator: Alexander Bickel, a Yale Law School professor, argued for the *New York Times*.

Bickel: Mr. Chief Justice, may it please the Court.

I don't, for a moment, argue that the president doesn't have full inherent power to establish a system of classification; that he doesn't have the fullest inherent power to administer that system and its procedures within the executive branch. He has his means of guarding security at the source. In some measure, he's aided by the criminal sanction, but in any event he has full inherent power. And the scope of judicial review of the exercise of that power will presumably vary with the case in which it comes up.

Narrator: Bickel made a strategic concession.

Bickel: We concede—we have all along in this case conceded—for purposes of the argument, that the prohibition against prior restraint, like so much else in the Constitution, is not an absolute. But beyond that, Mr. Justice, our position is a little more complicated than that.

Rather, our position is twofold. First, on principles as we view them with the separation of powers, which we believe deny the existence of inherent presidential authority on which an injunction can be based, first on those. And, secondly, on First Amendment principles which are interconnected on both and which involve the question of a standard before one reaches the facts—a standard on which we differ greatly from the solicitor general.

Narrator: Bickel's support for the "immediate harm" standard for prior restraint led to questions.

Court: I take it, then, that you could easily concede that there may be documents in these forty-seven volumes which would satisfy the definition of "top secret" in the Executive Order and, nevertheless, would not satisfy your standard?

Bickel: That would be chiefly the reason that, as is notorious, classifications are imposed…

Court: No, no, my question was, let's concede for the moment that there are some documents…(Bickel: Which are properly?)…properly classified "top secret." You would say that does not necessarily mean that your standard is satisfied?

Bickel: That's correct, Mr. Justice. I would say that…

Court: Well, I think—I haven't read anything in any of your documents, or in any of these cases, which the newspapers suggest for a moment that there is *no* document in these forty-seven volumes which satisfies properly the definition of "top secret."

Bickel: Having read the submissions of the government, I am flatly persuaded that there's nothing in there. Because if there—nothing that would meet my standard in there for a statute or for independent executive action—because if there were it surely should have turned up by now.

Narrator: Justice Potter Stewart asked a tough question.

Stewart: Now, Mr. Bickel, it's understandably and inevitably true that in a case like this, particularly when so many of the facts are under seal, it's necessary to speak in abstract terms. (Bickel: Yes, sir.) But let me give you a hypothetical case. Let us assume that when the members of the Court go back and open up this sealed record, we find something there that absolutely convinces us that its disclosure would result in the sentencing to death of a hundred young men whose only offense had been that they were nineteen years old and had low draft numbers. What should we do?

Bickel: Mr. Justice, I wish there were a statute that covered it.

Stewart: Well, there isn't, we agree—or you submit—so I'm asking you in this case, what should we do? You would say the Constitution requires that it be published and that these men die. Is that it?

Bickel: No. No, I'm afraid I'd have, I'm afraid that my, the inclinations of humanity overcome the somewhat more abstract devotion to the First Amendment, in a case of that sort.

Narrator: Justice Hugo Black asked if Congress could impose prior restraint on the press.

Bickel: We don't face it in this case and I really don't know. I'd have to face that if I saw it—if I saw the statute—if I saw how definite it was.

Black: Why would the statute make a difference? Because the First Amendment provides that "Congress shall make no law abridging freedom of the press." (Bickel: Well…) And you can read that to mean Congress may make "some laws" abridging freedom of the press?

Bickel: No, sir—only in that I have conceded for purposes of this argument that some limitations, some impairment of the absoluteness of that prohibition, is possible. And I argue that whatever that may be—whatever that may be—it is surely at its very least when the president acts without statutory authority, because that inserts into it, as well as separation of powers…

Black: That's a very strange argument for the *Times* to be making, that the Congress can make all of this illegal by passing laws.

Bickel: Well, I didn't really argue that, Mr. Justice. At least I hope not.

Black: That was the strong impression you left in my mind.

Narrator: William Glendon argued for the *Washington Post*. Chief Justice Burger asked about the "immediate harm" standard.

Burger: Mr. Glendon, how does a government meet the burden of proof in the sense that Judge Gesell laid it down? That doesn't bring any battleships to the outer limits of New York Harbor, or set off any missiles, but would you say that it's not a very grave matter?

Glendon: Your Honor, I think if we are to place possibilities or conjecture against suspension or abridgment of the First Amendment, the answer is obvious. The fact, the possibility, the conjecture of the hypothesis, that diplomatic negotiations would be made more difficult or embarrassing, does not justify—and this is what we have in this case, I think, it's all we have—does not justify suspending the First Amendment.

Burger: You are now in the position of making demands on the First Amendment…(Glendon: That's right)…and you say the newspaper has a right to protect its sources, but the government does not?

Glendon: I see no conflict, Your Honor. I see no conflict at all. We're in the position of asking that there not be a prior restraint, in violation of the Constitution, imposed on us, and that equity should not do that. We are also in the position of saying that under the First Amendment we are entitled to protect our sources. And I find—frankly, I just don't find any conflict there, Your Honor.

Narrator: Glendon reminded the Court of the stakes in the case.

Glendon: It isn't just that the United States has been injured. Judge Gesell made a point, which I think is a very good one, and I think perhaps the government may forget, that the interests of the United States are the people's interest. And you're weighing here—and this is why, I suppose, we're here—you're weighing here an abridgment of the First Amendment, the people's right to know. And that may be an abstraction, but it's one that's kept this country and made it great for some two hundred years, and you're being asked to approve something that the government has never done before. We were told by the attorney general to stop publishing this news. We didn't obey that order, and we were brought into court, and we ended up being enjoined.

Narrator: Solicitor General Griswold spoke in rebuttal. Justices Thurgood Marshall and Hugo Black had questions.

Griswold: I think that if properly classified materials are improperly acquired, and that it can be shown that they do have an immediate, or current impact, on the security of the United States that there ought to be an injunction. Now I think it is relevant, at this point...

Marshall: Well, wouldn't we then be—the federal courts—be the censorship board? (Griswold: Uh, that's...) As to whether this does...

Griswold: That's a pejorative way to put it, Mr. Justice. I don't know what the alternative is.

Black: The First Amendment might be. [*laughter*]

Griswold: Yes, Mr. Justice. And we are, of course, fully supporting the First Amendment. We do not claim, or suggest, any exception to the First Amendment. And we do not agree with Mr. Glendon when he says that we have set aside the First Amendment, or that Judge Gesell or the two Courts of Appeals in this case have set aside the First Amendment by issuing the injunction which they have.
The problem in this case is the construction of the First Amendment. Now, Mr. Justice Black, your construction of that is well known, and I certainly respect it. You say that "no law" means "no law," and that should be obvious.

Black: I rather thought that.

Griswold: And I can only say, Mr. Justice, that to me it is equally obvious that "no law" does *not* mean "no law." And I would seek to persuade the Court that that is true.

Narrator: On June 30th, 1971, only four days after this argument, the Supreme Court decided the Pentagon Papers case. In a three-paragraph opinion, six justices agreed that the government had not met the First Amendment's "heavy presumption" against prior restraints on the press. This short opinion was all the majority agreed on.

Reflecting the nation's division over the Vietnam War, each of the nine justices wrote a separate opinion. Justice Hugo Black blasted the government for what he called "a flagrant, indefensible, and continuing violation of the First Amendment."

Only Justice William Douglas agreed with Black that the Constitution barred *any* prior restraint. Four justices would allow the government to restrain publication of material that would cause, as Justice Potter Stewart wrote, "direct, immediate, and irreparable damage" to the United States. But the Pentagon Papers had not caused such damage.

Chief Justice Burger led the three dissenters. He blamed the newspapers for rushing into print and pressuring the Courts. "Free from unwarranted deadlines and frenetic pressures," he wrote, judges might have found documents that justified prior restraint.

Freed from judicial orders to stop the presses, newspapers across the country resumed publication of the Pentagon Papers. The Vietnam War ended four years later with an American defeat. Some critics blame the press for "losing" the war. The Persian Gulf War in 1991 again raised First Amendment issues of military censorship and media access to war zones. As long as bombs fall and presses roll, the Constitution will take hits from both sides. Whether it survives is up to the American people.

EDITED SUPREME COURT OPINION
New York Times v. United States

PER CURIAM.

We granted certiorari in these cases in which the United States seeks to enjoin the *New York Times* and the *Washington Post* from publishing the contents of a classified study entitled "History of U.S. Decision-Making Process on Viet Nam Policy." *Post*, pp. 942, 943.

"Any system of prior restraints of expression comes to this Court bearing a heavy presumption against its constitutional validity." *Bantam Books, Inc. v. Sullivan*, 372 U.S. 58, 70 (1963)…The Government "thus carries a heavy burden of showing justification for the imposition of such a restraint." *Organization for a Better Austin v. Keefe*, 402 U.S. 415, 419 (1971). The District Court for the Southern District of New York in the *New York Times* case and the District Court for the District of Columbia and the Court of Appeals for the District of Columbia Circuit in the *Washington Post* case held that the Government had not met that burden. We agree.

The judgment of the Court of Appeals for the District of Columbia Circuit is therefore affirmed. The order of the Court of Appeals for the Second Circuit is reversed and the case is remanded with directions to enter a judgment affirming the judgment of the District Court for the Southern District of New York. The stays entered June 25, 1971, by the Court are vacated. The judgments shall issue forthwith.

So ordered.

MR. JUSTICE BLACK, with whom MR. JUSTICE DOUGLAS joins, concurring.

I adhere to the view that the Government's case against the *Washington Post* should have been dismissed and that the injunction against the *New York Times* should have been vacated without oral argument when the cases were first presented to this Court. I believe that every moment's continuance of the injunctions against these newspapers amounts to a flagrant, indefensible, and continuing violation of the First Amendment....In my view it is unfortunate that some of my Brethren are apparently willing to hold that the publication of news may sometimes be enjoined. Such a holding would make a shambles of the First Amendment.

Our Government was launched in 1789 with the adoption of the Constitution. The Bill of Rights, including the First Amendment, followed in 1791. Now, for the first time in the 182 years since the founding of the Republic, the federal courts are asked to hold that the First Amendment does not mean what it says, but rather means that the Government can halt the publication of current news of vital importance to the people of this country....

The Bill of Rights changed the original Constitution into a new charter under which no branch of government could abridge the people's freedoms of press, speech, religion, and assembly. Yet the Solicitor General argues and some members of the Court appear to agree that the general powers of the Government adopted in the original Constitution should be interpreted to limit and restrict the specific and emphatic guarantees of the Bill of Rights adopted later. I can imagine no greater perversion of history. Madison and the other Framers of the First Amendment, able men that they were, wrote in language they earnestly believed could never be misunderstood: "Congress shall make no law…abridging the freedom…of the press…." Both the history and language of the First Amendment support the view that the press must be left free to publish news, whatever the source, without censorship, injunctions, or prior restraints.

In the First Amendment the Founding Fathers gave the free press the protection it must have to fulfill its essential role in our democracy. The press was to serve the governed, not the governors. The Government's power to censor the press was abolished so that the press would remain forever free to censure the Government. The press was protected so that it could bare the secrets of government and inform the people. Only a free and unrestrained press can effectively expose deception in government. And paramount among the responsibilities of a free press is the duty to prevent any part of the government from deceiving the people and sending them off to distant lands to die of foreign fevers and foreign shot and shell. In my view, far from deserving condemnation for their courageous reporting, the *New York Times*, the *Washington Post*, and other newspapers should be commended for serving the purpose that the Founding Fathers saw so clearly. In revealing the workings of government that led to the Vietnam War, the newspapers nobly did precisely that which the Founders hoped and trusted they would do….

The word "security" is a broad, vague generality whose contours should not be invoked to abrogate the fundamental law embodied in the First Amendment. The guarding of military and diplomatic secrets at the expense of informed representative government provides no real security for our Republic. The Framers of the First Amendment, fully aware of both the need to defend a new nation and the abuses of the English and Colonial governments, sought to give this new society strength and security by providing that freedom of speech, press, religion, and assembly should not be abridged. This thought was eloquently expressed in 1937 by Mr. Chief Justice Hughes—great man and great Chief Justice that he was—when the Court held a man could not be punished for attending a meeting run by Communists.

"The greater the importance of safeguarding the community from incitements to the overthrow of our institutions by force and violence, the more imperative is the need to preserve inviolate the constitutional rights of free speech, free press and free assembly in order to maintain the opportunity for free political discussion, to the end that government may be responsive to the will of the people and that changes, if desired, may be obtained by peaceful means. Therein lies the security of the Republic, the very founda- tion of constitutional government." *De Jonge v. Oregon*, 299 U.S. 353, 365.

MR. CHIEF JUSTICE BURGER, dissenting.

So clear are the constitutional limitations on prior restraint against expression, that…we have had little occasion to be concerned with cases involving prior restraints against news reporting on matters of public interest. There is, therefore, little variation among the members of the Court in terms of resistance to prior restraints against publication. Adherence to this basic constitutional principle, however, does not make these cases simple. In these cases, the imperative of a free and unfettered press comes into collision with another imperative, the effective functioning of a complex modern government and specifically the effective exercise of certain constitutional powers of the Executive. Only those who view the First Amendment as an absolute in all circumstances—a view I respect, but reject—can find such cases as these to be simple or easy.

These cases are not simple for another and more immediate reason. We do not know the facts of the cases. No district judge knew all the facts. No court of appeals judge knew all the facts. No member of this Court knows all the facts.

Why are we in this posture, in which only those judges to whom the First Amendment is absolute and permits of no restraint in any circumstances or for any reason, are really in a position to act?

I suggest we are in this posture because these cases have been conducted in unseemly haste….The prompt setting of these cases reflects our universal abhorrence of prior restraint. But prompt judicial action does not mean unjudicial haste.

Here, moreover, the frenetic haste is due in large part to the manner in which the *Times* proceeded from the date it obtained the purloined documents. It seems reasonably clear now that the haste precluded reasonable and deliberate judicial treatment of these cases and was not warranted. The precipitate action of this Court aborting trials not yet completed is not the kind of judicial conduct that ought to attend the disposition of a great issue.

The newspapers make a derivative claim under the First Amendment; they denominate this right as the public "right to know"…

It is not disputed that the *Times* has had unauthorized possession of the documents for three to four months, during which it has had its expert analysts studying them, presumably digesting them and preparing the material for publication. During all of this time, the *Times*, presumably in its capacity as trustee of the public's "right to know," has held up publication for purposes it considered proper and thus public knowledge was delayed. No doubt this was for a good reason; the analysis of seven thousand pages of complex material drawn from a vastly greater volume of material would inevitably take time and the writing of good news stories takes time. But why should the United States Government, from whom this information was illegally acquired by someone, along with all the counsel, trial judges, and appellate judges be placed under needless pressure? After these months of deferral, the alleged "right to know" has somehow and suddenly become a right that must be vindicated instantly.

Would it have been unreasonable, since the newspaper could anticipate the Government's objections to release of secret material, to give the Government an opportunity to review the entire collection and determine whether agreement could be reached on publication?...

To me it is hardly believable that a newspaper long regarded as a great institution in American life would fail to perform one of the basic and simple duties of every citizen with respect to the discovery or possession of stolen property or secret government documents. That duty, I had thought—perhaps naively—was to report forthwith, to responsible public officers. This duty rests on taxi drivers, Justices, and the *New York Times*. The course followed by the *Times*, whether so calculated or not, removed any possibility of orderly litigation of the issues....

The consequence of all this melancholy series of events is that we literally do not know what we are acting on. As I see it, we have been forced to deal with litigation concerning rights of great magnitude without an adequate record, and surely without time for adequate treatment either in the prior proceedings or in this Court. It is interesting to note that counsel on both sides, in oral argument before this Court, were frequently unable to respond to questions on factual points. Not surprisingly they pointed out that they had been working literally "around the clock" and simply were unable to review the documents that give rise to these cases and were not familiar with them. This Court is in no better posture....

We all crave speedier judicial processes but when judges are pressured as in these cases the result is a parody of the judicial function.

BIBLIOGRAPHY

GELB, LESLIE H. "Today's Lessons from the Pentagon Papers." *Life*, September 17, 1971, p. 34

KONIG, HANS. "Did the Pentagon Papers Make Any Difference?" *Saturday Review*, June 10, 1972, p. 13.

McGOVERN, GEORGE, AND JOHN R. ROCHE. "The Pentagon Papers—A Discussion." *Political Science Quarterly* 87, no. 2 (June 1972): 173.

SCHRAG, PETER. *Test of Loyalty*. Touchstone, 1974.

"The Counter-Government and the Pentagon Papers." *National Review*, July 13, 1971, p. 739.

"The First Amendment on Trial." *Columbia Journalism Review*, September/October 1971, p. 7.

UNGAR, SANFORD J. *The Papers and the Papers*. Dutton, 1972.

R.A.V. *v.*
City of St. Paul,
Minnesota

505 U.S. 377 (1992)

Early in 1990, Russell and Laura Jones and their five children moved into the working-class neighborhood of Dayton's Bluff in St. Paul, Minnesota. The Jones' were black and most of their neighbors were white. In the early morning of June 21, 1990, the Jones' heard noises and discovered a crudely made cross burning in their front yard. The police arrested two teenagers and charged them under St. Paul's "hate crimes" ordinance, which made it unlawful to place on any property a symbol that might arouse "anger, alarm or resentment in others on the basis of race, color, creed, or gender." One teenager pleaded guilty; the other—known in juvenile court by his initials, R.A.V.—challenged the law as a content-based violation of the First Amendment. The Supreme Court unanimously agreed, although the justices were divided on what standard the Court should apply. The majority argued that *any* content-based limitation of speech is unconstitutional. Four justices would retain the "fighting words" exception to the First Amendment but voted to strike down the St. Paul ordinance as "overbroad" in banning some kinds of protected speech.

TRANSCRIPT OF EDITED AND NARRATED ARGUMENTS IN
R.A.V. v. City of St. Paul, Minnesota, 505 U.S. 377 (1992)

Counsel for petitioner: Edward J. Cleary, St. Paul, Minnesota
Counsel for respondent: Tom Foley, Ramsey County Attorney, St. Paul, Minnesota

Chief Justice Rehnquist: We'll hear argument now in 90-7675, *R.A.V. v. St. Paul, Minnesota*.

Narrator: It's December 4, 1991. We're in the chamber of the United States Supreme Court in Washington, D.C. Chief Justice William Rehnquist has called for argument a case that tests the outer limits of the First Amendment.

This case began at 290 Earl Street in St. Paul, Minnesota. Early in 1990, Russell and Laura Jones and their five children moved into the working-class neighborhood of Dayton's Bluff. The Jones' were black and most of their neighbors were white. In the early morning of June 21, 1990, the Jones' heard noises, went outside and discovered a burning cross in their front yard. It was crudely made from two wooden chair legs, wrapped in terry cloth. The Jones' were terrified and quickly called the police.

Within a few days, the police arrested two teenage boys, who both lived near the Jones' home. They were charged under a St. Paul ordinance, adopted in 1982, which made it a crime to place on any property any symbol, object, or words that might arouse, in the law's words, "anger, alarm or resentment in others on the basis of race, color, creed, or gender...." The law specified burning crosses and Nazi swastikas as prohibited symbols.

The St. Paul ordinance was one of many legal efforts to punish "hate crimes" during the 1980s. Legal challenges to such laws faced the obstacle of a 1942 Supreme Court ruling, upholding the conviction of Walter Chaplinsky, who called a New Hampshire policeman a "goddamn fascist" during a street-corner altercation. The *Chaplinsky* case set out a "fighting words" exception to the First Amendment's free speech clause. However, in 1969 the Supreme Court ruled that Clarence Brandenburg, a Ku Klux Klan leader in Ohio, could not be punished for advocating violence against blacks and Jews, without a showing of "imminent lawless action."

The *Chaplinsky* and *Brandenburg* cases form the legal backdrop for today's argument. One of the boys charged in the cross burning pleaded guilty under the "hate crime" law. A juvenile court judge assigned a St. Paul lawyer, Edward Cleary, to represent the other boy, identified by his initials as R.A.V. His full name was Robert A. Viktora. Cleary had little in common with his client, who adopted "skinhead" attire and admitted contact with racist groups. But Cleary believed the "hate crime" law violated the First Amendment, and he persuaded a state judge to strike down the law on free speech grounds. But the Minnesota Supreme Court reversed this decision, citing the *Chaplinsky* and *Brandenburg* cases for authority. The U.S. Supreme Court granted Cleary's petition for review, and Chief Justice Rehnquist welcomes him to the podium.

Rehnquist: Mr. Cleary.

Cleary: Mr. Chief Justice, and may it please the Court. Each generation must reaffirm the guarantee of the First Amendment with the hard cases. The framers understood the dangers of orthodoxy and standardized thought and chose liberty. We are once again faced with a case that will demonstrate whether or not there is room for the freedom for the thought that we hate, whether there is room for the eternal vigilance necessary for the opinions that we loathe.

     The conduct in this case is reprehensible, is abhorrent, and is well known by now. I'm not here to defend the alleged conduct, but as Justice Frankfurter said forty years ago, history has shown that the safeguards of liberty are generally forged in cases involving not very nice people. He might just as well have said, involving cases involving very ugly fact situations. I am here to discuss and to ask the Court to review the Minnesota Supreme Court's interpretation of a St. Paul ordinance.

Narrator: Justice Sandra O'Connor quickly asks Cleary to address the *Chaplinsky* and *Brandenburg* cases. He takes a cautious approach in responding.

O'Connor: And in essence what the Minnesota Supreme Court appears to have said is, we interpret the law as reaching only those exceptions that the Supreme Court has recognized to the First Amendment—fighting words, for instance, out of our prior *Chaplinsky* case. Now, do you agree that that's what they've done?

Cleary: I agree that the court attempted to narrow the ordinance and in doing so cited *Chaplinsky* and *Brandenburg* to this court.

O'Connor: Right, and in essence they said what that statute means is what the Supreme Court has permitted in *Brandenburg* and *Chaplinsky*.

Cleary: They did cite those cases, Your Honor. I do believe, however, that the expansive language that was used shows a much broader reach than what this Court indicated in those cases.

O'Connor: So you would ask us to somehow overturn those older holdings.

Cleary: No, I don't believe it's necessary to do that, Your Honor, to get to the position that I'm requesting.

Narrator: Asking the justices to overturn earlier decisions is always risky. Another question allows Cleary to suggest a way around *Chaplinsky*.

Court: Mr. Cleary, isn't one of your complaints that the Minnesota statute as construed by the supreme court of Minnesota punishes only some fighting words and not others?

Cleary: It is, Your Honor. That is one of my positions, that in doing so, even though it is a subcategory, technically, of unprotected conduct, it is still picking out an opinion, a disfavored message, and making that clear through the state. It's a paternalistic idea, and the problem we have is that the government must not betray neutrality, and I believe it does, even when it picks out a subcategory.

Narrator: Cleary had shied away from asking the justices to overturn the *Chaplinsky* decision, which defined "fighting words" as "those which by their very utterance inflict injury" on others. Questions on this issue move Cleary to shift his position on *Chaplinsky*.

Court: With respect just to the words that injure, where would you draw the line on what is permissible?

Cleary: I believe, Your Honor, that the—I'll be very honest. I think that's a very hard line to draw, and I think that's perhaps the crux of this case to a certain degree, is the offensiveness idea and how—

Court: Is it hard enough so that in fact we have to say that that was simply a mistaken statement and disavow it and leave *Chaplinsky* with the fighting words category as alone subject to punishment?

Cleary: No, I don't believe so. I believe that the Court must draw the line in favor of the individual right of self-expression. I think that if the line—

Court: Well, I agree, but aren't you really coming to the point of saying that the *Chaplinsky* reference to words that injure was in fact, at least by today's standards, an erroneous reference and we should disavow *Chaplinsky* to that extent?

Cleary: I am.

Narrator: Cleary argues that the First Amendment does not permit laws to discriminate between "good" and "bad" attitudes or viewpoints toward minorities and women.

Cleary: The debate in this case is not about the wisdom of eradicating intolerance, the debate is about the method of reaching that goal. I believe that the city council officials in this case and in other communities are very well meaning, and that's usually the case, but the problem is that I believe these type of laws cross the line from the Fourteenth Amendment duty of the state to not participate in any racist state action or any intolerant state action, in that sense, with the First Amendment right of self-expression, even if it be intolerant, provided it does not cross the line of illegal conduct itself. I believe the danger in a law like this is that it does pick out viewpoints, that it is viewpoint-discriminatory.

Narrator: Minnesota has a law that punishes "terroristic threats" against others. Cleary faces questions about applying such a law to his client.

Court: Could this conduct be punished by a narrowly drawn statute that proscribes threats that cause violence? Could that state a cause of action against your client?

Cleary: I believe it could.

Court: On these facts?

Cleary: I believe it could. I believe, I have never argued that—again, that the conduct alleged in this case could not be addressed by viewpoint-neutral laws, but this type of a law leaves open the possibility for viewpoint discrimination, and it opens up, again, the selective enforcement idea.

Narrator: Cleary reminds the justices that the First Amendment was designed to protect free speech against fear and hysteria.

Cleary: Certainly in this current time there is a great deal of fear, and the First Amendment—and as it is construed and as it is before this Court, has to face the environment that we find ourselves in as a nation. Justice Brandeis once said that fear breeds repression and repression breeds hate. I believe that this is the hour of danger for the First Amendment in that there are many groups that would like to encroach upon its principles with well-meaning intentions, but in doing so, they are still punishing the content of the communication and they are doing so in a discriminatory manner, and the government is betraying a neutral principle in the sense that they are allowing that to happen and they are partaking in that.

Narrator: The Court ruled in 1989 that flag-burning was protected by the First Amendment, in *Texas v. Johnson*. Chief Justice Rehnquist dissented in that case, but he asks Cleary how the decision applies to cross burning. Cleary cites other "symbolic speech" cases—allowing red flags and black armbands as protest symbols—in his reply.

Rehnquist: The Court's opinion in *Texas* against *Johnson* suggested that there couldn't be a fighting symbol at any rate, per se, did it not?

Cleary: That's correct, Chief Justice. I think that the Court's holding in *Texas v. Johnson* supports the petitioners' position in this case, and I also would point out that I do not think that the dissents are necessarily inconsistent with the petitioners' position on this law. I would say that is particularly true because of the fact that this Court put a great emphasis on the unique nature of the American flag and in doing so, I believe, acknowledged the *Stromberg* red flag of the thirties, the black armband in the sixties, in *Tinker*, and was mindful of the fact that once that door is opened, that it could lead to a ban on symbolic behavior in such a fashion that a great deal of expression would be prohibited.

Narrator: Tom Foley is the county attorney in St. Paul. He defends the city's "hate crime" law, and endorses the *Chaplinsky* and *Brandenburg* rulings as precedent.

Foley: Mr. Chief Justice, and may it please the Court. The First Amendment was never intended to protect an individual who burns a cross in the middle of the night in the fenced yard of an African-American family's home. The city of St. Paul has the right to prohibit and prosecute such conduct. The ordinance at issue in this case has been interpreted by the Minnesota Supreme Court to prohibit only conduct that inflicts injury, tends to incite an immediate breach of the peace, or provokes imminent lawless action.

And unless this Court is willing to abandon its holdings in *Chaplinsky* and *Brandenburg*, holdings that it has upheld for the last fifty years, this ordinance must be upheld.

Narrator: Foley outlines his argument, and immediately runs into questions from Justice O'Connor.

Foley: In this oral argument I'm going to touch on four propositions. First is the purpose of the ordinance. Second, that the ordinance has been narrowly construed by the Minnesota Supreme Court only to apply to fighting words. Third, that the ordinance as construed is not overbroad or vague. And fourth, that the ordinance does not interfere with legitimate First Amendment rights.

O'Connor: Well, Mr. Foley, would you address the concern expressed by your opponent that that ordinance is limited to only fighting words that arouse anger, alarm, or resentment on the basis of race, color, creed, or religion or gender and not other fighting words that could cause the same reaction in people? The argument is that the statute is underinclusive.

Foley: Your Honor, it's our position that the statute is not underinclusive, that this is a fighting words case, that this is unprotected conduct under the First Amendment, and that the city of St. Paul has the right to determine which harms it can proscribe within the limits of its jurisdiction.

O'Connor: Well, certainly it is limited by subject matter or content of the fighting words that are spoken, is it not? In that sense it is a content-based ordinance.

Foley: Your Honor, it's our position that it is not a content-based ordinance, that it certainly could be used to be a content-neutral ordinance.

O'Connor: Well, but it doesn't cover fighting words that are not limited to words on the basis of race, color, creed, religion, or gender.

Foley: That's correct, Your Honor.

Narrator: Picking up where Justice O'Connor ended, Justice Scalia turns up the heat on Foley.

Scalia: If you want to prohibit fighting words, prohibit fighting words. But why pick only if you use fighting words for these particular purposes: race, color, creed, religion, and gender? What about other fighting words?

Foley: I think the city has an absolute right and purpose to try to regulate the harm that goes on to its citizens. And certainly this bias-motivated conduct and violence is much more harmful and has more harmful impacts to its citizens—

Scalia: That's a political judgment. I mean, you may feel strongest about race, color, creed, religion, or gender. Somebody else may feel strong as to about philosophy, about economic philosophy, about whatever. You picked out five reasons for causing somebody to breach the peace. But there are a lot of other ones. What's your basis for making that subjective discrimination?

Foley: Your Honor, the city of St. Paul is attempting to fashion responses to violence that it deems necessary to prohibit and will add additional harms to be regulated as it finds them. Under this particular ordinance, it seemed that this is a particular harm going on that is necessary within the city of St. Paul to prohibit and regulate.

Scalia: It doesn't have to add anything. You could just drop the words and, you know, just say that arouses anger, alarm, or resentment in others, period, or shall be guilty of a misdemeanor. It didn't have to say arouses anger, alarm, or resentment on the basis of race, color, creed, religion, or gender. You don't need that for *Chaplinsky*. If it's a fighting word, it's a fighting word. They could get the cross burning, they could get all sorts of activities.

Foley: Your Honor, I think it's the city's position that this is a fighting words case, that the ordinance has been sufficiently narrowed by the Minnesota Supreme Court. And you could reread that ordinance under these facts to say that whoever, based on race, places an object or symbol with the intent to inflict injury, incite immediate violence, or provoke imminent lawless action is guilty of a crime. And I think that the Minnesota Supreme Court's narrowing of that ordinance is sufficient to uphold its constitutionality under the *Chaplinsky* and *Brandenburg* holdings of this Court.

Scalia: Well, are you saying that because they can prevent or punish all fighting words, they can select any category within the broad scope of fighting words for it to be singled out?

Foley: Yes, Your Honor.

Narrator: Foley tries to move on, but his claim that St. Paul can pick and choose the groups to protect from hate crimes provokes another round of questions from Justice Scalia.

Foley: I think it is important to look at bias-motivated violence, which is significantly more harmful on the impact than similar criminal conduct not similarly motivated. The burning of the cross and the African-American family is not the equivalent of a simple trespass or minor arson, either to the targeted victims or to the community in which it occurred.

Scalia: Well, you say bias-motivated, but it depends on what your biases are. If a family with a mentally deficient child should move into the neighborhood or if there should be established in the neighborhood a home for the mentally ill, and someone should burn a cross on the lawn of that home or institution with a sign that says, mentally ill out, that would not be covered by this ordinance, isn't that correct?

Foley: I don't believe under the facts that you described that it would.

Scalia: It's the wrong kind of bias. It's—at least until they come around to adding—which may well be the next one, gender, religion, gender, or disability, until they come around to adding that, it's the wrong kind of bias and therefore you can't—

Foley: It's probably not addressed under this particular ordinance. There are other alternative criminal laws that may apply to that particular situation.

Scalia: Why is that? I mean, if you are concerned about breaches of the public peace, if it's a fighting words problem, why is it okay for the state to have the public peace broken for that reason? It's only these, other reasons they are worried about, why is that? That seems to me like the rankest kind of subject matter discrimination.

Foley: Well, there are many reasons that cities and state legislatures look to a particular wrong that they are attempting to address, and I don't think they address all of those wrongs at the same time, and they attempt to get as many of them as they can, and they do address in a content-based—under certain circumstances, certain harms that they want to address and including—

Scalia: It wasn't hard to write this in such a way that it wouldn't discriminate in that fashion. They just had to drop out, on the basis of race, color, creed, religion, or gender, but those are the only things that they seemed to be concerned about.

Foley: I think the Minnesota Supreme Court addressed or made reference to that issue when it said that the particular city ordinance could have been drawn a little bit better, but then went on to clearly narrow the impact of that ordinance and narrowed it only to apply to fighting words. And in the context of the facts of this case, the burning of the cross, the historical context of a burning cross in the middle of the night is a precursor to violence and hatred in this country.

Narrator: Foley concludes with a reminder of the impact of hate crimes on victims like the Jones family.

Foley: In the case of bias-motivated crimes, there is a compelling state purpose to deal with what is a cancer on society, and it will, unless effectively dealt with, spread throughout the community. Bias motivated crimes have a devastating effect on the particular target victims and equally profound effect on all members of the minority that is indirectly targeted and a pervasive effect on the community as a whole.

Given the historical experience of African-Americans, a burning cross targeted at a black family under the circumstances outlined is an unmistakable threat. Terroristic conduct such as this can find no protection in the Constitution. Thank you, Your Honors.

Narrator: On June 22, 1992—two years and one day after Robert Viktora burned a cross in the front yard of the Jones family—the Supreme Court ruled that St. Paul's "hate crimes" ordinance violated the First Amendment. The decision was unanimous, but the justices agreed on hardly anything in this hard case. The four separate opinions in *R.A.V. v. St. Paul* exposed the deep—almost bitter—divisions within the Court over the troubling issue of hate speech.

Justice Antonin Scalia had peppered both lawyers with questions during oral argument. He left no doubt that he considered the law an impermissible content-based regulation of speech. In his opinion for the Court, Scalia took a hard line. Singling out for punishment any category of speech, based on its viewpoint or message, violates the First Amendment. No matter how offensive the message may be, creating "favored" and "disfavored" categories of speech turns the government into a censorship board. "The First Amendment," Scalia wrote, "does not permit St. Paul to impose special prohibitions on those speakers who express views on disfavored subjects." Scalia spoke in his opinion for Chief Justice Rehnquist and Justices Anthony Kennedy, David Souter, and Clarence Thomas.

The remaining four justices agreed that the ordinance violated the First Amendment. However, as Justice Byron White wrote, "our agreement ends there." White accused Scalia of tossing out the "fighting words" exception to protected speech in the *Chaplinsky* case. This category of speech, White stated, "is by definition worthless and undeserving of constitutional protection." Had the St. Paul city council enacted a more narrowly-drawn law, Justice White would have upheld Robert Viktora's conviction. But the law was "overbroad" in banning all speech that might arouse anger or resentment. The vice of the law, White wrote, was that it reaches beyond "fighting words" and "criminalizes a substantial amount of expression that—however repugnant—is shielded by the First Amendment."

The Court's decision in R.A.V. leaves the "fighting words" doctrine in limbo. The justices have not upheld a conviction based on *Chaplinsky*, but they haven't overruled this historic decision, preferring to leave it in their judicial arsenal. Back in St. Paul, the Court's decision changed very little. Robert Viktora got into trouble again, after a skinhead companion yelled "White Power" at a police officer. Viktora was fined $100 for scuffling with the officer. The Jones family still lives in their home on Earl Street, but there have been other cross burnings in the area. Racial tensions create a tinderbox in many American communities. The hard job, as Justice Scalia wrote, is to deal with these tensions "without adding the First Amendment to the fire."

EDITED SUPREME COURT OPINIONS
R.A.V. v. *City of St. Paul, Minnesota*
Argued December 4, 1991—Decided June 22, 1992

JUSTICE SCALIA delivered the opinion of the Court.

In the predawn hours of June 21, 1990, petitioner and several other teenagers allegedly assembled a crudely made cross by taping together broken chair legs. They then allegedly burned the cross inside the fenced yard of a black family that lived across the street from the house where petitioner was staying. Although this conduct could have been punished under any of a number of laws, one of the two provisions under which respondent city of St. Paul chose to charge petitioner (then a juvenile) was the St. Paul Bias-Motivated Crime Ordinance, St. Paul, Minn., Legis. Code §292.02 (1990), which provides:

"Whoever places on public or private property a symbol, object, appellation, characterization or graffiti, including, but not limited to, a burning cross or Nazi swastika, which one knows or has reasonable grounds to know arouses anger, alarm or resentment in others on the basis of race, color, creed, religion or gender commits disorderly conduct and shall be guilty of a misdemeanor." Petitioner moved to dismiss this count on the ground that the St. Paul ordinance was substantially overbroad and impermissibly content based and therefore facially invalid under the First Amendment. The trial court granted this motion, but the Minnesota Supreme Court reversed. That court rejected petitioner's overbreadth claim because, as construed in prior Minnesota cases…. the modifying phrase "arouses anger, alarm or resentment in others" limited the reach of the ordinance to conduct that amounts to "fighting words," *i.e.,* "conduct that itself inflicts injury or tends to incite immediate violence…," *In re Welfare iS R. A. V.:,* 464 N. W. 2d 507, 510 (Minn. 1991) (citing *Chaplinsky v. New Hampshire,* 315 U.S. 568, 572 (1942)), and therefore the ordinance reached only expression "that the First Amendment does not protect."… The court also concluded that the ordinance was not impermissibly content based because, in its view, "the ordinance is a narrowly tailored means toward accomplishing the compelling governmental interest in protecting the community against bias-motivated threats to public safety and order." *Ibid.* We granted certiorari…

The First Amendment generally prevents government from proscribing speech, see, *e.g., Cantwell v. Connecticut,* 310 U.S. 296, 309–311 (1940), or even expressive conduct, see, *e.g., Texas v. Johnson,* 491 U.S. 397, 406 (1989), because of disapproval of the ideas expressed. Content-based regulations are presumptively invalid.

From 1791 to the present, however, our society, like other free but civilized societies, has permitted restrictions upon the content of speech in a few limited areas, which are "of such slight social value as a step to truth that any benefit that may be derived from them is clearly outweighed by the social interest in order and morality." *Chaplinsky, supra,* at 572. We have recognized that "the freedom of speech" referred to by the First Amendment does not include a freedom to disregard these traditional limitations….

We have sometimes said that these categories of expression are "not within the area of constitutionally protected speech."…or that the "protection of the First Amendment does not extend" to them…

Such statements must be taken in context, however, and are no more literally true than is the occasionally repeated shorthand characterizing obscenity "as not being speech at all," Sunstein, Pornography and the First Amendment, 1986 Duke L. J. 589, 615, n. 46. What they mean is that these areas of speech can, consistently with the First Amendment, be regulated *because of their constitutionally proscribable content* (obscenity, defamation, etc.)—not that they are categories of speech entirely invisible to the Constitution, so that they may be made the vehicles for content discrimination unrelated to their distinctively proscribable content. Thus, the government may proscribe libel; but it may not make the further content discrimination of proscribing only libel critical of the government….

The proposition that a particular instance of speech can be proscribable on the basis of one feature (*e.g.,* obscenity) but not on the basis of another (*e.g.,* opposition to the city government) is commonplace and has found application in many contexts. We have long held, for example, that nonverbal expressive activity can be banned because of the action it entails, but not because of the ideas it expresses—so that burning a flag in violation of an ordinance against outdoor fires could be punishable, whereas burning a flag in violation of an ordinance against dishonoring the flag is not....

And just as the power to proscribe particular speech on the basis of a non-content element (*e.g.*, noise) does not entail the power to proscribe the same speech on the basis of a content element; so also, the power to proscribe it on the basis of one content element (*e.g.*, obscenity) does not entail the power to proscribe it on the basis of *other* content elements.

In other words, the exclusion of "fighting words" from the scope of the First Amendment simply means that, for purposes of that Amendment, the unprotected features of the words are, despite their verbal character, essentially a "nonspeech" element of communication....

When the basis for the content discrimination consists entirely of the very reason the entire class of speech at issue is proscribable, no significant danger of idea or viewpoint discrimination exists. Such a reason, having been adjudged neutral enough to support exclusion of the entire class of speech from First Amendment protection, is also neutral enough to form the basis of distinction within the class. To illustrate: A State might choose to prohibit only that obscenity which is the most patently offensive in its *prurience, i.e.*, that which involves the most lascivious displays of sexual activity. But it may not prohibit, for example, only that obscenity which includes offensive *political* messages....

Another valid basis for according differential treatment to even a content-defined subclass of proscribable speech is that the subclass happens to be associated with particular "secondary effects" of the speech, so that the regulation is "justified without reference to the content of the...speech."...

A State could, for example, permit all obscene live performances except those involving minors. Moreover, since words can in some circumstances violate laws directed not against speech but against conduct (a law against treason, for example, is violated by telling the enemy the Nation's defense secrets), a particular content-based subcategory of a proscribable class of speech can be swept up incidentally within the reach of a statute directed at conduct rather than speech....

Applying these principles to the St. Paul ordinance, we conclude that, even as narrowly construed by the Minnesota Supreme Court, the ordinance is facially unconstitutional. Although the phrase in the ordinance, "arouses anger, alarm or resentment in others," has been limited by the Minnesota Supreme Court's construction to reach only those symbols or displays that amount to "fighting words," the remaining, unmodified terms make clear that the ordinance applies only to "fighting words" that insult, or provoke violence, "on the basis of race, color, creed, religion or gender." Displays containing abusive invective, no matter how vicious or severe, are permissible unless they are addressed to one of the specified disfavored topics. Those who wish to use "fighting words" in connection with other ideas—to express hostility, for example, on the basis of political affiliation, union membership, or homosexuality—are not covered. The First Amendment does not permit St. Paul to impose special prohibitions on those speakers who express views on disfavored subjects....

In its practical operation, moreover, the ordinance goes even beyond mere content discrimination, to actual viewpoint discrimination. Displays containing some words—odious racial epithets, for example—would be prohibited to proponents of all views. But "fighting words" that do not themselves invoke race, color, creed, religion, or gender—aspersions upon a person's mother, for example—would seemingly be usable *ad libitum* in the placards of those arguing in *favor* of racial, color, etc., tolerance and equality, but could not be used by those speakers' opponents....

The content-based discrimination reflected in the St. Paul ordinance comes within neither any of the specific exceptions to the First Amendment prohibition we discussed earlier nor a more general exception for content discrimination that does not threaten censorship of ideas. It assuredly does not fall within the exception for content discrimination based on the very reasons why the particular class of speech at issue (here, fighting words) is proscribable. As explained earlier,...the reason why fighting words are categorically excluded from the protection of the First Amendment is not that their content communicates any particular idea, but that their content embodies a particularly intolerable (and socially unnecessary) *mode* of expressing *whatever* idea the speaker wishes to convey. St. Paul has not singled out an especially offensive mode of expression—it has not, for example, selected for prohibition only those fighting words that communicate ideas in a threatening (as opposed to a merely obnoxious) manner. Rather, it has proscribed fighting words of whatever manner that communicate messages of racial, gender, or religious intolerance. Selectivity of this sort creates the possibility that the city is seeking to handicap the expression of particular ideas. That possibility would alone be enough to render the ordinance presumptively invalid, but St. Paul's comments and concessions in this case elevate the possibility to a certainty....

Finally, St. Paul and its *amici* defend the conclusion of the Minnesota Supreme Court that, even if the ordinance regulates expression based on hostility towards its protected ideological content, this discrimination is nonetheless justified because it is narrowly tailored to serve compelling state interests. Specifically, they assert that the ordinance helps to ensure the basic human rights of members of groups that have historically been subjected to discrimination, including the right of such group members to live in peace where they wish. We do not doubt that these interests are compelling, and that the ordinance can be said to promote them....

The dispositive question in this case, therefore, is whether content discrimination is reasonably necessary to achieve St. Paul's compelling interests; it plainly is not. An ordinance not limited to the favored topics, for example, would have precisely the same beneficial effect. In fact the only interest distinctively served by the content limitation is that of displaying the city council's special hostility towards the particular biases thus singled out. That is precisely what the First Amendment forbids. The politicians of St. Paul are entitled to express that hostility—but not through the means of imposing unique limitations upon speakers who (however benightedly) disagree.

Let there be no mistake about our belief that burning a cross in someone's front yard is reprehensible. But St. Paul has sufficient means at its disposal to prevent such behavior without adding the First Amendment to the fire.

The judgment of the Minnesota Supreme Court is reversed, and the case is remanded for proceedings not inconsistent with this opinion.

It is so ordered.

JUSTICE WHITE, with whom JUSTICE BLACKMUN and JUSTICE O'CONNOR join, and with whom JUSTICE STEVENS joins except as to PartI-A, concurring in the judgment.

I agree with the majority that the judgment of the Minnesota Supreme Court should be reversed. However, our agreement ends there.

This case could easily be decided within the contours of established First Amendment law by holding, as petitioner argues, that the St. Paul ordinance is fatally overbroad because it criminalizes not only unprotected expression but expression protected by the First Amendment....

Today, however, the Court announces that earlier Courts did not mean their repeated statements that certain categories of expression are "not within the area of constitutionally protected speech."...

The present Court submits that such clear statements "must be taken in context" and are not "literally true."...

To the contrary, those statements meant precisely what they said: The categorical approach is a firmly entrenched part of our First Amendment jurisprudence. Indeed, the Court in *Roth* reviewed the guarantees of freedom of expression in effect at the time of the ratification of the Constitution and concluded, "In light of this history, it is apparent that the unconditional phrasing of the

First Amendment was not intended to protect every utterance." 354 U.S., at 482–483.

Nevertheless, the majority holds that the First Amendment protects those narrow categories of expression long held to be undeserving of First Amendment protection—at least to the extent that lawmakers may not regulate some fighting words more strictly than others because of their content. The Court announces that such content-based distinctions violate the First Amendment because "[t]he government may not regulate use based on hostility—or favoritism—towards the underlying message expressed."…Should the government want to criminalize certain fighting words, the Court now requires it to criminalize all fighting words.

To borrow a phrase: "Such a simplistic, all-or-nothing-at-all approach to First Amendment protection is at odds with common sense and with our jurisprudence as well."…

It is inconsistent to hold that the government may proscribe an entire category of speech because the content of that speech is evil,…but that the government may not treat a subset of that category differently without violating the First Amendment; the content of the subset is by definition worthless and undeserving of constitutional protection.

Although I disagree with the Court's analysis, I do agree with its conclusion: The St. Paul ordinance is unconstitutional. However, I would decide the case on overbreadth grounds.

We have emphasized time and again that overbreadth doctrine is an exception to the established principle that "a person to whom a statute may constitutionally be applied will not be heard to challenge that statute on the ground that it may conceivably be applied unconstitutionally to others, in other situations not before the Court."…

A defendant being prosecuted for speech or expressive conduct may challenge the law on its face if it reaches protected expression, even when that person's activities are not protected by the First Amendment. This is because "the possible harm to society in permitting some unprotected speech to go unpunished is outweighed by the possibility that protected speech of others may be muted."…

I agree with petitioner that the ordinance is invalid on its face. Although the ordinance as construed reaches categories of speech that are constitutionally unprotected, it also criminalizes a substantial amount of expression that—however repugnant—is shielded by the First Amendment.

JUSTICE BLACKMUN, concurring in the judgment.

I regret what the Court has done in this case. The majority opinion signals one of two possibilities: It will serve as precedent for future cases, or it will not. Either result is disheartening.

In the first instance, by deciding that a State cannot regulate speech that causes great harm unless it also regulates speech that does not (setting law and logic on their heads), the Court seems to abandon the categorical approach, and inevitably to relax the level of scrutiny applicable to content-based laws. As JUSTICE WHITE points out, this weakens the traditional protections of speech. If all expressive activity must be accorded the same protection, that protection will be scant. The simple reality is that the Court will never provide child pornography or cigarette advertising the level of protection customarily granted political speech. If we are forbidden to categorize, as the Court has done here, we shall reduce protection across the board. It is sad that in its effort to reach a satisfying result in this case, the Court is willing to weaken First Amendment protections.

In the second instance is the possibility that this case will not significantly alter First Amendment jurisprudence but, instead, will be regarded as an aberration—a case where the Court manipulated doctrine to strike down an ordinance whose premise it opposed, namely, that racial threats and verbal assaults are of greater harm than other fighting words. I fear that the Court has been distracted from its proper mission by the temptation to decide the issue over "politically correct speech" and "cultural diversity," neither of which is presented here. If this is the meaning of today's opinion, it is perhaps even more regrettable.

I see no First Amendment values that are compromised by a law that prohibits hoodlums from driving minorities out of their homes by burning crosses on their lawns, but I see great harm in preventing the people of Saint Paul from specifically punishing the race-based fighting words that so prejudice their community.

I concur in the judgment, however, because I agree with JUSTICE WHITE that this particular ordinance reaches beyond fighting words to speech protected by the First Amendment.

Texas *v.* Johnson

491 U.S. 397 (1989)

During the 1984 Republican National Convention in Dallas, Texas, Gregory Lee Johnson joined a demonstration against the Reagan administration's policies. At the end of the march, while protesters chanted, Johnson burned an American flag. He was convicted of "desecration of a venerated object" protected by Texas law and sentenced to a year in prison. Johnson appealed, claiming that his actions were protected by the First Amendment as symbolic political speech. In 1989, the Supreme Court ruled by one vote that the state's interest in protecting the flag as a symbol of national unity does not justify restrictions of political expression. "We do not consecrate the flag by punishing its desecration," Justice William Brennan wrote, "for in doing so we dilute the freedom that this cherished symbol represents." The next year, the Court also rejected a congressional attempt to punish flag burners.

TRANSCRIPT OF EDITED AND NARRATED ARGUMENTS IN
Texas v. Johnson, 491 U.S. 397 (1989)

Counsel for petitioner: Kathi Alyce Drew, Dallas, Texas
Counsel for respondent: William Kunstler, New York, New York

Chief Justice Rehnquist: Number 88-155, Texas versus Gregory Lee Johnson.

Narrator: It's March 21st, 1989. Chief Justice William Rehnquist has called a case that involves the symbol of our country: the American flag. The flag stands beside the Justices in the courtroom. It flies over the Capitol; over the White House; at the Tomb of the Unknown Soldier. Millions of Americans have pledged their allegiance to the flag and to the principles it symbolizes: liberty and justice for all.

But, does that liberty include the right to burn the flag? Can a state punish acts of flag desecration with criminal penalties? Does the free speech clause of the First Amendment protect those who destroy our national symbol? These questions provoke heated answers on both sides.

Justice Hugo Black once wrote that "emotions bubble and tempers flare" when protest spills into the streets. This case began in the streets of Dallas, Texas, on a hot August day. The 1984 Republican National Convention attracted thousands of delegates and hundreds of demonstrators. One small protest group, the Revolutionary Communist Youth Brigade, marched through downtown Dallas. Gregory Johnson led the march and shouted slogans—some obscene—over a bullhorn. When his group reached City Hall, Johnson held up an American flag, soaked it with lighter fluid, and set it on fire. While the flag burned, protesters chanted, "Red, white, and blue, we spit on you!"

The flag burning drew a crowd. One man, Daniel Walker, gathered up the charred remains, took them home, and buried them in his backyard. Prosecutors said Gregory Johnson violated a Texas law punishing anyone who "desecrates" a state or national flag. The state must prove the act "will seriously offend one or more persons" who observe it. Walker told the jury the flag burning offended his feelings. The prosecutor also claimed Johnson breached the peace. Johnson posed a danger to Texas, he said, "by what he does and the way he thinks." The jurors agreed and sentenced Johnson to a year in prison.

The state's highest court struck down his conviction. The judges ruled that flag burning was a form of "symbolic speech." They applied three legal tests; Texas failed each one. First, the state had not shown a "compelling interest" in protecting the flag. Second, states cannot punish the content of speech, however offensive. Third, even if Johnson caused "serious offense" to Daniel Walker, hurt feelings alone do not breach the peace. Kathi Drew, an assistant district attorney in Dallas, argues the state's appeal.

Drew: Mr. Chief Justice, and may it please the Court.

The issue before this Court is whether the public burning of an American flag which occurred as part of a demonstration with political overtones is entitled to First Amendment protection.

For purposes of this argument today and with the Court's indulgence, the state will assume the symbolic speech standard and proceed directly to the question of Texas's compelling interests in regulating this type of conduct.

Throughout the course of the appellate history in this case, Texas has advanced two compelling state interests. One is the preservation of the flag as a symbol of nationhood and national unity. The second is the preservation [*sic*] of a breach of the peace.

I would like to address first the nationhood interest. We believe that preservation of the flag as a symbol of nationhood and national unity is a compelling and valid state interest. We feel very certain that Congress has the power to both adopt a national symbol and to take steps to prevent the destruction of that symbol, to protect the symbol.

Narrator: Justice Antonin Scalia broke in.

Scalia: Why does the—why did the defendant's actions here destroy the symbol? His actions would have been useless unless the flag was a very good symbol for what he intended to show contempt for. His action does not make it any less a symbol.

Drew: Your Honor, we believe that if a symbol over a period of time is ignored or abused that it can, in fact, lose its symbolic effect.

Scalia: I think not at all. I think when somebody does that to the flag, the flag becomes even more a symbol of the country. I mean, it seems to me you're running quite a different argument—not that he's destroying its symbolic character, but that he is showing disrespect for it, that you not just want a symbol, but you want a venerated symbol, and you don't make that argument because then you're getting into a sort of content preference. I don't see how you can argue that he's making it any less of a symbol than it was.

Drew: Your Honor, I'm forced to disagree with you. Because I believe that every desecration of the flag carried out in the manner that he did here—and certainly I don't think there can be any question that Mr. Johnson is a hard-core violator of this statute—if his actions in this case, under the facts of this case, do not constitute flag desecration, then I really am not quite certain what *would* constitute flag desecration.

Scalia: They desecrate the flag indeed, but do they make it—do they destroy the symbol? Do they make it any less symbolic of the country? That's the argument I thought you were running, that we have a right to have a national symbol. And if you let the people desecrate the flag, we won't have a national symbol. I don't see how that follows. We may not have a respected national symbol, but that's a different argument. Now, if you want to run that argument that we have the right to insist upon respect for the flag, that's a different argument.

Drew: Texas is not suggesting that we can insist on respect. We are suggesting that we have the right to preserve the physical integrity of the flag so that it may serve as a symbol because its symbolic effect is diluted by certain flagrant public acts of flag desecration.

Narrator: Justice Sandra O'Connor shifted from Gregory Johnson to Daniel Walker. She forced a concession from Drew.

O'Connor: I thought this statute only applied if the desecration were done in a way that the actor knows will offend one or more other people likely to discover it.

Drew: That is correct, Your Honor.

O'Connor: There is that little added requirement, is there not?

Drew: Yes, Your Honor, that is correct.

O'Connor: Well, I thought that the Court had held that it's firmly settled under the Constitution, that the public expression of ideas may not be prohibited merely because the ideas are themselves offensive to some of their hearers.

Drew: That's correct, Your Honor.

O'Connor: And this statute seems to try to achieve exactly that.

Drew: I don't believe that it does, Your Honor, because I believe that the pivotal point is, in a way, how is the conduct effectuated, how is it done, not what an individual may be trying to say, not how onlookers perceive the action, not how the crowd reacts, but how is it done. If you take your flag into your basement in the dead of night, soak it with lighter fluid and ignite it, you probably have not violated this statute, because the Texas statute is restricted to certain limited forms of flag desecration.

Narrator: Justice Scalia continued his debate with Drew.

Scalia: What is the juridical category you're asking us to adopt in order to say we can punish this kind of speech? Just an exception for flags? It's just a—there's just a flag exception of the First Amendment?

Drew: To a certain extent, we have made that argument in our brief. With respect to the symbolic speech standard, we believe that there are compelling state interests that will in a balancing posture override this individual's symbolic speech rights, and that preserving the flag as a symbol, because it is such a national property, is one of those.

Scalia: I understand that. But we up to now have never allowed such an item to be declared a national symbol and to be usable symbolically only in one direction, which is essentially what you're arguing. You can honor it all you like, but you can't dishonor it as a sign of disrespect for the country.

Drew: No, Your Honor. We're not arguing that at all. (Scalia: Oh?) Not at all. We are in no way arguing that one cannot dishonor the flag or that one cannot demonstrate disrespect for the flag. Individuals have that right. What we are arguing is that you may not publicly desecrate a flag, regardless of the motivation for your action.

Narrator: Justice O'Connor started another exchange.

O'Connor: Do you suppose Patrick Henry and any of the Founding Fathers ever showed disrespect to the Union Jack?

Drew: Quite possibly, Your Honor.

O'Connor: You think they had in mind then in drafting the First Amendment that it should be a prosecutable offense?

Drew: Of course, Your Honor, one has no way of knowing whether it would be or not.

Scalia: I think your response is that they were willing to go to jail, just as they were when they signed the Declaration.

Court: They were hoping they wouldn't get caught. [*laughter*]

Drew: Yes, Your Honor, I believe the classic line is: "We hang together or separately."

Court: That's right.

Narrator: Drew concluded.

Drew: I'd like to turn very briefly, if I may, to the breach of the peace interest. We do feel that preventing a breach of the peace is a legitimate state interest. And, indeed, the Texas court of criminal appeals recognized that preventing a breach of the peace is a legitimate state interest. Again, the Texas legislature has made a judgment in this area that public desecration is likely to lead to violence, that it can lead to violence. And I think the record in this case is abundantly clear that it is merely fortuitous; it is our good luck that a breach of the peace did not occur as a result of this particular flag desecration.

I think the flag is this nation's cherished property, that every individual has a certain interest. The government may maintain a residual interest, but so do the people. And you protect the flag because it is such an important symbol of national unity.

Narrator: William Kunstler argues for Gregory Johnson. He has defended many controversial clients. Kunstler jumps on Drew's concession to Justice O'Connor.

Kunstler: Mr. Chief Justice, may it please the Court.

Some of the steam has been taken out of me by some of the questions and some of the responses and the concession by the state. The state now apparently concedes that you can write out of the statute what Justice O'Connor referred to, the question of whether the actor knows or means that what he's doing will seriously offend one or more persons likely to observe or destroy [*sic*], or discover his particular act.

That's out of the statute, apparently, according to the argument, because in the reply brief and today she has said essentially what is in the reply brief. Like Gertrude Stein, "A rose is a rose," they now say, "A flag burning is a flag burning." And they read out of the statute under which he was convicted and which went to the jury and the charge on the question of seriously offend, that's all out as far as Ms. Drew is concerned. But it's *not* out as far as this Court is concerned. That's what the conviction was about, that's what the argument to the jury was about, that's what the charge was about.

I think that what you have here is a statute that depends solely and exclusively on communicative impact on the audience, whether they're there or they read it in the newspaper or they see it on the screen in the evening.

Narrator: Kunstler raised two questions. Is the flag a sacred symbol? And just what *is* a flag?

Kunstler: And when you use the word "desecrate," you don't mean really in essence praising the flag. Desecrate has a meaning, and I just looked in *Webster's Second International* about it, and desecrate means "to divest of a sacred character or office, to divert from a sacred purpose, to violate the sanctity of, to profane, the opposite of consecrate."

It's used all over for commercial purposes. I notice that Barbara Bush wore a flag scarf, for example. There are flag bikinis, there are flag everything. There are little cocktail flags that you put into a hot dog or meatball and then throw in the garbage pail. They're flags under the Texas statute, something made out of cloth, but I think there are all sorts of flags used commercially. I'm not sure in my heart whether I think there's any control over the use of the flag, not on the criminal side anyway.

By the way, "national flag" does not just mean the American flag. There is a presidential flag—they don't put it in capitals—there is a presidential flag that is flown. The secretary of state has a flag that's a national flag. There are many national flags. I counted seventeen national flags. Each department here in Washington has a flag. They're national flags, and the state of Texas would also include those as national flags, certainly the president's flag. So, I think that the word "national" flag needs definition in itself.

Narrator: Under Supreme Court precedent, speech cannot be punished unless it poses a "clear and present danger" to society. Kunstler attacked the Texas law.

Kunstler: I think you must at least show some clear and present danger, some imminence. The statute here is not limited to an imminent breach, by the way. It doesn't say imminent breach of the peace at all. It just says "likely" or "might" or "the actor could reasonably believe that someone might be seriously offended by it."

The Texas court of appeals treated this, I think, in its opinion. It said, "This statute is so broad that it may be used to punish protected conduct which has no propensity to result in breaches of the peace." Serious offense does not always result in a breach of the peace. The protest in this case did not lead to violence. And, I might add, in this protest they had policemen right along with them, undercover police officers. The crowd was not a large crowd. They estimate between 100, 110, and Texas went on to say, as with most other protests of this nature, police were present at the scene.

A witness was obviously seriously offended by appellant's conduct because he gathered the burned flag and buried it at his home. Nevertheless so seriously offended, this man was not moved to violence. Serious offense occurred, but there was no breach of the peace, nor does the record reflect that the situation was potentially explosive. One cannot equate serious offense with incitement to breach the peace.

Narrator: Another Supreme Court precedent—*West Virginia v. Barnette*—ruled that schools could not force students to salute the flag. Kunstler debated the case with Chief Justice Rehnquist.

Kunstler: With reference to the nationhood and national unity, which Ms. Drew raised and which is filled in the brief, both the reply brief and the main brief of the state, I think—I thought *Barnette* set that to rest. I thought when Justice Jackson said that, "If there is any fixed star in our constitutional constellation, it is that no official, high or petty, can prescribe what shall be orthodox in politics, nationalism…"

Rehnquist: Well, the facts of *West Virginia v. Barnette* were quite different from this. There the students were required to salute the flag.

Kunstler: And here, Chief Justice, you're asking—people are required *not* to do something.

Rehnquist: Yes.

Kunstler: And I think that's a comparable situation. We order you—we can't order you to salute the flag, we can't order you to do all these obeisances with reference to the flag. Can we order you *not* to do something to show something about the flag?

   Can you say you can't force them to salute the flag or pledge allegiance to the flag, but can you then say we can force them *not* to show other means of disrespect for the flag, other means of protest over the flag by saying you can't burn the flag? I think they're the same, in all due deference. I don't know if I've convinced you, but…

Rehnquist: Well, you may have convinced others. [*laughter*]

Narrator: Kunstler summed up.

Kunstler: I would just like to end my argument—I think this is a fundamental

First Amendment case, that the First Amendment to the written Constitution is in jeopardy by statutes like this. And I wanted to essentially close with two remarks. One, Justice Jackson said in *Barnette*, "Those who begin coercive elimination of dissent soon find themselves eliminating dissenters. Compulsory unification of opinion achieves only the unanimity of the graveyard. The First Amendment was designed to avoid these ends by avoiding these beginnings." And I think that's an important statement over the years from Justice Jackson.

And I understand that this flag has serious important meanings. The Chief has mentioned many times that it's not just pieces of material, blue and white and red. That it has real meaning to real people out there. But that does not mean that it may have different meanings to other people out there and that they may not under the First Amendment show their feelings by what Texas calls desecration of a venerated object.

I think it's a most important case. I sense that it goes to the heart of the First Amendment, to hear things or to see things that we hate tests the First Amendment more than seeing or hearing things that we like. It wasn't designed for things we like. They never needed a First Amendment. This statute, or this amendment was designed so that the things we hate can have a place in the marketplace of ideas and can have an area where protest can find itself. I submit that this Court should on whatever ground it feels right, should affirm the Texas court of criminal appeals with reference to this statute and this conviction. Thank you very much.

Narrator: On June 21st, 1989, the Justices struck down the Texas law by a vote of five-to-four. Justice William Brennan wrote for the majority. He agreed that "there is a special place reserved for the flag in this nation." It is because of that special place that burning a flag conveys a powerful message, however hateful to most Americans. Gregory Johnson was punished, Brennan said, "because of the content" of his message. The Constitution does not permit such punishment. Brennan put the case in these words: "If there is a bedrock principle underlying the First Amendment, it is that the Government may not prohibit the expression of an idea because society finds the idea…offensive." Brennan suggested an answer to Johnson. "We can imagine no more appropriate response to burning a flag than waving one's own."

This was a hard case for Justices on both sides. The Court's newest member, Anthony Kennedy, joined the majority with a brief concurrence. "The hard fact," he said, "is that sometimes we must make decisions we do not like. We make them because they are right, right in the sense that the law and the Constitution, as we see them, compel the result."

The four dissenters disagreed. Chief Justice Rehnquist did not see the flag as "just another symbol," Johnson's act as just another message. The flag was more than special to Rehnquist. Millions of Americans, he said, regard the flag "with an almost mystical reverence." He cited the Marines who raised the flag over Iwo Jima in World War Two. The government tells Americans, Rehnquist said, "they must fight and perhaps die for the flag." States can certainly protect it from burning.

The Court's decision ignited a political fire storm. President George Bush called for a constitutional amendment to overrule the Court. Congress declined to tamper with the Constitution, but it passed a federal law against flag burning. Once again, Gregory Johnson burned a flag, this time on the Capitol steps. Once again, he was arrested. And once again, the Supreme Court struck down the law.

Early in this century, Justice Oliver Wendell Holmes made a profound statement. "We live by symbols," he said. But symbols only reflect our values. And America's basic values—liberty and justice for all—are embodied in our Constitution.

EDITED SUPREME COURT OPINIONS
Texas v. Gregory Lee Johnson

JUSTICE BRENNAN delivered the opinion of the Court.

After publicly burning an American flag as a means of political protest, Gregory Lee Johnson was convicted of desecrating a flag in violation of Texas law. This case presents the question whether his conviction is consistent with the First Amendment. We hold that it is not.

While the Republican National Convention was taking place in Dallas in 1984, respondent Johnson participated in a political demonstration dubbed the "Republican War Chest Tour." As explained in literature distributed by the demonstrators and in speeches made by them, the purpose of this event was to protest the policies of the Reagan administration and of certain Dallas-based corporations. The demonstrators marched through the Dallas streets, chanting political slogans and stopping at several corporate locations to stage "die-ins" intended to dramatize the consequences of nuclear war. On several occasions they spray-painted the walls of buildings and overturned potted plants, but Johnson himself took no part in such activities. He did, however, accept an American flag handed to him by a fellow protestor who had taken it from a flag pole outside one of the targeted buildings.

The demonstration ended in front of Dallas City Hall, where Johnson unfurled the American flag, doused it with kerosene, and set it on fire. While the flag burned, the protestors chanted, "America, the red, white, and blue, we spit on you." After the demonstrators dispersed, a witness to the flag burning collected the flag's remains and buried them in his backyard. No one was physically injured or threatened with injury, though several witnesses testified that they had been seriously offended by the flag burning.

Of the approximately one hundred demonstrators, Johnson alone was charged with a crime. The only criminal offense with which he was charged was the desecration of a venerated object in violation of Tex. Penal Code Ann. st42.09 (a)(3) (1989). After a trial, he was convicted, sentenced to one year in prison, and fined two thousand dollars....

The State of Texas conceded for purposes of its oral argument in this case that Johnson's conduct was expressive conduct...Johnson burned an American flag as part—indeed, as the culmination—of a political demonstration that coincided with the convening of the Republican Party and its renomination of Ronald Reagan for President. The expressive, overtly political nature of this conduct was both intentional and overwhelmingly apparent. At his trial, Johnson explained his reasons for burning the flag as follows: "The American Flag was burned as Ronald Reagan was being renominated as President. And a more powerful statement of symbolic speech, whether you agree with it or not, couldn't have been made at that time. It's quite a juxtaposition. We had new patriotism and no patriotism."... In these circumstances, Johnson's burning of the flag was conduct "sufficiently imbued with elements of communication...to implicate the First Amendment."...

The State offers two separate interests to justify this conviction: preventing breaches of the peace, and preserving the flag as a symbol of nationhood and national unity. We hold that the first interest is not implicated on this record and that the second is related to the suppression of expression.

Texas claims that its interest in preventing breaches of the peace justifies Johnson's conviction for flag desecration. However, no disturbance of the peace actually occurred or threatened to occur because of Johnson's burning of the flag. Although the State stresses the disruptive behavior of the protestors during their march toward City Hall,...it admits that "no actual breach of the peace occurred at the time of the flag burning or in response to the flag burning."... The State's emphasis on the protestors' disorderly actions prior to arriving at City Hall is not only somewhat surprising given that no charges were brought on the basis of this conduct, but it also fails to show that a disturbance of the peace was a likely reaction to Johnson's conduct. The only evidence offered by the State at trial to show the reaction to Johnson's actions was the testimony of several persons who had been seriously offended by the flag burning....

The State's position, therefore, amounts to a claim that an audience that takes serious offense at particular expression is necessarily likely to disturb the peace and that the expression may be prohibited on this basis. Our precedents do not countenance such a presumption. On the contrary, they recognize that a principal "function of free speech under our system of government is to invite dispute. It may indeed best serve its high purpose when it induces a condition of unrest, creates dissatisfaction with conditions as they are, or even stirs people to anger." *Terminiello v. Chicago*, 337 U.S. 1, 4 (1949)…

Texas' focus on the precise nature of Johnson's expression, moreover, misses the point of our prior decisions: their enduring lesson, that the Government may not prohibit expression simply because it disagrees with its message, is not dependent on the particular mode in which one chooses to express an idea. If we were to hold that a State may forbid flag burning wherever it is likely to endanger the flag's symbolic role, but allow it wherever burning a flag promotes that role—as where, for example, a person ceremoniously burns a dirty flag—we would be saying that when it comes to impairing the flag's physical integrity, the flag itself may be used as a symbol—as a substitute for the written or spoken word or a "short cut from mind to mind"—only in one direction. We would be permitting a State to "prescribe what shall be orthodox" by saying that one may burn the flag to convey one's attitude toward it and its referents only if one does not endanger the flag's representation of nationhood and national unity….

It is not the State's ends, but its means, to which we object. It cannot be gainsaid that there is a special place reserved for the flag in this Nation, and thus we do not doubt that the Government has a legitimate interest in making efforts to "preserve the national flag as an unalloyed symbol of our country." *Spence*, 418 U.S., at 412. We reject the suggestion, urged at oral argument by counsel for Johnson, that the Government lacks "any state interest whatsoever" in regulating the manner in which the flag may be displayed….

To say that the Government has an interest in encouraging proper treatment of the flag, however, is not to say that it may criminally punish a person for burning a flag as a means of political protest. "National unity as an end which officials may foster by persuasion and example is not in question. The problem is whether under our Constitution compulsion as here employed is a permissible means for its achievement." *Barnette*, 319 U.S., at 640….

The way to preserve the flag's special role is not to punish those who feel differently about these matters. It is to persuade them that they are wrong…. And, precisely because it is our flag that is involved, one's response to the flag burner may exploit the uniquely persuasive power of the flag itself. We can imagine no more appropriate response to burning a flag than waving one's own, no better way to counter a flag burner's message than by saluting the flag that burns, no surer means of preserving the dignity even of the flag that burned

than by—as one witness here did—according its remains a respectful burial. We
do not consecrate the flag by punishing its desecration, for in doing so we dilute
the freedom that this cherished emblem represents.

Johnson was convicted for engaging in expressive conduct. The State's
interest in preventing breaches of the peace does not support his conviction
because Johnson's conduct did not threaten to disturb the peace. Nor does the
State's interest in preserving the flag as a symbol of nationhood and national
unity justify his criminal conviction for engaging in political expression. The
judgment of the Texas Court of Criminal Appeals is therefore

Affirmed.

JUSTICE KENNEDY, concurring…

The case before us illustrates better than most that the judicial power is
often difficult in its exercise. We cannot here ask another branch to share responsibility, as when the argument is made that a statute is flawed or incomplete. For
we are presented with a clear and simple statute to be judged against a pure command of the Constitution. The outcome can be laid at no door but ours.

The hard fact is that sometimes we must make decisions we do not like.
We make them because they are right, right in the sense that the law and the
Constitution, as we see them, compel the result. And so great is our commitment to the process that, except in the rare case, we do not pause to express dis-
taste for the result, perhaps for fear of undermining a valued principle that dic-
tates the decision. This is one of those rare cases.

Our colleagues in dissent advance powerful arguments why respondent
may be convicted for his expression, reminding us that among those who will be
dismayed by our holding will be some who have had the singular honor of carrying the flag in battle. And I agree that the flag holds a lonely place of honor in an
age when absolutes are distrusted and simple truths are burdened by unneeded
apologetics.

With all respect to those views, I do not believe the Constitution gives us
the right to rule as the dissenting members of the Court urge, however painful
this judgment is to announce. Though symbols often are what we ourselves
make of them, the flag is constant in expressing beliefs Americans share, beliefs
in law and peace and that freedom which sustains the human spirit. The case
here today forces recognition of the costs to which those beliefs commit us. It is
poignant but fundamental that the flag protects those who hold it in contempt.
For all the record shows, this respondent was not a philosopher and perhaps did
not even possess the ability to comprehend how repellent his statements must
be to the Republic itself. But whether or not he could appreciate the enormity

of the offense he gave, the fact remains that his acts were speech, in both the technical and the fundamental meaning of the Constitution. So I agree with the Court that he must go free.

CHIEF JUSTICE REHNQUIST, with whom JUSTICE WHITE and JUSTICE O'CONNOR join, dissenting.

In holding this Texas statute unconstitutional, the Court ignores Justice Holmes' familiar aphorism that "a page of history is worth a volume of logic."...For more than two hundred years, the American flag has occupied a unique position as the symbol of our Nation, a uniqueness that justifies a governmental prohibition against flag burning in the way respondent Johnson did here.

At the time of the American Revolution, the flag served to unify the Thirteen Colonies at home, while obtaining recognition of national sovereignty abroad....

The American flag played a central role in our Nation's most tragic conflict, when the North fought against the South. The lowering of the American flag at Fort Sumter was viewed as the start of the war....The Southern States, to formalize their separation from the Union, adopted the "Stars and Bars" of the Confederacy. The Union troops marched to the sound of "Yes We'll Rally Round The Flag Boys, We'll Rally Once Again." President Abraham Lincoln refused proposals to remove from the American flag the stars representing the rebel States, because he considered the conflict not a war between two nations but an attack by eleven States against the National Government....By war's end, the American flag again flew over "an indestructible union, composed of indestructible states."...

In the First and Second World Wars, thousands of our countrymen died on foreign soil fighting for the American cause. At Iwo Jima in the Second World War, United States Marines fought hand-to-hand against thousands of Japanese. By the time the Marines reached the top of Mount Suribachi, they raised a piece of pipe upright and from one end fluttered a flag. That ascent had cost nearly six thousand American lives....

During the Korean War, the successful amphibious landing of American troops at Inchon was marked by the raising of an American flag within an hour of the event. Impetus for the enactment of the Federal Flag Desecration Statute in 1967 came from the impact of flag burnings in the United States on troop morale in Vietnam....

The flag symbolizes the Nation in peace as well as in war. It signifies our national presence on battleships, airplanes, military installations, and public buildings from the United States Capitol to the thousands of county courthouses and city halls throughout the country. Two flags are prominently placed

in our courtroom. Countless flags are placed by the graves of loved ones each year on what was first called Decoration Day, and is now called Memorial Day....

The American flag, then, throughout more than two hundred years of our history, has come to be the visible symbol embodying our Nation. It does not represent the views of any particular political party, and it does not represent any particular political philosophy. The flag is not simply another "idea" or "point of view" competing for recognition in the marketplace of ideas. Millions and millions of Americans regard it with an almost mystical reverence regardless of what sort of social, political, or philosophical beliefs they may have. I cannot agree that the First Amendment invalidates the Act of Congress, and the laws of forty-eight of the fifty States, which make criminal the public burning of the flag....

The Court concludes its opinion with a regrettably patronizing civics lecture, presumably addressed to the members of both Houses of Congress, the members of the forty-eight state legislatures that enacted prohibitions against flag burning, and the troops fighting under that flag in Vietnam who objected to its being burned: "The way to preserve the flag's special role is not to punish those who feel differently about these matters. It is to persuade them that they are wrong."...The Court's role as the final expositor of the Constitution is well established, but its role as a platonic guardian admonishing those responsible to public opinion as if they were truant school children has no similar place in our system of government.... Uncritical extension of constitutional protection to the burning of the flag risks the frustration of the very purpose for which organized governments are instituted. The Court decides that the American flag just another symbol, about which not only must opinions pro and con be tolerated, but for which the most minimal public respect may not be enjoined. The government may conscript men into the Armed Forces where they must fight and perhaps die for the flag, but the government may not prohibit the public burning of the banner under which they fight. I would uphold the Texas statute as applied in this case.

BIBLIOGRAPHY

BERNS, WALTER. "Flag-Burning and Other Modes of Expression." *Commentary* 88, no. 4 (October 1989): 37.

BUCKLEY, WILLIAM F. "The Court and the Flag Decision." *National Review*, August 4, 1989, p. 13.

GARBUS, M. "The 'Crime' of Flag Burning." *Nation*, March 20, 1989, p. 369.

LOEWY, A. H. "The Flag Burning Case." *North Carolina Law Review* 68 (November 1989): 165.

TUSHNET, MARK V. "The Flag Burning Episode." *University of Colorado Law Review* 61, no. 1 (Winter 1990): 39.

WOOD, JAMES E., JR. "Making the Nation's Flag a Sacred Symbol." *Journal of Church and State* 31, no. 3 (Autumn 1989): 375.

Tinker *v.* Des Moines

393 U.S. 503 (1969)

In 1965, Mary Beth Tinker was an eighth grader at Warren Harding Junior High in Des Moines, Iowa. In December, she and students from other schools decided to support a Christmas truce and bombing halt in the Vietnam War by wearing black armbands to school. Hearing of this plan, the Des Moines public school principals immediately enacted a policy prohibiting students from wearing armbands, claiming that protest would lead to disruption. They subsequently suspended five students who wore armbands. Mary Beth Tinker challenged the policy as violating the free speech clause of the First Amendment. In 1969, the Supreme Court ruled that the Constitution guarantees public school students a right to symbolic, nondisruptive political expression. Students, Justice Abe Fortas wrote, do not "shed their constitutional rights to freedom of speech or expression at the schoolhouse gate."

Counsel for petitioners: Dan Johnston, Des Moines, Iowa
Counsel for respondents: Allen Herrick, Des Moines, Iowa

Narrator: It's November 12th, 1968. Chief Justice Earl Warren has called for argument a case—*"Tinker v. Des Moines"*—that stemmed from domestic conflict over the Vietnam War. For the past four years, since Congress authorized President Lyndon Johnson to unleash bombing attacks on North Vietnam, the war split the nation into hawks and doves. Support for the war eroded as thousands of American troops came home in body bags. Johnson's critics—both hawks and doves—shot down his reelection plans. Just a week before this argument, Richard Nixon was narrowly elected President, promising a "secret plan" to end the war.

The *Tinker* case began in America's heartland, the farm country of Iowa, in December 1965. In broadest terms, it placed free speech claims under the Constitution's First Amendment against the powers of government. More narrowly, it questioned the authority of school officials to censor symbolic speech in classrooms. And finally, it challenged the right of Des Moines principals to suspend five students, including Mary Beth Tinker, for wearing black armbands to class. A federal judge upheld the suspensions, ruling that the armbands, in his words, "would be likely to disturb the disciplined atmosphere required for any classroom." Mary Beth's lawyer, Dan Johnston, argues her appeal to the Supreme Court.

Warren: Mr. Johnston.

Johnston: Mr. Chief Justice, and may it please the Court.

The conduct of the students essentially was this. That at Christmastime in 1965, they decided that they would wear small black armbands to express certain views which they had in regard to the war in Vietnam. Specifically, the views were that they mourned the dead of both sides, both civilian and military in that war, and they supported the proposal that had been made by United States Senator Robert Kennedy that the truce which had been proposed for that war over the Christmas period be made an open-ended or an indefinite truce. This was the purpose that the students gave for wearing the armbands during this period.

During this period of time, of course, there were school days and they wore the armbands to school. Prior to the time when any of these petitioners wore the armbands to school, it came to the attention of the school authorities that perhaps there would be some students who would express views related to the war in Vietnam in this manner during school time.

Narrator: Johnston explained what happened when school officials were informed of the armband protest.

Johnston: The principals of the secondary schools, the high schools, and perhaps the junior high schools in the City of Des Moines public school system met prior to the time that any of the armbands had been worn and enacted a policy which was not written but which was agreed upon among themselves, that no student could wear an armband in the Des Moines public school system for this purpose; that if the student came to school wearing the armband he would be asked to remove it; failing that, the student's parents would be contacted and their assistance would be solicited in getting the students to remove the armbands; failing that, the students would be sent home—would be in effect suspended from school until such time as they were willing to return to school without the armbands.

Narrator: Johnston introduced the Justices to his three clients.

Johnston: The three students who are petitioners in this case—Christopher Eckhardt, who was sixteen and in the tenth grade at Roosevelt High School in Des Moines at the time; John Tinker, who was fifteen and in the eleventh grade at another high school; Mary Beth Tinker, who was thirteen and in the eighth grade—determined that in spite of the policy that had been announced through the schools, they would wear the armbands as a matter of conscience to express the views that they had.

Narrator: The vice-principal suspended Chris Eckhardt even before he got to his first class. Mary Beth Tinker, at Warren Harding Junior High, was next.

Johnston: Mary Beth Tinker also wore her armband on that first day. However, she wore it throughout the entire morning without any incident related to it that in any way disrupted the school or distracted. She wore it at lunch and she wore it—where there was, by the way, some conversation between herself and other students in the lunchroom about why she was wearing the armband and whether or not she should be wearing it—and then wore it into the first class in the afternoon. And it was in the first class in the afternoon that she was called to the office and the procedure was followed for contacting her parents, apparently asking her to remove it, and she did remove the armband and then returned to class. However, in spite of the fact that she had removed the armband and was returned to class, she was later called out of class and suspended nevertheless.

Narrator: Justice Byron White broke in.

White: What if the student had gotten up from the class he went to and delivered the message orally that his armband was intended to convey and insisted on doing it all through the hour?

Johnston: In that case, Your Honor, we would not be here, even if he insisted on doing it only for a second, because he would clearly be—although he would be expressing his views, he would be doing something else.

White: Why did they wear the armband to class, to express that message?

Johnston: To express the message, yes.

White: To everybody in the class?

Johnston: To everyone in the class, yes, Your Honor.

White: Everybody while they were listening to some other subject matter was supposed to be looking at the armband and taking in that message?

Johnston: Well, to the extent that they would see it. But I don't believe there was any—I don't believe that the…

White: Well, they were intended to see it, weren't they?

Johnston: They were intended to see it in a way that would not be distracting…

White: And to understand it.

Johnston: And to understand it.

White: And to absorb that message…

Johnston: And to absorb the message…

White: While they're studying arithmetic or mathematics, they're supposed to be taking in this message about Vietnam?

Johnston: Well, except that, Your Honor, I believe that the method that the students chose in this particular instance was specifically designed in such a way that it would not cause that kind of disruption.

Narrator: Justice White pressed Dan Johnston on classroom disruption.

White: Again, why did they wear the armband?

Johnston: They wore the armband to…

White: …convey a message.

Johnston: …convey the message; that's right.

White: They anticipated students would see it and understand it and think about it?

Johnston: That's correct.

White: And when they did it in class, they intended the students to do it *in* class?

Johnston: I think it's a fair assumption that the method of expression…

White: They intended the students to think about it outside of class but not in class?

Johnston: I think they intended, I think they chose a message, chose a method of expression, Your Honor, which would not be distracting…

White: …physically; it wouldn't make a noise, it wouldn't cause a commotion, but don't you think it would cause some people to direct their attention to the armband and the Vietnam War and think about that, rather than what they were thinking about, supposed to be thinking about in the classroom?

Johnston: I think perhaps, Your Honor, it might for a few moments have done that, and I think it perhaps might have distracted some students, just as many other things do in the classroom which are allowed, from time to time.

Narrator: Johnston accused the school board of violating the First Amendment.

Johnston: Our contention is that the policy as it was adopted, it was a broad policy which did not distinguish, not in any way was directed toward disruption or distraction. It is a policy which will not stand the test of freedom of expression under the First Amendment.

Narrator: Another justice moved to the *method* of expressing a message.

Court: Suppose it had been a big button—Stop the Bombing.

Johnston: Well, as a matter of fact, a number of political buttons were worn at this school.

Court: That is, I'm for Humphrey, or I'm for Wallace?

Johnston: I'm for Humphrey—well, we didn't have at that time—I'm for Humphrey, or I'm for Nixon, I'm for Goldwater. The record also shows that...

Court: Suppose it was just, Stop the Bombing?

Johnston: That, to me, would not be the sort of thing which would be designed to disrupt the class.

Court: Suppose it was a placard, with a message?

Johnston: The situation, I think, and the problem that we have, is this specific regulation, directed only toward one specific kind of conduct. The difficulty we have with this particular policy as it was enacted is that there was no indication, no testimony by teachers, by administrators or anyone else, of any reason to believe that it would be disruptive. And when the students in fact did wear the armbands, the record quite clearly shows that it was not in fact disruptive.

Narrator: Chief Justice Warren pushed Johnston on the disruption issue.

Warren: I suppose you would concede that if it started fistfights, or something of that kind, and disrupted the school, that the principal could prevent the use of them?

Johnston: The suggestion I believe we're making, Your Honor, is that there should not be any special rule for freedom of expression cases for schools. I would like to make a distinction, if I may, between the, an expression of an opinion which might itself disrupt a class, and the expression of an opinion which might cause someone else to disrupt the class. And I believe those are perhaps two separate cases. I would also like to make a distinction between the expression of an opinion which is coupled with something else, like marching in the hallway, or standing up in the class and making a speech about the war in Vietnam during mathematics class. That kind of thing, I think the court can prohibit.

Narrator: Dan Johnston concluded.

Johnston: I should not think that there would have to be a special rule for schools or any other part of our society for the First Amendment. Now the evidence of disruption might be different. But as far as the principles applied, we'd like to have the same principles applied in the school or perhaps especially in the school that are applied elsewhere.

Narrator: Allan Herrick represented the school board. Born at the end of the nineteenth century, he reflected the values of an older generation.

Herrick: The respondents believe that there are two basic issues involved here. The first, Do school administrators or school boards have to wait until violence, disorder, and disruption break out and the scholarly discipline of the school is disrupted, or may they act when in good faith, in their reasonable discretion and judgment, disorder and disruption of the scholarly atmosphere of the schoolroom will result unless they act firmly and promptly?

The second issue, it seems to me, is that this Court must determine how far it wants to go under the constitutional amendments for free speech in reviewing every decision of every school district made in good faith, in its reasonable discretion and judgment, as necessary to maintain order and a scholarly, disciplined atmosphere within the classroom.

A third issue might be added. Are disturbances or threatened disturbances in the schools to be measured by identical standards with disturbances or threatened disturbances on the streets?

Narrator: Herrick defended the school board's decision to ban the armbands.

Herrick: Now, it's the position of the respondents that the decision of the school administration and of the school board, made in good faith, under the circumstances existing when that decision was made, was the reasonable exercise of discretion on the part of the school authorities and did not deprive petitioners of their constitutional right of free speech.

Narrator: Herrick cited a recent Supreme Court decision upholding criminal convictions of black students who marched to support jailed sit-in demonstrators. Justice Thurgood Marshall had defended black students as a civil rights lawyer.

Herrick: The case of *Adderly versus the State of Florida* seems particularly pertinent, where the students went from the university to the jail grounds to protest the arrest of students who had been arrested the day before, and their claim was…

Marshall: Mr. Herrick, how many students were involved in the *Addersly* [*sic*] case?

Herrick: In the *Adderly* case?

Marshall: Uh, huh. Several hundred, wasn't it?

Herrick: It was quite a large number.

Marshall: How many were involved in this one?

Herrick: Well, there were….That's a question, Your Honor, what do you mean by "involved"?

Marshall: How many were wearing armbands?

Herrick: Well, there were five suspended for wearing armbands.

Marshall: Well, were any wearing armbands who were not suspended?

Herrick: Yes, I think there were two.

Marshall: That makes seven.

Herrick: They weren't excepted, and I'll refer to that a little later; they were…

Marshall: Seven out of eighteen thousand, and the school board was afraid that seven students wearing armbands would disrupt eighteen thousand. Am I correct?

Herrick: I think, if the Court please, that that doesn't give us the entire background that builds up to what was existing in the Des Moines schools at the time the armbands were worn.

Narrator: Three months before this argument, antiwar rallies at the Democratic Party convention in Chicago provoked a violent police response. It shocked the nation. Herrick tried to link the Des Moines protestors to a controversial group, Students for a Democratic Society, that sponsored the Chicago rallies and earlier antiwar marches.

Herrick: In the background of this case, in November of 1965, the petitioner, Christopher Eckhardt, with his mother, who was president of the Des Moines chapter of the Women's International League for Peace and Freedom, had come to Washington, D.C., to participate with the Students for a Democratic Society, Dr. Spock, and others, in the march, which I'm sure this Court's familiar with, from the White House to the Washington Monument.

Now, that was in November, I think, about the Thanksgiving holiday. On Saturday, December 11th, 1965, following this march, a group which included students related to the Students for a Democratic Society, and some adults, met at the Eckhardt home, and one of the proposals that developed at this meeting was the wearing of these black armbands.

Narrator: Herrick quoted the trial judge's opinion in the *Tinker* case.

Herrick: "The Vietnam war and the involvement of the United States therein has been the subject of a major controversy for some time. When the armband regulation involved herein was promulgated, debate over the Vietnam War had become vehement in many localities. A protest march against the war had recently been held in Washington, D.C. A wave of draft card burning incidents protesting the war had swept the country. At that time, two highly publicized draft card burning cases were pending in this court. Both individuals supporting the war and those opposing it were quite vocal in expressing their views. This was demonstrated during the school board's hearing on the arm-band regulation."

And that appears also in the record. I think some two hundred had gathered who were, many of them, outsiders, at the time of the school board hearing. At this hearing the school board voted in support of the rule prohibiting the wearing of the black armbands, the wearing of armbands, in school premises. It is against this background the Court must review the reasonableness of the regulation.

Narrator: During the armband controversy, a Des Moines soldier, Private James

Flagg, died in Vietnam. Herrick said his death created an "explosive situation" in the schools. Justice Marshall raised sharp questions.

Herrick: This thing had been extensively exploited in the press. We had a situation here where it was explosive.

Marshall: And that explosive situation was that they had a meeting in Washington, D.C. What else besides that?

Herrick: All right. This is page 70, at the top of the Appendix. "A former student at one of our high schools was killed in Vietnam. Some of his friends are still in school. It was felt that if any kind of a demonstration existed, it might evolve into something which would be difficult to control."

Marshall: Do we have a city in this country that hasn't had someone killed in Vietnam?

Herrick: No, I think not, Your Honor, but I don't think it would be an explosive situation in most cases. But if someone is going to appear in court with an armband here, protesting the thing, that it could be explosive. That is the situation we find ourselves in.

Marshall: It *could* be.

Herrick: What?

Marshall: It *could* be. Is that your position? And there is no evidence that it *would* be? Is that the rule you want us to adopt?

Herrick: No, not at all, Your Honor.

Narrator: Herrick asked the Justices to tell Mary Beth Tinker where she could *not* wear her armband.

Herrick: Not at every time, not at every place, and particularly not under the circumstances that existed in this case, not in the school room at a time when it might result in disruption and might even result in violence.

    Now, in substance, if we understand the petitioners' position in this case, it is that the school officials are powerless to act until the disruption occurs. Respondents believe that should not be the rule. Sometimes an ounce of preven-

tion is a lot better than a pound of cure, and I think the subsequent history of
such activities bear out the judgment of the school officials in their discretion.

Narrator: Three months later, on February 24th, 1969, Mary Beth Tinker won
the right to wear her black armband. Justice Abe Fortas wrote the opinion in the
seven-to-two decision. Neither students nor teachers, he wrote, "shed their constitutional rights to freedom of speech or expression at the schoolhouse gate."
In Fortas's words, public schools "may not be enclaves of totalitarianism."

    "Fear or apprehension of disturbance" cannot overcome the First Amend-
ment. He admitted that speech on controversial issues may start arguments
or cause disturbance. But in his words, "our Constitution says we must take
this risk."

    The Court's oldest member, Hugo Black, was known for his absolute
defense of the First Amendment. But he rebelled in the *Tinker* case, endorsing,
in his words, "the old-fashioned slogan that 'children are to be seen not heard.'"
He warned that the Court's approval of armbands marked "the beginning of a
new revolutionary era of permissiveness in this country."

    Since the *Tinker* decision, the Supreme Court has trimmed the First
Amendment rights of students. In 1988, a five-to-four majority ruled that officials could censor articles in school newspapers that—in Justice Byron White's
words—are "unsuitable for immature audiences." In *Hazelwood School District
v. Kuhlmeier* he cited Justice Black's dissent in the Tinker case.

    Mary Beth Tinker is proud of her stand in junior high. She now works as a
VA hospital nurse and treats Vietnam veterans. And she's still a peace activist.
"I'm really proud that we had a part in ending the crazy Vietnam war," she says.

EDITED SUPREME COURT OPINIONS
Tinker v. Des Moines

MR. JUSTICE FORTAS delivered the opinion of the Court.

    First Amendment rights, applied in light of the special characteristics of
the school environment, are available to teachers and students. It can hardly be
argued that either students or teachers shed their constitutional rights to freedom of speech or expression at the schoolhouse gate. This has been the unmistakable holding of this Court for almost fifty years....

    In *West Virginia v. Barnette,*...this Court held that under the First Amend-
ment, the student in public school may not be compelled to salute the flag.
Speaking through Mr. Justice Jackson, the Court said:

> "The Fourteenth Amendment, as now applied to the States, protects the
> citizen against the State itself and all of its creatures—Boards of Educa-

tion not excepted. These have, of course, important, delicate, and highly discretionary functions, but none that they may not perform within the limits of the Bill of Rights. That they are educating the young for citizenship is reason for scrupulous protection of Constitutional freedoms of the individual, if we are not to strangle the free mind at its source and teach youth to discount important principles of our government as mere platitudes." 319 U.S., at 637.

On the other hand, the Court has repeatedly emphasized the need for affirming the comprehensive authority of the States and of school officials, consistent with fundamental constitutional safeguards, to prescribe and control conduct in the schools....Our problem lies in the area where students in the exercise of First Amendment rights collide with the rules of the school authorities.

The problem posed by the present case does not relate to regulation of the length of skirts or the type of clothing, to hair style, or deportment....It does not concern aggressive, disruptive action or even group demonstrations. Our problem involves direct, primary First Amendment rights akin to "pure speech."

The school officials banned and sought to punish petitioners for a silent, passive expression of opinion, unaccompanied by any disorder or disturbance on the part of petitioners. There is here no evidence whatever of petitioners' interference, actual or nascent, with the schools' work or of collision with the rights of other students to be secure and to be let alone. Accordingly, this case does not concern speech or action that intrudes upon the work of the schools or the rights of other students.

Only a few of the eighteen thousand students in the school system wore the black armbands. Only five students were suspended for wearing them. There is no indication that the work of the schools or any class was disrupted. Outside the classrooms, a few students made hostile remarks to the children wearing armbands, but there were no threats or acts of violence on school premises.

The District Court concluded that the action of the school authorities was reasonable because it was based upon their fear of a disturbance from the wearing of the armbands. But, in our system, undifferentiated fear or apprehension of disturbance is not enough to overcome the right to freedom of expression. Any departure from absolute regimentation may cause trouble. Any variation from the majority's opinion may inspire fear. Any word spoken, in class, in the lunchroom, or on the campus, that deviates from the views of another person may start an argument or cause a disturbance. But our Constitution says we must take this risk,...and our history says that it is this sort of hazardous freedom—this kind of openness—that is the basis of our national strength and of the independence and vigor of Americans who grow up and live in this relatively permissive, often disputatious, society.

In order for the State in the person of school officials to justify prohibition of a particular expression of opinion, it must be able to show that its action was caused by something more than a mere desire to avoid the discomfort and unpleasantness that always accompany an unpopular viewpoint. Certainly where there is no finding and no showing that engaging in the forbidden conduct would "materially and substantially interfere with the requirements of appropriate discipline in the operation of the school," the prohibition cannot be sustained....

It is also relevant that the school authorities did not purport to prohibit the wearing of all symbols of political or controversial significance. The record shows that students in some of the schools wore buttons relating to national political campaigns, and some even wore the Iron Cross, traditionally a symbol of Nazism. The order prohibiting the wearing of armbands did not extend to these. Instead, a particular symbol—black armbands worn to exhibit opposition to this nation's involvement in Vietnam—was singled out for prohibition. Clearly, the prohibition of expression of one particular opinion, at least without evidence that it is necessary to avoid material and substantial interference with schoolwork or discipline, is not constitutionally permissible.

In our system, state-operated schools may not be enclaves of totalitarianism. School officials do not possess absolute authority over their students. Students in school as well as out of school are "persons" under our Constitution. They are possessed of fundamental rights which the State must respect, just as they themselves must respect their obligations to the State. In our system, students may not be regarded as closed-circuit recipients of only that which the State chooses to communicate. They may not be confined to the expression of those sentiments that are officially approved. In the absence of a specific showing of constitutionally valid reasons to regulate their speech, students are entitled to freedom of expression of their views....

We reverse and remand for further proceedings consistent with this opinion.

Reversed and remanded.

MR. JUSTICE BLACK, dissenting.

While the record does not show that any of these armband students shouted, used profane language, or were violent in any manner, detailed testimony by some of them shows their armbands caused comments, warnings by other students, the poking of fun at them, and a warning by an older football player that other, nonprotesting students had better let them alone. There is also evidence that a teacher of mathematics had his lesson period practically "wrecked" chiefly by disputes with Mary Beth Tinker, who wore her armband for her "demonstration." Even a casual reading of the record shows that this arm-band did divert students' minds from their regular lessons, and that talk, comments, etc., made John Tinker "self-conscious" in attending school with his armband. While the absence of obscene remarks or boisterous and loud disorder perhaps justifies the Court's statement that the few armband students did not actually "disrupt" the classwork, I think the record overwhelmingly shows that the armbands did exactly what the elected school officials and principals foresaw they would, that is, took the students' minds off their classwork and diverted them to thoughts about the highly emotional subject of the Vietnam War. And I repeat that if the time has come when pupils of state-supported schools, kindergartens, grammar schools, or high schools, can defy and flout orders of school officials to keep their minds on their own schoolwork, it is the beginning of a new revolutionary era of permissiveness in this country fostered by the judiciary....

Change has been said to be truly the law of life but sometimes the old and the tried and true are worth holding. The schools of this Nation have undoubtedly contributed to giving us tranquility and to making us a more law-abiding people. Uncontrolled and uncontrollable liberty is an enemy to domestic peace. We cannot close our eyes to the fact that some of the country's greatest problems are crimes committed by the youth, too many of school age. School discipline, like parental discipline, is an integral and important part of training our children to be good citizens—to be better citizens. Here a very small number of students have crisply and summarily refused to obey a school order designed to give pupils who want to learn the opportunity to do so. One does not need to be a prophet or the son of a prophet to know that after the Court's holding today some students in Iowa schools and indeed in all schools will be ready, able, and willing to defy their teachers on practically all orders. This is the more unfortunate for the schools since groups of students all over the land are already running loose, conducting break-ins, sit-ins, lie-ins, and smash-ins. Many of these student groups, as is all too familiar to all who read the newspapers and watch the television news programs, have already engaged in rioting, property seizures, and destruction. They have picketed schools to force students not to cross their picket lines and have too often violently attacked earnest but frightened students who wanted an education that the pickets did not want them to get. Students engaged in such activities are apparently confident that they know far more about how to operate public school systems than do their parents, teachers, and elected school officials. It is no answer to say that the particular students here have not yet reached such high points in their demands to attend classes in order to exercise their political pressures. Turned loose with lawsuits for damages and injunctions against their teachers as they are here, it is nothing but wishful thinking to imagine that young, immature students will not soon believe it is their right to control the schools rather than the right of the States that collect the taxes to hire the teachers for the benefit of the pupils. This case, therefore, wholly without constitutional reasons in my judgment, subjects all the public schools in the country to the whims and caprices of their loudest-mouthed, but maybe not their brightest, students. I, for one, am not fully persuaded that school pupils are wise enough, even with this Court's expert help from Washington, to run the 23,390 public school systems in our fifty States. I wish, therefore, wholly to disclaim any purpose on my part to hold that the Federal Constitution compels the teachers, parents, and elected school officials to surrender control of the American public school system to public school students. I dissent.

BIBLIOGRAPHY

CUTLIP, JAMES. "Symbolic Speech, High School Protest and the First Amendment." *Journal of Family Law* 9, no. 1 (1969): 119.

"Free to Speak Out—With Limits" *Senior Scholastic* 94, no. 7 (March 14, 1969): 14.

IRONS, PETER. *The Courage of Their Convictions*, ch. 10. Penguin, 1990.

NAHMOD, S. H. "Beyond Tinker..." *Harvard Civil Rights-Civil Liberties Law Review* 5 (April 1970): 278.

"School Protest: Is It a 'Right'?" *U.S. News & World Report*, March 10, 1969, p. 12.

SHEPLEY, JAMES R. "Demonstrations, Not Disruption." *Time*, March 7, 1969, p. 47.

United States *v.* O'Brien

391 U.S. 367 (1968)

The Vietnam War heated up American national politics and local passions in the 1960s. One small but vocal and visible group of protesters demonstrated their opposition to the war by burning their draft cards. On March 31, 1966, David O'Brien and three companions stood on the steps of the South Boston courthouse in Massachusetts and set their cards on fire. Their act inflamed a hostile crowd, and Boston police stood by as onlookers assaulted O'Brien and the other card burners. FBI agents hustled the protesters inside the courthouse and then arrested them for violating a newly-passed federal law that made it illegal to "destroy or mutilate" draft cards. O'Brien was convicted and sentenced to a prison term of up to six years. He based his Supreme Court appeal on claims that his act was a protected form of "symbolic speech" and that Congress was motivated by hostility to war protesters. With only one dissenter, the Court upheld O'Brien's conviction. Chief Justice Earl Warren wrote that burning draft cards frustrated the "smooth and efficient operation" of the draft system, and that the Court would not probe the motives of lawmakers.

Counsel for petitioner: Solicitor General Erwin Griswold, Washington, D. C.
Counsel for respondent: Marvin Karpatkin, New York City

Chief Justice Earl Warren: Number 232 and 233, *United States*, Petitioner, versus *David Paul O'Brien*, and *David Paul O'Brien*, Petitioner, versus the *United States*.

Narrator: It's January 24, 1968. We're in the chamber of the United States Supreme Court in Washington, D.C. Chief Justice Earl Warren has called for argument a case that fills the quiet courtroom with echoes of noisy and disruptive protests against the Vietnam War.

The legal question in this case is abstract and complex: what forms of "symbolic speech" are protected by the First Amendment? The real question has a human face: should David O'Brien go to prison for burning his draft card to protest the war?

This case began on March 31, 1966, on the steps of the South Boston Courthouse in Massachusetts. Four young men—neatly dressed in suits and ties—stood together, surrounded by reporters, Boston police, FBI agents, and a hostile crowd. As cameras clicked and spectators shouted, David O'Brien and his three companions touched flames to their draft cards and burned them. Angry spectators then attacked the protesters without police intervention. O'Brien and his friends were rescued by FBI agents, who interrogated and then arrested them.

The year before O'Brien's arrest, Congress amended the draft law to impose criminal penalties on anyone who "knowingly destroys" or "knowingly mutilates" a Selective Service card. The Congressman who sponsored the amendment said it was aimed at "beatniks" and "Communist stooges" whose antiwar protests, he warned, would "destroy American freedom." O'Brien was tried, convicted and sentenced to prison for up to six years. A federal appeals court reversed the draft-card burning conviction, ruling that the congressional action violated the First Amendment. But the judges also held that O'Brien was guilty of "nonpossession" of his card, although he had not been charged with this offense. Both sides appealed, and the Supreme Court granted review on both issues.

Solicitor General Erwin Griswold, a former Harvard Law School dean, argues for the United States. Chief Justice Warren welcomes him to the podium. Griswold briefly reviews the facts.

Chief Justice Warren: Mr. Solicitor General?

Griswold: May it please the Court:

The evidence at the trial was not in dispute. It showed that the defendant, and three others, burned small white cards on the steps of the South Boston Courthouse own March 31, 1966, in the presence of a sizeable crowd.

Immediately after the event, and after he had been advised of his right to remain silent and to have counsel, the defendant told an agent of the Federal Bureau of Investigation—and this is on page 11 of the record—"I asked him what he had done; what he had burned," said the agent. "He told me he had burned a Selective Service certificate, and that he knew it was a violation of Federal law, but that he had his own beliefs and his own philosophy why he did it. And he produced the charred remains of the Selective Service certificate, which he showed me, and it was in an envelope.

Narrator: The government's brief claimed that O'Brien's action was not protected speech, but unlawful conduct. Griswold expands on this argument.

Griswold: On its face there can be no constitutional question about the statute. It forbids the doing of an act: "knowingly destroys, knowingly mutilates."

The contention is made, however, that in the circumstances of this case the act constitutes symbolic speech; and that Congress cannot proscribe it because that would violate the First Amendment's prohibition of laws abridging the freedom of speech. Of course it is clear that there can be symbolic speech. Or to put it another way, that acts may in effect be speech, though they are not vocal, oral, by voice—a nod, a shake of the head, a wink, a raising of an eyebrow at an auction sale, a gesture such as thumbs-down—may be modes of communication; and one can readily think of circumstances under which Congress could not forbid them, as, for example, in the case of an address delivered by hand signals to an audience of deaf persons.

But it does not follow from this that all acts are the equivalent of speech, or that Congress cannot forbid them even though there is an element of communication in them. I suppose that assaulting an official of the Selective Service System could be thought of as symbolic speech, or breaking a window of this Court building, under certain circumstances. In a sense, refusing to report for induction could be argued to be symbolic speech. It seems equally clear that all of these acts can be made unlawful by Congress.

Narrator: Justice Potter Stewart's question leads Griswold to flag-burning laws, two decades before the Court struck them down.

Stewart: Well, I suppose somebody who had the very sincere belief that the laws against robbery were all wrong could not express that belief by going around and robbing houses, because that would be injuring other people. But here, you don't have any of that quality, do you?

Griswold: We don't have that quality, but we do maintain that there was a valid reason for the enactment of this statute. Not aesthetics, to be sure, but one related to the effective operation of the Selective Service System, which is within the power expressly granted to Congress to raise and support armies and to enact all laws necessary and proper to carry out the aforegoing powers.

Let me see if I can help to answer your question by turning to another one, which is more emotional, the flag. Neither side here has made much reference to the flag, I suppose because it comes close to the line. Of course the flag is a symbol, and burning, or defiling a flag, could be regarded as symbolic speech. As things have developed in this country, legislation with respect to desecration of the flag has been almost entirely left to the states. Nearly every state has such a statute.

Can there be any doubt about the validity of such a statute? I would have thought not. And similar legislation has been applied in many state decisions. Of course a draft card is not a flag; nevertheless it can be regarded as a symbol of public authority. I suppose that the fact that it is such a symbol is what makes it attractive to burn. Is it not clear that maintaining public authority—not suppression of speech, but simply maintaining authority—is a proper exercise of Government, and specifically is something which Congress could properly regard as necessary and proper to the effective exercise of its undoubted power to raise and support armies.

Narrator: Griswold suggests that O'Brien had other ways of protesting the war.

Griswold: Congress did not forbid dissent. It could not do that. O'Brien was free, at all times, to express dissent by speech from the courthouse steps, or on the street corners, by letters to the editor, by pamphlet, by radio and television. This case does not involve a question of the line between speech and no speech, where the answer would be clear in favor of speech. For the contention of the defendant is not that he can speak—which, of course, he can—but, rather, that he can do acts, despite the fact that they had been forbidden by that formal action of the representatives of the people in Congress assembled which we call a statute.

Narrator: Griswold concludes that O'Brien brought his prison term on himself, however sincere and nonviolent his protest against the war.

*Griswold:*Whatever feelings of compassion or regret one may have for the defendant and his situation, it's clear that he violated the law. We submit that the law was validly made, and it is not fairly to be regarded as an abridgement of freedom of speech when it does not involve speech in any way, and when all avenues of speech remain open to the defendant.

Congress could conclude that the law it passed bears the proper relation to the maintenance of effective self-government. We submit that the judgment of the Court of Appeals holding the statute unconstitutional should be reversed.

Narrator: David O'Brien spoke for himself at trial. An experienced First Amendment lawyer, Marvin Karpatkin, speaks for him in the Supreme Court. Chief Justice Warren welcomes Karpatkin. Justice Abe Fortas has the first question.

Chief Justice Warren : Mr. Karpatkin?

Karpatkin: Mr. Chief Justice, may it please the Court:

First, I believe it is clear…that the verbal conduct or symbolic act, or whatever words one chooses to use, on the part of David O'Brien, was intended as an act of dissent, as an act of expression of dissent to Government foreign policy, to government military policy, to the war in Vietnam, and to the drafting of young men to serve in that war. I think it must also be conceded that this symbolic speech or verbal conduct on O'Brien's part attracted attention—attracted the attention of the media, attracted attention of the media audiences, attracted the attention of a hostile crowd—

Fortas: What do you mean, "verbal conduct"? That's not what we're talking about here, is it?

Karpatkin: Mr. Justice Fortas, I—

Fortas: We're talking about the burning of the draft card. And now you can say that that is symbolic First Amendment expression, if you want to, but we're not talking about verbal—we're not talking about anything he uttered here, are we?

Mr. Karpatkin: No, Mr. Justice Fortas. We're talking about the act of public demonstration on the part of O'Brien in publicly setting fire to his Selective Service certificate under the circumstances for which he did it. I use the word "verbal conduct" synonymously with "symbolic speech." And I believe that there may be some cases that support it, but I won't press that point.

Narrator: Chief Justice Warren poses a difficult question.

Warren: Suppose a soldier over in Vietnam, in front of a large crowd of soldiers, broke his weapon and said it was a protest against the War and the foreign policy of the Government. Would that be symbolic speech?

Karpatkin: Mr. Chief Justice, I don't know whether that would or wouldn't be symbolic speech.

Warren: Well, we have to go a little farther than just this particular case, do we not?

Karpatkin: We certainly do not argue, as the Government in its brief suggests, that under our theory anything which communicates is protected, and that anything which communicates an idea is protected. We don't argue that the dumping of garbage is protected, or that political assassination is protected, or that any other of the fanciful notions which the Government seems to charge us with, is protected.

Warren: Where do you draw the line?

Karpatkin: We would like to suggest, Mr. Chief Justice, that the line should be drawn in accordance with the proper application of the "clear and present danger" test. However, we feel that even if the Court would choose to apply the ad hoc balancing test, that the various values which are placed in the balance on both sides are such that this statute could not survive constitutional scrutiny.

Narrator: Karpatkin disputes the government's claim that the draft system cannot function properly without O'Brien's card. Justice Fortas has another question.

Karpatkin: It is well known that the Selective Service System keeps elaborate records at its national headquarters, and emergency records of other kinds as well. Now I suggest that perhaps the reason why the Solicitor General was not more explicit in stating these reasons is that some of them are so fanciful as perhaps not to be worthy of mentioning in this Court. And I notice that two of those which have been suggested in the lower courts have not been suggested in this Court; namely, that in the event of an earthquake, disaster, or other flood or something of the nature of a flood, it would be possible for there to be a quick reconstruction of the records before men would be ordered to report to a certain place by radio or television. And the final suggestion which was made in the arguments below, but thankfully not in this Court, was that in the event of an enemy missile attack and a call-up by radio, why, persons could be ordered to report to certain places in accordance with their draft classifications, and that would serve a valid governmental purpose.

The only other purpose which it was suggested it would serve was that when a registrant goes to his local board, in the event he may have forgotten his number or forgotten the address of his board, why, it may assist in this identification if he has the card in his possession. Now it seems to me that if that is all that the Government can offer in support of this, it is a very, very light balance, indeed.

Fortas: I thought it was an enforcement device, to help identify people who have registered.

Karpatkin: But enforcement of what, Mr. Justice Fortas?

Fortas: Selective Service registration. No?

Karpatkin: There does not seem to be—it does not seem to play any role in the enforcement of the Selective Service laws. No mention of it can be found in any of the volumes and volumes of material which Selective Service has published, and the Selective Service System has been administering the Selective Service laws since 1940. I think it is most surprising indeed that not only was no Selective Service testimony presented to Congress, but any time in the course of all this litigation, in the trial courts and the appellate courts. Able attorneys for the Government have not been able to come forward with even a single statement on the part of any Selective Service official or Defense Department official, or governmental official, showing that this serves any purpose at all.

Narrator: Karpatkin argues that Congress had an improper motive in punishing antiwar protesters who destroy their draft cards.

Karpatkin: David O'Brien was neither indicted nor tried nor convicted for non-possession. He was indicted, tried, and convicted for burning, we respectfully submit before this Court, and there is a special area of constitutional questions which arise because of the manner of enactment of this statute. And I do not, with respect, believe that this can be avoided, notwithstanding the suggestion by the Solicitor General that the distinction between Congressional motive and Congressional purpose is elusive to the Government.

I believe that the entire legislative history which we have set forth as an appendix brief—and we have done it deliberately because we don't wish to be open to the suggestion that we are picking and choosing—demonstrates beyond any question that the only Congressional purpose here was the purpose of stamping out dissent, of stamping out this particular form of expression of dissent. The Government, indeed, so acknowledged it, and the Solicitor General acknowledged it in part of his argument, that the Government was seeking to punish contumacious conduct. The Government acknowledges that. It says that perhaps some of the purposes were less constitutionally justified than others. The Government acknowledges that at least one of the purposes was to declare draft card burning insulting and unpatriotic.

Narrator: Karpatkin ends by linking David O'Brien with sit-down strikers for labor unions and sit-in demonstrators for civil rights.

Karpatkin: I can just say, in summation—I have, alas, not been able to reach other points which I hoped I would have an opportunity to reach—that just as decisions of this Court have referred to peaceful picketing as the workingman's means of communication…and just as the sit-in has been called the "poor man's printing press," I would like to respectfully suggest that perhaps the act of an obscure pacifist who wants to engage in a dramatic anti-war act of burning his draft card makes draft card burning the war protester's TV transmitter.

Thank you very much.

Narrator: The Supreme Court decided this case on May 27, 1968. Only one justice dissented from the ruling that upheld David O'Brien's conviction and sent him to federal prison. Chief Justice Earl Warren assigned the opinion to himself, hoping to blunt the criticism he knew would come from First Amendment stalwarts. Even the Court's law clerks—most of them young men of draft age—opposed the decision. One scholar wrote that the clerks "engaged in virtual guerilla warfare" to weaken Warren's opinion.

Warren tried hard not to trample on the First Amendment. He took a careful path around the Court's precedents, and devoted just one paragraph to the "symbolic speech" question. Warren wrote that "when 'speech' and 'non-speech' elements are combined in the same course of conduct, a sufficiently important governmental interest in regulating the nonspeech element can justify incidental limitations on First Amendment freedoms."

Following this long sentence, Warren dismissed O'Brien's free speech claim in a few words. Burning his draft card, Warren wrote, "wilfully frustrated" the government's interest in "the smooth and efficient functioning of the Selective Service System." Those who watched O'Brien burn his card saw a statement against the draft in the flames. The Chief Justice looked only at the ashes: "For this noncommunicative impact of his conduct, and for nothing else, he was convicted."

Warren also dismissed O'Brien's claim that Congress was motivated to punish antiwar dissenters. "Inquiries into congressional motives or purposes are a hazardous matter, he wrote. The Court would not strike down a law because of what "a handful of congressmen said about it" during the debate. Warren left out the heated statements of those who vowed to punish "open defiance" of the draft law.

David O'Brien's open defiance of Congress sent him to prison. But the Court's decision did not slow down the growing antiwar movement. Hundreds of young men burned their draft cards, thousands of men and women marched against the war, and the draft finally expired with the war's end. Draft cards are now a relic of those painful years.

EDITED SUPREME COURT OPINIONS
United States v. O'Brien
Argued January 24, 1968—Decided May 27, 1968

MR. CHIEF JUSTICE WARREN delivered the opinion of the Court.

On the morning of March 31, 1966, David Paul O'Brien and three companions burned their Selective Service registration certificates on the steps of the South Boston Courthouse. A sizable crowd, including several agents of the Federal Bureau of Investigation, witnessed the event; immediately after the burning, members of the crowd began attacking O'Brien and his companions. An FBI agent ushered O'Brien to safety inside the courthouse. After he was advised of his right to counsel and to silence, O'Brien stated to FBI agents that he had burned his registration certificate because of his beliefs, knowing that he was violating federal law. He produced the charred remains of the certificate, which, with his cannonade, were photographed.

For this act, O'Brien was indicted, tried, convicted, and sentenced in the United States District Court for the District of Massachusetts. He did not contest the fact that he had burned the certificate. He stated in argument to the jury that he burned the certificate publicly to influence others to adopt his antiwar beliefs, as he put it, "so that other people would reevaluate their positions with Selective Service, with the armed forces, and reevaluate their position in the culture of today, to hopefully consider my position."

The indictment upon which he was tried charged that he "willfully and knowingly did mutilate, destroy, and change by burning…[his] Registration Certificate (Selective Service System Form No. 2); in violation of Title 50, App.,

United States Code, Section 462(b)." Section 462 (b) is part of the Universal Military Training and Service Act of 1948. Section 462 (b)(3), one of six numbered subdivisions of § 462 (b), was amended by Congress in 1965, 79 stat. 586 (adding the words italicized below), so that at the time O'Brien burned his certificate an offense was committed by any person, "who forges, alters, *knowingly destroys, knowingly mutilates,* or in any manner changes any such certificate...." (Italics supplied.)

In the District Court, O'Brien argued that the 1965 Amendment prohibiting the knowing destruction or mutilation of certificates was unconstitutional because it was enacted to abridge free speech, and because it served no legitimate legislative purpose. The District Court rejected these arguments, holding that the statute on its face did not abridge First Amendment rights, that the court was not competent to inquire into the motives of Congress in enacting the 1965 Amendment, and that the Amendment was a reasonable exercise of the power of Congress to raise armies.

On appeal, the Court of Appeals for the First Circuit held the 1965 Amendment unconstitutional as a law abridging freedom of speech. At the time the Amendment was enacted, a regulation of the Selective Service System required registrants to keep their registration certificates in their "personal possession at all times." 32 CFR § 1617.1 (1962). Willful violations of regulations promulgated pursuant to the Universal Military Training and Service Act were made criminal by statute. 50 U.S. C. App. § 462 (b)(6). The Court of Appeals, therefore, was of the opinion that conduct punishable under the 1965 Amendment was already punishable under the nonpossession regulation, and consequently that the Amendment served no valid purpose; further, that in light of the prior Regulation, the Amendment must have been "directed at public as distinguished from private destruction." On this basis, the court concluded that the 1965 Amendment ran afoul of the First Amendment by singling out persons engaged in protests for special treatment. The court ruled, however, that O'Brien's conviction should be affirmed under the statutory provision, 50 U.S.C. App. § 462 (b)(6), which in its view made violation of the nonpossession regulation a crime, because it regarded such violation to be a lesser included offense of the crime defined by the 1965 Amendment....

O'Brien first argues that the 1965 Amendment is unconstitutional as applied to him because his act of burning his registration certificate was protected "symbolic speech" within the First Amendment. His argument is that the freedom of expression which the First Amendment guarantees includes all modes of "communication of ideas by conduct," and that his conduct is within this definition because he did it in "demonstration against the war and against the draft."

We cannot accept the view that an apparently limitless variety of conduct can be labeled "speech" whenever the person engaging in the conduct intends thereby to express an idea. However, even on the assumption that the alleged communicative element in O'Brien's conduct is sufficient to bring into play the First Amendment, it does not necessarily follow that the destruction of a registration certificate is constitutionally protected activity. This Court has held that when "speech" and "nonspeech" elements are combined in the same course of conduct, a sufficiently important governmental interest in regulating the nonspeech element can justify incidental limitations on First Amendment freedoms. To characterize the quality of the governmental interest which must appear, the Court has employed a variety of descriptive terms: compelling; substantial; subordinating; paramount, cogent, strong. Whatever imprecision inheres in these terms, we think it clear that a government regulation is sufficiently justified if it is within the constitutional power of the Government; if it furthers an important or substantial governmental interest; if the governmental interest is unrelated to the suppression of free expression; and if the incidental restriction on alleged First Amendment freedoms is no greater than is essential to the furtherance of that interest. We find that the 1965 Amendment to § 12(b)(3) of the Universal Military Training and Service Act meets all of these requirements, and consequently that O'Brien can be constitutionally convicted for violating it....

O'Brien's argument to the contrary is necessarily premised upon his unrealistic characterization of Selective Service certificates. He essentially adopts the position that such certificates are so many pieces of paper designed to notify registrants of their registration or classification, to be retained or tossed in the wastebasket according to the convenience or taste of the registrant. Once the registrant has received notification, according to this view, there is no reason for him to retain the certificates. O'Brien notes that most of the information on a registration certificate serves no notification purpose at all; the registrant hardly needs to be told his address and physical characteristics. We agree that the registration certificate contains much information of which the registrant needs no notification. This circumstance, however, does not lead to the conclusion that the certificate serves no purpose, but that, like the classification certificate, it serves purposes in addition to initial notification. Many of these purposes would be defeated by the certificates' destruction or mutilation.

The many functions performed by Selective Service certificates establish beyond doubt that Congress has a legitimate and substantial interest in preventing their wanton and unrestrained destruction and assuring their continuing availability by punishing people who knowingly and wilfully destroy or mutilate them. And we are unpersuaded that the preexistence of the nonpossession regulations ill any way negates this interest....

Equally important, a comparison of the regulations with the 1965 Amendment indicates that they protect overlapping but not identical governmental interests, and that they reach somewhat different classes of wrongdoers. The gravamen of the offense defined by the statute is the deliberate rendering of certificates unavailable for the various purposes which they may serve. Whether registrants keep their certificates in their personal possession at all times, as required by the regulations, is of no particular, concern under the 1965 Amendment, as long as they do not mutilate or destroy the certificates so as to render them unavailable. Although as we note below we are not concerned here with the nonpossession regulations, it is not inappropriate to observe that the essential elements of nonpossession are not identical with those of mutilation or destruction. Finally, the 1965 Amendment, like § 12 b) which it amended, is concerned with abuses involving *any* issued Selective Service certificates, not only with the registrant's own certificates. The knowing destruction or mutilation of someone else's certificates would therefore violate the statute but not the nonpossession regulations.

We think it apparent that the continuing availability to each registrant of his Selective Service certificates substantially furthers the smooth and proper functioning of the system that Congress has established to raise armies. We think it also apparent that the Nation has a vital interest in having a system for raising armies that functions with maximum efficiency and is capable of easily and quickly responding to continually changing circumstances. For these reasons, the Government has a substantial interest in assuring the continuing availability of issued Selective Service certificates.

It is equally clear that the 1965 Amendment specifically protects this substantial governmental interest. We perceive no alternative means that would more precisely and narrowly assure the continuing availability of issued Selective Service certificates than a law which prohibits their wilful mutilation or destruction.... The 1965 Amendment prohibits such conduct and does nothing more. In other words, both the governmental interest and the operation of the 1965 Amendment are limited to the noncommunicative aspect of O'Brien's conduct. The governmental interest and the Scope of the 1965 Amendment are limited to preventing harm to the smooth and efficient functioning of the Selective Service System. When O'Brien deliberately rendered unavailable his registration certificate, he wilfully frustrated this governmental interest. For this noncommunicative impact of his conduct, and for nothing else, he was convicted....

In conclusion, we find that because of the Government's substantial interest in assuring the continuing availability of issued Selective Service certificates, because amended § 462(b) is an appropriately narrow means of protecting this interest and condemns only the independent noncommunicative impact of conduct within its reach, and because the noncommunicative impact of O'Brien's act of burning his registration certificate frustrated the Government's interest, a sufficient governmental interest has been shown to justify O'Brien's conviction.

O'Brien finally argues that the 1965 Amendment is unconstitutional as enacted because what he calls the "purpose" of Congress was "to suppress freedom of speech." We reject this argument because under settled principles the purpose of Congress, as O'Brien uses that term, is not a basis for declaring this legislation unconstitutional.

It is a familiar principle of constitutional law that this Court will not strike down an otherwise constitutional Statute on the basis of an alleged illicit legislative motive....

Inquiries into congressional motives or purposes are a hazardous matter. When the issue is simply the interpretation of legislation, the Court will look to statements by legislators for guidance as to the purpose of the legislature, because the benefit to sound decision-making in this circumstance is thought sufficient to risk the possibility of misreading Congress' purpose. It is entirely a different matter when we are asked to void a statute that is, under well-settled criteria, constitutional on its face, on the basis of what fewer than a handful of Congressmen said about it. What motivates one legislator to make a speech about a statute is not necessarily what motivates scores of others to enact it, and the stakes are sufficiently high for us to eschew guesswork. We decline to void essentially on the ground that it is unwise legislation which Congress had the undiluted power to enact form if the same or another legislator made a "wiser" speech about it....

We think it not amiss, in passing, to comment upon O'Brien's legislative-purpose argument. There was little floor debate on this legislation in either House. Only Senator Thurmond commented on its substantive features in the Senate....

In the House debate only two Congressmen addressed themselves to the Amendment—Congressmen Rivers and Bray....

The bill was passed after their statements without any further debate by a vote of 393 to 1. It is principally on the basis of the statements by.these three Congressmen that O'Brien makes his congressional-"purpose" argument. We note that if we were to examine legislative purpose in the instant case, we would be obliged to consider not only these statements but also the more authoritative reports of the Senate and House Armed Services Committees. The portions of those reports explaining the purpose of the Amendment are reproduced in the Appendix in their entirety. While both reports make clear a concern with

the "defiant" destruction of so-called "draft cards" and with "open" encourage-
ment to others to destroy their cards, both reports also indicate that this concern stemmed from an apprehension that unrestrained destruction of cards
would disrupt the smooth functioning of the Selective Service System.

Since the 1965 Amendment to § 12(b)(3) of the universal Military Training
and Service Act is constitutional as enacted and as applied, the Court of
Appeals should have affirmed the judgment of conviction entered by the District Court. Accordingly, we vacate the judgment of the Court of Appeals, and
reinstate the judgment and sentence of the District Court. This disposition
makes unnecessary consideration of O'Brien's claim that the Court of Appeals
erred in affirming his conviction on the basis of the nonpossession regulation.

It is so ordered.

MR. JUSTICE DOUGLAS, dissenting.

The Court states that the constitutional power of Congress to raise and
support armies is "broad and sweeping" and that Congress' power "to classify
and conscript manpower for military service is "beyond question."' This is
undoubtedly true in times when, by declaration of Congress, the Nation is in a
state of war. The underlying and basic problem in this case, however, is whether
conscription is permissible in the absence of a declaration of war. That question
has not been briefed nor was it presented in oral argument; but it is, I submit, a
question upon which the litigants and the country are entitled to a ruling....

It is time that we made a ruling. This case should be put down for reargument....on the question of the constitutionality of a peacetime draft...